International Political Theory Series

Series Editor: **Gary Browning**, Professor of Politics, Department of International Relations, Politics and Sociology, Oxford Brookes University, UK

The *Palgrave International Political Theory Series* provides students and scholars with cutting-edge scholarship that explores the ways in which we theorise the international.

Political theory has by tradition implicitly accepted the bounds of the state, and this series of intellectually rigorous and innovative monographs and edited volumes takes the discipline forward, reflecting both the burgeoning of IR as a discipline and the concurrent internationalization of traditional political theory issues and concepts. Offering a wide-ranging examination of how international politics is to be interpreted, the titles in the series thus bridge the IR–political theory divide.

The aim of the series is to explore international issues in analytic, historical and radical ways that complement and extend common forms of conceiving international relations such as realism, liberalism and constructivism.

Titles include:

Keith Breen and Shane O'Neill (*editors*)
AFTER THE NATION
Critical Reflections on Nationalism and Postnationalism

Gary Browning, Raia Prokhovnik and Maria Dimova-Cookson (*editors*)
DIALOGUES WITH CONTEMPORARY POLITICAL THEORISTS

Gary Browning
GLOBAL THEORY FROM KANT TO HARDT AND NEGRI

Tony Burns and Simon Thompson (*editors*)
GLOBAL JUSTICE AND THE POLITICS OF RECOGNITION

Alexandros Kioupkiolis
FREEDOM AFTER THE CRITIQUE OF FOUNDATIONS
Marx, Liberalism, Castoriadis and Agonistic Autonomy

Michaela Neacsu
HANS J. MORGENTHAU'S THEORY OF INTERNATIONAL RELATIONS
Disenchantment and Re-Enchantment

Antony O'Loughlin
OVERCOMING POSTSTRUCTURALISM
Rawls, Kratochwil and the Structure of Normative Reasoning in International Relations

Raia Prokhovnik and Gabriella Slomp (*editors*)
INTERNATIONAL POLITICAL THEORY AFTER HOBBES
Analysis, Interpretation and Orientation

Howard Williams
KANT AND THE END OF WAR
A Critique of Just War Theory

Huw Lloyd Williams
ON RAWLS, DEVELOPMENT AND GLOBAL JUSTICE
The Freedom of Peoples

Stephen Winter
TRANSITIONAL JUSTICE IN ESTABLISHED DEMOCRACIES
A Political Theory

International Political Theory Series
Series Standing Order ISBN 978–0–230–20538–3 hardcover
978–0–230–20539–0 paperback
(*outside North America only*)

You can receive future titles in this series as they are published by placing a standing order. Please contact your bookseller or, in case of difficulty, write to us at the address below with your name and address, the title of the series and the ISBNs quoted above.

Customer Services Department, Macmillan Distribution Ltd, Houndmills, Basingstoke, Hampshire RG21 6XS, England

Overcoming Poststructuralism

Rawls, Kratochwil and the Structure of Normative Reasoning in International Relations

Antony O'Loughlin
Solicitor in England and Wales and the British Virgin Islands, Mishcon de Reya

palgrave
macmillan

First published 2014 by
PALGRAVE MACMILLAN

Palgrave Macmillan in the UK is an imprint of Macmillan Publishers Limited, registered in England, company number 785998, of Houndmills, Basingstoke, Hampshire RG21 6XS.

Palgrave Macmillan in the US is a division of St Martin's Press LLC, 175 Fifth Avenue, New York, NY 10010.

Palgrave Macmillan is the global academic imprint of the above companies and has companies and representatives throughout the world.

ISBN 978–1–137–38072–2

This book is printed on paper suitable for recycling and made from fully managed and sustained forest sources. Logging, pulping and manufacturing processes are expected to conform to the environmental regulations of the country of origin.

A catalogue record for this book is available from the British Library.

Library of Congress Cataloging-in-Publication Data
O'Loughlin, Antony, 1981–
Overcoming poststructuralism : Rawls, Kratochwil and the structure of normative reasoning in international relations / Antony O'Loughlin.
pages cm — (International political theory series)
Summary: "The theorisation of international relations has progressed considerably in recent years to the point that a dialogue between the concurrent disciplines of International Relations (IR), political theory and international law has started to emerge. There is, however, much work still to be done in establishing what could be termed an 'International Theory' – one which contains the potential to transcend arbitrary disciplinary and methodological boundaries (particularly where the subject matter of the respective disciplines – working out a conception of normative reason appropriate to application in considerations of international justice and human rights – is trans-disciplinary in nature). This insightful contemporary critique considers the poststructuralist challenge to the very foundations and methodological commitments of traditional IR theory, as developed by R.B.J. Walker and Richard Ashley in the 1990s and beyond – as well as the various ways in which the discipline has sought to respond to such a pervasive attack on its most cherished beliefs. This study not only brings into question the central tenets of traditional IR theory, but also uses the political thought and theories of key thinkers including John Rawls, Friedrich Kratochwil and Peri Roberts to posit an account of normative reasoning which overcomes the challenges presented by a poststructuralist perspective" — Provided by publisher.
ISBN 978–1–137–38072–2 (hardback)
1. International relations—Philosophy. 2. Poststructuralism I. Title.
JZ1305.O56 2014
327.101—dc23 2014020357

Contents

Introduction: The 'Enormous Creative Potential of Practical Reason' 1

Part I The Challenge – Poststructuralism and IR's Responses

1 Inside/Outside: Walker, Ashley and the Poststructuralist Critique of IR 15

2 Overcoming the Poststructuralist Critique? Ontology and Epistemology in the Constructivist Theories of Wendt and Kratochwil 40

3 Constitutive Political Theory: Mervyn Frost and the Role of Norms in International Political Theory 72

Part II The Solution – Constructing Normative Reason

4 Beyond Coherence: Rawls' Conception of Public Reason 93

5 Contemporary Moral Foundationalism: Buchanan's Conception of Normative Reasoning and the Role of Institutions in Political Justification 118

6 Philosophical Constructivism and Critical Constructivism Combined: Kratochwil's Account of the Conditions of Practical Reasoning and the Rawlsian Conception of Public Reason 143

7 The Concept of the Reasonable in International Political Justification: A Rejoinder to the Poststructuralist Critique 182

Conclusion: Poststructuralism and Beyond 244

Notes 246

References 276

Index 280

Introduction: The 'Enormous Creative Potential of Practical Reason'[1]

This book is concerned with constructivism in international relations. Specifically, it is concerned with the ability of a constructivist account of the structure of normative reasoning to ground a theory of international relations capable of overcoming the poststructuralist challenge to the traditional foundations and methodology developed and adopted by the discipline of IR. While the book begins with a detailed analysis of this challenge and a consideration of the means by which IR has attempted to answer it, this is primarily an account of the conditions of international relations analysed through the lens of international political theory, but one which incorporates crucial theoretical features developed within the more mainstream discipline of IR. Ultimately, what I set out to do is to dispel the idea that the disciplines operate in necessarily distinct spaces (and that they can therefore effectively speak past one another) and instead offer an account of international relations grounded on a conception of normative reasoning capable of 'combining' the various elements and theoretical tools of each discipline, which I consider crucial to a *true* understanding of the nature of world politics.

I intentionally leave the word 'constructivism' unqualified above. There are two broad accounts of the nature and conditions of international relations which can properly be called 'constructivist':

1. *Social* constructivism, which I argue constitutes one of the means by which the discipline of IR sought to respond to critical challenges to the assumptions and methodological commitments around which it had traditionally oriented itself. The two positions I consider herein are the 'conventional' constructivism of Alexander Wendt (which I consider to characterise IR's attempt to respond to its critics while remaining

essentially loyal to the key ontological and methodological commitments it had long adhered to) and the more 'holistic' form of social constructivism (and accompanying theories of social epistemology and normative reasoning) developed with much sophistication by Friedrich Kratochwil.

2. *Philosophical* constructivism, originating within the discipline of political theory and most closely associated (in its contemporary *political* form) with the work of John Rawls. While I ultimately consider certain concepts drawn from the framework of Rawlsian constructivism to be the most effective means of grounding a *legitimate* account of international relations, I also consider that there are crucial elements of a cohesive and complete account of the nature of international politics, in particular the characteristics and structure of normative, practical and institutional reasoning in IR, which cannot be understood through the lens of philosophical constructivism alone. For this reason, my book advocates a response to the challenge of poststructuralism built around the most fundamental concepts employed by Rawls, but with the vital addition of those elements of Kratochwil's and others' theories which I consider to be crucial to a 'complete' understanding of the characteristics of practical reasoning in the context of international relations.

While theorists such as Kratochwil and Rawls are essentially concerned with the same subject matter – the nature and conditions of practical reason as a means to the construction of normatively significant and *justified* structures in domestic politics and international relations – it is striking that neither engages with the other's position to any great extent. This, I believe, can in large part be attributed to the fact that, traditionally, the disciplines of International Relations and political theory (even where the latter spoke to international considerations) have essentially operated as if the other did not exist. Perhaps consciously, the methodologies and research agendas of the distinct disciplines, with their respective focuses on positivistic analyses and philosophical explanations, were historically almost prima facie unable or unwilling to engage one another. Explaining and understanding international phenomena was the preserve of International Relations, normative justificatory theory and philosophical conceptions of right and justice the hallmark of political theory.

More recently, as Wendt and Snidal observe in an important 2009 article,[2] a degree of synthesis and amalgamation has occurred among the 'international disciplines'. This is the case, claim Wendt and Snidal, due to the shedding of the 'intellectual prejudices' of political theorists and philosophers 'in favour of domestic politics'[3] (which, they claim, rendered international normative considerations an afterthought of 'subsidiary works' as opposed to the 'great ones' concerned with domestic issues) – meaning that a far greater focus has been afforded to international questions than was previously the case, as well as the more recent emphasis on the role of ideas and ideational factors in international social structures, the introduction of 'explicitly normative concepts such as appropriateness and legitimacy'[4] into the IR lexicon and the acknowledgement of 'the role of scholars not merely as observers of world politics but as critics and, through ideas, even shapers of international outcomes'[5] among IR theorists (meaning that 'the level of theoretical sophistication within IR is much higher now than it was four decades ago'[6]). Thus, claim Wendt and Snidal, a genuine International Theory has emerged, oriented around the 'distinct disciplinary communities' of IR, International Political Theory and the resurgence of theoretical work in International Law.[7]

The lingering problem, however, and the raison d'être behind Wendt and Snidal's piece, is the fact that 'different theoretical communities are not engaging each other in ways that could be mutually productive'.[8] Thus, they claim:

> In contrast to the at least sporadic trade (and warfare) between theoretical approaches that takes place within the discipline-defined boundaries of IT, serious engagement across disciplines is almost non-existent. Thus, instead of one set of conversations around an international issue among normative, positive, and legal theorists, there are three separate sets of conversations going on, each within its own, relatively self-contained, disciplinary 'silo'. These silos constitute the primary universe of discourse about the international for their members, defining expectations both professionally (in the sense of the prominence of journals and presses and thus the incentive structure for publication), and intellectually in the sense of what constitutes good work or 'the literature' in a given domain (i.e. even if good work outside the silo bears on the problem).[9]

Wendt and Snidal do acknowledge the fact that, in contemporary debates, there is 'some fluidity' between discourses, particularly '[a]t the level of individual scholars'.[10] However, 'significant intellectual impediments remain', evident in 'citation patterns that continue to be heavily weighted toward work in one's home discipline'.[11] Thus:

> While we do not imagine that the diversity of [International Theory – i.e. its positive, normative and legal elements] can be reduced to a single conversation, or that this is even a desirable goal, there is nevertheless something important for these fields to talk about: the areas where their concerns overlap.[12]

The areas of overlap between the supposedly distinct elements of 'International Theory' – positive, normative and legal – are of crucial importance for my book. Given the inherent nature of contemporary international relations, it does not appear to me to be possible to truly understand and theorise about world politics without a sophisticated understanding of the ways in which the normative, legal, institutional and practical elements of international relations are connected. My most fundamental claim herein is therefore that the 'distinct' elements of theorising about international relations, and their inherently intertwined nature, can be properly understood and (equally importantly) legitimately justified through a complex conception of practical reason within the context of international normative structure. Kratochwil develops such a conception; Rawls provides the philosophical framework within which the conception can be embedded, contextualised and, crucially, afforded a robust normative justification.

I do not claim that this book unlocks the key to a truly unified 'International Theory' (to employ Wendt and Snidal's claim). I primarily approach the study of international politics from the perspective of political theory. What I set out to consider, however, is the most effective means of overcoming a particular challenge to the theoretical analysis of the nature of international relations – namely, the challenge of poststructuralism. I want to consider the ways in which IR has attempted to speak to attacks on its most fundamental assumptions (both substantive and methodological) in order to ascertain whether the discipline of IR contains the tools necessary to overcome such challenges. This will involve, initially, revisiting the challenge propounded by poststructuralism – and by Richard Ashley and R.B.J. Walker in particular – to the discipline of IR in the 1990s and the (at the time) radical responses offered by IR[13] in an attempt to overcome this attack on the very heart of the discipline (namely, the very foundations by which IR assumed that its theoretical knowledge could be deemed authoritative) which I consider through a comparative analysis of conventional and critical constructivism.[14] My argument is that, although the poststructuralists presented the discipline of IR with a far-reaching and ultimately devastating challenge, it did little to move beyond that challenge to a constructive account of how a consideration of international relations ought to proceed in a legitimate and justifiable manner ('from *de*construction to *re*construction', to coin a phrase adopted by Friedrichs and Kratochwil[15]). The paucity of *re*constructive poststructuralist theory can clearly be attributed to the deconstructive method which characterises the approach. If one challenges the very possibility of authoritative and legitimate theoretical knowledge in an absolute manner – as Walker and Ashley essentially set out to do – one is left with little by way of resources by which to ground reconstructive possibility aside from 'anti-foundationalism' (as Walker and Ashley themselves expound) or else the *pragmatism* of theorists such as Friedrichs and Kratochwil. While the latter are not themselves poststructuralists, the piece in question seeks to move beyond 'epistemological deadlock' (which, it claims, adequately captures the state of the debates regarding social-scientific methodology) through the identification of a sound pragmatic approach to the ontological and epistemological issues thrown up by the conclusions of post-positivistic theory:

> We suggest that a coherent pragmatic approach consists of two elements: the recognition of knowledge generation as a social and discursive activity, and the orientation of research toward the generation of useful knowledge.[16]

Therefore, a 'pragmatic' approach to the question of anchoring the foundations of theoretical knowledge requires an *intersubjective* understanding of the production of knowledge and requires that questions of *practicality* (i.e. how to generate practically beneficial theoretical knowledge) drive the research agenda. Friedrichs and Kratochwil claim that *if* the idea that the categories of knowledge are conditioned by the reason of the observing subject is accepted, questions of epistemology must be engaged:

> Insofar as the subject is deeply implicated in the constitution of the object, it is impossible to derive concepts and theoretical assertions directly from 'the facts'. If the objects of experience are not simply 'out there,' to understand the world we have to reflect on the categories we use.

> Since it is clear that these categories are part of the human mind and not a property of the objective world, ontological realism is in trouble and an epistemological alternative is required. Any such alternative will highlight the constitution of what we perceive as the world through our cognitive endowment and conceptual instruments.[17]

The assertion that the commitments of a social-scientific methodology which privileges the status of an independent and objectively discernible set of facts and logical propositions can no longer be legitimately sustained is akin to the conclusions of Walker's and Ashley's poststructuralism, which (as we will see in Chapter 1) ultimately proclaims the impossibility of *any* legitimate foundation for knowledge. For Friedrichs and Kratochwil, however,

> questioning conventional methodology has nothing to do with 'nihilism' [i.e. in a theoretical sense]. Instead, it obliges us to critically examine alternative criteria that can lend force to our assertions. It is a fallacy to assume that without universally valid, timeless, and unshakeable foundations 'everything becomes relative' and 'anything goes'.[18]

This is a critical point and one that feeds into the substance of my book. Given the work that has been undertaken in IR and political theory over the last two decades to dispel the idea that either social or moral 'facts' exist independently of the agents who participate in both action and observation (whether by poststructuralism or alternative versions of critical theory), the idea of constructivism, which *in both senses* listed above is premised on the idea that a sufficiently sophisticated and inclusive conception of practical reason can offer a legitimate alternative to the traditional categories of foundationalism (both normative and ontological), assumes primary importance. I do not claim that constructivism is the *only* plausible solution to the problems with traditional IR theory identified by poststructuralism. Other forms of reconstructive normative theory (such as contemporary moral foundationalism[19]) are viable rejoinders to the poststructuralist challenge in their own right. My claim, however, is that the aim of philosophical constructivism – that is, to construct a robust and *legitimate* account of the nature and conditions of world politics through sophisticated conceptions of the justifying power of practical reason – imbues the theoretical model with a philosophical rigour and normative legitimacy which, in my contention, most forcefully transcends the challenge of poststructuralism.

I want to explore the idea that the very conditions of practical reasoning, and a conception of reasonableness more broadly, can do a tremendous amount of work in unlocking the essence of international relations. Such requires, I believe, a complex understanding of how the various strands of reasoning about practical issues in world politics – the legal, institutional and moral questions which face any true form of International Theory – can be combined within an appropriate philosophical framework which *can* present a reconstructive alternative to the anti-foundationalist conclusions of poststructuralism. My central contention is that the conditions of practicality, and an appropriate conception of reasonableness, can provide a legitimate justification for a conception of normative reasoning which combines a Rawlsian account of the idea of public reason with a Kratochwilian account of practical reason (the latter incorporating novel arguments as to why legal, institutional and moral reasoning can be subsumed within the ambit of practical reasoning with norms). By structuring a conception of normative reasoning in this way, I claim, a sophisticated understanding of international relations can be constructed through robust and legitimate means, with the potential to account for the complex ways in which the various elements of normative reasoning (legal, institutional, moral, practical) interact and cohere within a cohesive and justificatory philosophical framework.

I do not claim to offer a comprehensive trans-disciplinary analysis of international politics, law, morality and structure. Nor do I present a unified account of the realisation of all normative facets of international political theory (e.g. a categorical expression of principles of political justice; a fully developed theory of human rights). Nor, finally, do I suggest that the account of normative reasoning I explore and espouse herein is the only means by which to transcend poststructuralism. What I set out to achieve is a reanalysis of a particularly vociferous challenge to the traditional discipline of IR, and the responses inspired by such a challenge which I consider to most adequately capture a true understanding of the nature of world politics, from the perspective of contemporary debates. In particular, I want to consider the nature of contemporary international relations from a standpoint at which it is possible to combine a *philosophical* constructivism with a holistic *social*-constructivist account of the conditions of practical reason, in order to present a *viable* theory which combines important elements of the various theorists I consider, in order to ground a 'combined', trans-disciplinary, constructivist response. My claim that the ideas of reasonableness, public reason and the conditions of practicality provide the driving force behind a legitimate and appropriate account of the nature of international relations leads me to consider the conceptions of reasonableness and normative reason which form the subject matter of my book in close detail. A deep and detailed analysis of these elements of constructivism will, I believe, ground a sophisticated understanding of the most fundamental nature of contemporary international relations and, as Friedrichs and Kratochwil state, will 'release the enormous creative potential of practical reason and make it work for international relations scholarship'.[20]

Chapter-by-chapter outline

It may be helpful to set out in brief overview the various theoretical approaches I examine in each chapter as I articulate and attempt to find a robust solution to the challenge of poststructuralism.

In Chapter 1 I set out, in detail, the poststructuralist positions (primarily those of Ashley and Walker) which, I say, represent a far-reaching, viable challenge to the fundamental tenets of traditional IR theory. I set out the challenge in detail and consider the various theoretical techniques employed by traditional IR, which poststructuralism seeks to deconstruct. I also consider the antifoundationalist conclusions which Walker and Ashley draw in light of the challenges and critique they expound.

In Chapter 2 I go on to consider IR's most cohesive response to the challenge of poststructuralism – namely, the social constructivism of Alexander Wendt. Wendt's constructivism did much to challenge the structural-determinist assumptions on which the classic doctrines of IR – such as Realism and Idealism – were predicated. However, the fact that he attempted to combine a 'holist ontology' with a commitment to a scientific methodology means that Wendt's theory exemplifies a 'conventional' form of social constructivism – he challenges the deterministic elements of traditional IR theory from within its own methodological and epistemological frames of reference. This falls short, I claim, of truly overcoming the poststructuralist challenge. I then go on to consider the 'critical' constructivism of Friedrich Kratochwil. Kratochwil challenges Wendt's commitment to a conceptual distinction between ontology and epistemology, opting instead for an *intersubjective* understanding of the creation of structure and meaning in international relations. Kratochwil's theory is, I claim, genuinely far-reaching and contains far more critical potential by which to move beyond the stultifying disciplinary and methodological constraints which IR imposed on itself (even in responding to challenges to *precisely* these disciplinary and methodological constraints). However, the great benefit of considering these responses to poststructuralism *from the perspective of political theory (or, rather, from a perspective which can offer trans-disciplinary analyses)* is that, through such a perspective, it becomes clear that the problem with Kratochwil's theory *in itself* is that it cannot provide an appropriate philosophical framework by which claims to *moral*[21] authority can be afforded adequate justification *beyond* the context of normative structure. Given that, as I claim, a conception of normative reasoning must be contextualised and justified through an appropriate philosophical framework, it becomes imperative to broaden the remit of analysis and consider potential responses to the poststructuralist challenge provided by political theory.

In Chapter 3 I do just this – I consider the ability of a *constitutive* political theory, expounded by Mervyn Frost, to ground a robust, critical theory by which to transcend poststructuralism's nihilistic conclusions. Frost's normative theory is anchored around what he calls the 'settled norms of contemporary international relations' (claims to sovereignty; human rights, etc.), from which, he claims, an appropriate background theory can be derived which can offer a deep understanding of the nature of contemporary international relations. Frost argues that his chosen theory – the 'constitutive theory of individuality' – is the best and most coherent 'fit' with the most fundamental norms of contemporary international life, and is thus the most appropriate and justified means by which to ground an understanding of world politics. In the chapter I consider whether an understanding of international relations premised on, and derived from, the 'settled norms' really offers the most robust means by which to overcome the challenge of poststructuralism. I conclude that a 'coherence-based' form of philosophical justification does not contain the theoretical and critical strength required to truly circumvent the challenge expounded by Walker and Ashley.

Chapter 4 opens Part II of my book – an analysis of various positions on the nature and conditions of normative reasoning. In Chapter 4 I consider the ability of philosophical constructivism (specifically, Rawlsian political constructivism) to provide robust and legitimate means by which normative structure in international relations can be contextualised and justified. As stated above, my crucial claim is that the driving forces behind political constructivism are the related ideas of reasonableness and public/practical reason. The chapter comprises an extended exposition and consideration of Rawls' account of reasonableness, and the idea of public reason, in his *Political Liberalism*[22] and

The Law of Peoples[23] (concepts which will be familiar to any scholar of Rawls but which is vital groundwork to what follows herein). Rawls' ideas of reasonableness and public reason arguably represent the most sophisticated and fully developed accounts in the contemporary literature, and any analysis of contemporary political constructivism (Rawls' term for the *freestanding* form of philosophical constructivism he develops in *Political Liberalism* and *The Law of Peoples*) should (and usually does) begin with an analysis of Rawls.

I then go on in Chapter 5 to consider the critique of Rawls, and the *institutional* conception of human rights, adopted by Allen Buchanan. Buchanan's theory provides a sophisticated and comprehensive understanding of human rights theory which develops out of a consideration and critique of Rawls' ideas in *The Law of Peoples*. Crucially, Buchanan offers the key insight that, given the status of human rights in the contemporary legal and practical landscape of world politics, any comprehensive understanding of the nature of international relations *must* include an institutional component as part of its justificatory element, with an appropriate conception of institutional reasoning and sophisticated social epistemology. These arguments for an institutional justificatory component are convincing, and I certainly wish to take them seriously and explore means of adopting them herein. However, I ultimately argue that the normative basis for Buchanan's theoretical model functions in a foundationalist manner and *assumes* the acceptance of various liberal predicates on the part of his intended audience. While there is much value in an analysis of Buchanan's theory, and while Buchanan's foundationalist moral assumptions will certainly appeal to his explicit target audience (i.e. those who already accept the unjustified moral claims he asserts in developing his conception of normative justification), I ultimately contend that a combined constructivist conception of normative reasoning, backed by a sophisticated account of the concept of the reasonable, grounds a more robust and (in wide international terms) *legitimate* means by which to overcome the charges laid at International Relations by poststructuralism.

The final account of normative reason I focus on (in Chapter 6) is that of Kratochwil. The chapter is challenging (as any consideration of Kratochwil's complex theoretical position would be) but extremely fruitful. I consider in close detail Kratochwil's conception of practical reasoning which, based as it is on the conditions of reasoning with intersubjective norms, and the contextualising presence of *topoi*, commonplaces and analogies, subsumes conceptions of legal, moral and institutional reasoning within its general ambit. Kratochwil's account of the conditions of practical reasoning is instructive in that it allows the various facets of International Theory to be subsumed within one overriding theory of the nature of normative reason. I also argue that it can be effectively combined with the Rawlsian conception of public reason I previously examined. I work through the implications of this combined account of normative reason and argue that, by combining the Kratochwilian conception with the Rawlsian account, normative reason is imbued with a more fully fleshed-out account of the *moral* dimension of practical reason, and can be contextualised within a philosophical framework which, I contend, is appropriate for application to International Theory.

Finally, in Chapter 7 I consider in greater detail the Rawlsian concept of the reasonable which, I have argued, can form the basis on which a theoretical structure can be built and which contains the tools necessary to transcend the poststructuralist challenge. I begin with a reanalysis of the concept of the reasonable in Rawls, and focus in particular on the in-depth consideration and ultimate critique afforded to Rawls' idea of the burdens of judgement by Catriona McKinnon. McKinnon's work in political constructivism goes to the heart of Rawls' crucial conception of reasonableness, and her deep consideration of the 'demandingness' of the requirement that agents accept the burdens of judgement allows her to consider an alternative account of political constructivism oriented around a conception of self-respect. I consider McKinnon's constructivism, and the account of self-respect on which her theory is premised, in detail as I want to explore the strength of her argument that the requirement that agents respect the burdens of judgement renders Rawls' conception of reasonableness too demanding (in the technical sense adopted by McKinnon – i.e. a requirement of uniformity of belief in the reasons behind an acceptance of reasonable pluralism). McKinnon's arguments concerning self-respect, and her 'many flowers' interpretation of the reasons behind the fact of reasonable pluralism, are, I argue, built on acceptance of a substantive, 'primary good'-style argument as to the inherent value of self-respect and also necessitate complex considerations of attribute and evaluative preference to be built into McKinnon's conception of the agent.

I consider whether McKinnon is correct in her claim that her alternative conception of reasonableness grounds a form of political constructivism which is *less* demanding (in her sense) on agents than Rawls' conception (and, therefore, *more* appropriate to an understanding of international relations). By way of comparison, I consider the interpretation of Rawls' conception of reasonableness developed by Peri

Roberts. Roberts works out minimalistic conceptions of reasonableness and practical reason linked to the 'constraints of practicality' – the idea that practical reasoning should recognise and be responsive to the conditions within which it operates. His central claim is that a conception of practical reason (and a corresponding conception of reasonableness) can be developed from an account of the minimal requirements of practicality which can nevertheless ground an objective and authoritative means by which to construct justified principles of justice. Roberts considers arguments as to the potential limitations on reasoning (theoretical, practical and motivational, the latter of which incorporates an argument developed by Thomas Scanlon as to the inherent motivational qualities of reasons which I also wish to adopt) and provides convincing responses to them all. He then develops an account of the authority of reasoning which, I believe, renders his reading of Rawlsian constructivism *appropriate* and *legitimate* in grounding a theory of international relations, and which is to be preferred (in the context of a rejoinder to poststructuralism) to McKinnon's 'many flowers' account.

I conclude by claiming that, through a combination of the various elements of the theories I have considered, an inclusive and unified understanding of international relations can be built on a minimal but robust conception of reasonableness. The 'combined' conception of normative reasoning I describe in Chapter 6 can be supported by such, and thus the challenge of poststructuralism can, through a trans-disciplinary consideration of the inherent nature and conditions of practical reason within the normative structures of IR, and an appropriate conception of the reasonable, be effectively overcome.

Part I

The Challenge – Poststructuralism and IR's Responses

1
Inside/Outside: Walker, Ashley and the Poststructuralist Critique of IR

Richard Ashley claimed in 1996 that

> [i]f ever there was a field of discourse whose parties' every performance presupposes the necessity of thinking, acting and narrating political life in the service of some sovereign centre of decision that can at once represent and derive its powers from a familiar territory of its exclusionary being, international relations is surely it.[1]

This presupposition, though seemingly innocuous, became the target of poststructuralist attempts to problematise and recast the most inherent assumptions found within the field of International Relations theory which, I contend, has lost none of its potency in the intervening decade and a half. Specifically, the work of Richard Ashley and R.B.J. Walker (among others) is designed to expose the imaginative limitations of traditional attempts to categorise the domain of world politics through a radical attack on the foundationalist methodologies incorporated by a discipline co-existent with the modernist project. The pervasive nature of this postmodern critique stems from the targeting and deconstruction of those characterisations of world politics whose self-evidence seems indisputable, specifically, the world as a system of bounded sovereign states, the anarchical nature of the spaces between these states and the necessarily self-serving, calculating actions of the states which flow from this anarchy. While these characterisations are generally identified with the doctrine of Realism, postmodern theory is not confined to an attack on the traditionally dominant theory of IR: basic concepts of sovereignty, universalism and foundationalism, and the ahistorically privileged position granted to them, not only by Realism but also by more normative international theory, are fundamentally challenged.

These challenges allow an illumination into the ways in which IR theory itself becomes a form of power politics, through the creation of dichotomous extremes. As Cochran claims:

> In directing this critique to the constructions of contemporary international theory, these writers problematise the dominant understanding of IR as a world of sovereign states which demarcate inside from outside, order from anarchy, and identity and difference. More generally, they challenge the notion of sovereignty as an ahistorical, universal, transcendent concept, be it applied to the sovereign state, the sovereign individual or a sovereign truth.[2]

Taken to its extreme, this critique denies the very possibility of obtaining a privileged position from which to make universal claims about international politics or ethical judgement. Without state sovereignty, the traditional distinction between international and political theory (or the inside/outside distinction) cannot be maintained; without the sovereign individual, the traditional privileging of what Ashley calls the 'heroic' ideal of rational man is ungrounded, and without the possibility of sovereign truth, the epistemological privileging of some forms of knowledge above others is unjustified. In short, without sovereignty, political space is endless.

My purpose here is to elucidate this poststructuralist challenge to IR theory. It is not a challenge which is universally accepted as having any real importance amidst the debates of IR; Chris Brown, for example, dismisses Walker's work as an exercise in complication for complication's sake.[3] As I will go on to say, however, the postmodern challenge contains elements which go to the heart of IR theory, and which work to explain the tendency of IR to simplify, conservatise and at times exclude fundamental characteristics of world politics. Specifically, the contention that IR theory in actuality forms part of the historical fabrication of the domain it attempts to understand serves to critically reassess the creation of those apparently self-evident truths which traditional theory, particularly Realism, has served to perpetuate. Moreover, Realism's reliance on a perceived continuum (or, in Ashley's phrase, a 'monologue') of work which supposedly reinforces the central tenets of power politics through timeless political wisdom[4] is frustrated by both Walker[5] and William Connolly[6] through an attempt to identify those elements of the thinkers relied on by Realism which do not correspond with their supposedly rigid espousal of the 'realities' of power politics. This is a fascinating project which forms part of the poststructuralist attempt to highlight the historicised and contingent nature of all attempts to locate a sovereign point of reference or a fixed notion of textual interpretation, and the relation between them.[7] Walker, in particular, espouses a powerful critique and reanalysis of the concept of sovereignty as applied to the state, arguing that the apparently unquestionable presence of state sovereignty in any discussion of international relations arises from the universalisation of a particular spatiotemporal conception of sovereignty which turns out in actuality to be the product of a contingent historical imagination. If this critique of the concept of sovereignty is accepted, radical implications follow for the traditional distinction between international and political theory, with the opening up of the possibilities of political space and the blurring of the inside/outside dichotomy.

My claim is that the postmodernist critique of sovereignty and authoritative theoretical knowledge offers a relevant challenge to the more traditional theoretical approaches found in IR, and that this challenge necessitates the radical overhaul of the foundations relied on by these approaches, including examples of more normative IR theory. I specifically select the work of Walker and Ashley, as opposed to alternative versions of critical theory, as a means by which to consider the most vociferous and far-reaching theoretical challenge felt by the discipline of IR to date. The fact that the poststructuralism of Walker and Ashley has not been universally accepted as a legitimate challenge to the foundations of IR, I contend, means that systematic attempts to engage with and ultimately overcome the critique set down by these theorists have not been as comprehensive and forthcoming as is warranted by what I argue is a valid and radical attack on the discipline's most fundamental assumptions and commitments. Moreover, I want to suggest that the methodologies employed by certain IR theorists to try to overcome challenges such as this (particularly 'conventional' constructivism, which I will explore in Chapter 2), while containing much that is useful in opening the closed categories of traditional theory, represents a theoretical discourse still tied to those concepts it attempts to critique. In particular, Alexander Wendt's[8] brand of agency-focused constructivism formulates its own theoretical identity in terms of its relationship with Realism, thus perpetuating those dichotomies of inside/outside, domestic/international that poststructuralist theory seeks to problematise and ceding much ground to the Realist theory purportedly being criticised. More radical versions of constructivism, such as critical and holistic varieties,[9] gain far more critical purchase on the very foundations of Realism, but I will argue that it is precisely because they begin to develop theories which can effectively cohere with the more philosophical conceptions of international relations that they manage to overcome the gravitational pull of traditional characterisations of the nature of world politics. My central purpose will be to dispute the conclusion of poststructuralism that its critique of the wide concept of sovereignty (that is, sovereignty as applied to *any* attempt to privilege certain epistemological or ontological forms) necessarily leads to an acknowledgement of the impossibility of *any* legitimate means by which to ground an authoritative account of the conditions of international relations. Certain international political theories can function as a response to the poststructuralist challenge to IR by reformulating the possibility of sovereign knowledge through predicates which take seriously the poststructuralist insistence on contingency and the avoidance of the unjustified privileging of foundations which themselves turn out to be contingent. Chief among these, I will argue, is Rawls' constructivist formulation of the concepts of the reasonable and public reason. Rawls' constructivism is developed as a response to the contingency present in world politics (what Rawls conceives of as the 'fact of reasonable pluralism') – and recognises the intellectual violence done by attempting to deny that contingency and to assert one unequivocal metaphysical foundation to the construction of meaning and understanding in IR – but is not therefore resigned to an all-out scepticism about the possibility of grounding a critical yet legitimate construction of an understanding of world politics. The possibility of grounding a robust and legitimate normative theory of international relations, however minimal, will always remain a contentious issue between philosophical constructivism and postmodernism, but it is my intention to attempt to espouse a conception of the reasonable and an account of the conditions of practical reasoning which may avoid poststructuralist accusations of illegitimacy. The framework of Rawlsian constructivism, rooted in a conception of the reasonable, and working in conjunction with the more sophisticated and critical forms of constructivism in IR (most notably, I argue, the unique account of normative structure and the conditions of practical reasoning developed in complex detail by Friedrich Kratochwil) gives rise to an understanding of the nature of international relations which, I will argue, contains the tools necessary to genuinely overcome the critique directed at the discipline of International Relations by Walker and Ashley.

Knowledge as power

Walker claims:

> Theories of international relations...are interesting less for the substantive explanations they offer about political conditions in the modern world than as expressions of the limits of the contemporary political imagination when confronted with persistent claims about and evidence of fundamental historical and structural transformation.[10]

The years since *Inside/Outside* was published have done little to alter Walker's central complaint about the nature of theorising about international relations. In his 2010 book *After the Globe, Before the World,*[11] Walker claims:

> It is not that there is nothing to commend among at least some of the literatures claiming to be either politically realistic or ethically inspirational, especially those that find some way of refusing the overdetermining rhetorics counterposing the realistic to the normative. Nevertheless, both sorts of literatures have a bad habit of ignoring or crudely oversimplifying questions about what it means to claim political authority, and more specifically, what it means to make a claim to the forms of authority expressed by the modern sovereign state, and to knowledge about the forms of authority expressed by the modern sovereign state.[12];

And:

> [W]e are often overwhelmed by too much information, but also underwhelmed by scholarly traditions competing to interpret too many uneven and contradictory trends, often on the basis of overinflated claims about our capacity to decipher the causal secrets of the modern world and an underappreciation both of the clichéd character of the theoretical categories through which we are asked to make sense of empirical data, and of what it means to challenge the principles of modern sovereignty and subjectivity that are at work in these categories.[13]

Central to the poststructuralist methodology is an explicit analysis of the relationship between theory, history and power. An important point to note is that, in its critique of modernity, poststructuralism does not originate from an external point 'outside' of or independent to that which it criticises; hence the prefix 'post'. Its theoretical identity is constructed in relation to the subject matter of the critique, due to the acceptance by poststructuralism that modernist logic is not a definite theoretical voice with fixed boundaries, but an attempt to systematise a contingent world through the construction of sovereignty. The purpose or 'point' of the poststructuralist critique is to make explicit that which is implicit in International Relations theory.[14] This involves the dissection of the presumption, inherent in scientific methodologies within traditional IR, that the role of theory is to observe and explain an independent data set, a practice detached and separate from its subject matter, a complete break between theory and practice. Such a presumption is consistent with the self-perception inherent in much neo-Realist thought that it enjoys a consistent textual history through which its central propositions are reemphasised by an essentially homogenous literature. This perception is maintained, as poststructuralism claims, through a filtering process designed to attribute fixed textual meaning by the systematic universalisation of elements of a theory that support those propositions, and a systematic exclusion from consideration of those that do not. This process serves to turn the supposed 'heroes' of neo-Realism into, in Gregory's term, 'wraith-like caricatures',[15] writers whose sole conclusions are the espousal of Realism's particular brand of power politics.

The homogenisation of theory into a timeless political voice identifies a key modernist practice which poststructuralism seeks to fundamentally undermine. The elucidation of this process of logocentrism (a phrase lifted by Ashley from Jacques Derrida) provides a useful point of departure in considering the wide poststructuralist critique of international theory, which can then be applied to the specific practices of the cannon of IR. This procedure is directly related to the central tenets of the poststructuralist critique: the privileging of a sovereign point of reference and the normalisation of predicates which constrain and order a world which is essentially open and contingent. It is also directly related to the practice of narrow textual reading which excludes historicity or ambiguity from sources which poststructuralism claim are essentially historicised and ambiguous. The poststructuralist response to logocentrism – intertextuality – allows a useful point from which to feed into the narrow poststructuralist critique of sovereign practices in IR theory.

The procedure of logocentrism is elucidated in Ashley's seminal 'Living on Border Lines':

> the expectation that all interpretation and practice must secure recognition and power by appeal to some identical consciousness, principle of interpretation, or necessary subjectivity having at least two qualities. First, it is regarded as a central interpretive orientation – a coherent sovereign voice, if you will – that supplies a unified rational meaning and direction to the interpretation of the spatial and temporal diversity of history. Second, as a sovereign voice, this principle is itself regarded as a pure and originary presence – an unproblematic, extrahistorical identity, in need of no critical accounting.[16]

This explanation perfectly captures the processes of rationalisation and normalisation identified with the project of modernity and evident within the traditional development of IR theory. It applies to the project of ordering and interpreting history in a manner which systematises apparently random, system-less events in conformity with an overarching principle, universal criterion or fixed grounding. The power of this grounding-point to provide order and rationality to history, once established, allows it to achieve an authoritative status in that it becomes the referential point of history, systematising the overwhelming range of events and categorisations into fixed points in relation to the unifying ground. Poststructuralism claims that this process relies on the creation of opposing categories which rely for their conceptual identity on their negation relationship with the other. In other words, the modernist project of rationalisation necessarily creates a transcendental sovereign viewpoint, which comes to regard itself as being self-evident, through its opposition to a state of irrationality:

> It [logocentrism] inclines a participant to identify his voice of interpretation and practice with a subjective standpoint, a sovereign independent centre, from which one side in such oppositions can be seen as a higher reality, belonging to the domain of logos, or pure and indecomposable presence in need of no explanation.[17]

The sovereign voice created by this procedure is invariably that which tends towards rationalisation, hence, the creation of a dichotomy infused with hierarchy. This methodology, expressed in the dichotomy between domestic/international, then serves to *create* the very subject matter it purports to analyse, through the diametric relationship between the two apparently distinct spaces and the supposedly anarchical negation of the first, privileged term as located in the second. In this way, theory becomes a form of power politics, in its establishment of fixed boundaries and distinctions, by the imposition of a conception of sovereignty which it then insists is self-evident. As Walker and Ashley, in a discussion of the experience of marginality within modernist frames of reference, claim:

> [P]eople here confront arbitrary cultural practices that work to discipline ambiguity and impose effects of identity and meaning by erecting exclusionary boundaries that separate the natural and necessary domicile of certain being from the contingencies and change events that the self must know as problems, difficulties, and dangers to be exteriorised and brought under control. Here, in other words, power is not negative and repressive but positive and productive. Practices of power do not deny the autonomy of subjects already present so much as they work to impose and fix ways of knowing and doing that shall be recognised as natural and necessary to autonomous being. They work to produce effects of presence, of identity, of a territorial ground and origin of meaning. And they work by discriminately reading and representing ambiguous circumstances to impose differences between that which may be counted as the certainty of presence and that which must be regarded as the absence beyond its bounds.[18]

Poststructuralist methodology in relation to this practice is to explicate this form of knowledge–power relation, and crucially, its relation (or anti-relation) to both history and politics. Logocentrism, claims poststructuralism, is committed to the characterisation of history and politics as the negative constituent of a dichotomous relation with sovereignty. The sovereign reference point which the modernist project is concerned to identify and espouse is in direct opposition to the categories of history and politics which constrain human action through their limitless possibilities and endless contingency, and which the role of theory is to transcend:

> Given an undecidable diversity of contesting interpretive possibilities, a logocentric discourse is inclined to impose closure by resorting to one or another fixed standard of interpretation that is itself accorded the status of a pure and identical presence – a standpoint and standard supposedly occupying a place outside of history and

> beyond politics from which it is possible to give voice to a singular interpretation of the historical and political differences perceived.[19]

Poststructuralism seeks to challenge this inclination both through textual, and historical, reanalysis. *Intertextuality*, as it has been described, is a reanalysis designed to expose the modernist-based processes by which a particular textual interpretation comes to be characterised as authoritative, and the corresponding effect this has on the categories of analysis of the social world. As Der Derian claims:

> an intertextual strategy attempts to understand the placement and displacement of theories, how one theory comes to stand above and silence other theories, but also how theory as a knowledge practice has been historically and often arbitrarily separated from 'events', that is, the materially inspired practices comprising the international society.[20]

This deconstruction of the theory–practice divide has profound implications for the analysis of 'reality' in international relations. If the poststructuralist theorists succeed in their task of identifying an interdependence between the analysis and practice of international relations, they will also succeed in their claim that the arbitrary normalisation of a particular set of categories of analysis has profound implications not only for the theory of IR, but also the domain of world politics as interpreted as a practice.

This project is fundamentally linked to the textual reanalysis offered by poststructuralists. Textual deconstruction in intertextuality is designed to perform a number of inter-related tasks: to consider the practices which allow a particular theoretical discourse to obtain sovereign status; to open the closed categories of interpretation associated with a particular text or tradition; and, as stated above, to explicate the link between homogenisation in textual interpretation and practices of legitimisation. One particularly illuminating strand of intertextuality is concerned with the relation between legitimisation and the putatively homogenous tradition (or, as George refers to it, Tradition) of classical work. This Tradition, generally claiming Thucydides, Machiavelli and Hobbes among its number, is invoked by neo-Realists as an account of reality which transcends the contingencies of historicity and spatiality to form a universal monologue. Scientific methodology is highlighted and espoused, logic is invoked, and simplicity is admired. The presence of this canonical Tradition has become a crucial factor in the processes by which Realism, and the categories used by it, became the authoritative discourse in International Relations theory, as it is through the interpretation of these texts that the theoretical trends with which Realism comes to identify itself (state/anarchy, domestic/international etc.) are perpetuated through the apparently rigid interpretation available here. Walker emphasises the significance of the Tradition to the evolution of International Relations theory thus:

> Contemporary explorations of world politics commonly begin by invoking a tradition, a starting point from which historical trajectories, theoretical innovations and future aspirations may be charted and judged. Appeals to this tradition of political realism underwrite the rituals through which students are introduced to the theory of international relations, and thus disciplined both to think of the realities of relations between states as fundamentally different from life within states and to repudiate hopes for a future free from the tragic necessities of power politics.[21]

A number of poststructuralist theorists have attempted to draw attention to the stultifying interpretive method that this homogenising technique entails. Crucially, as George notes:

> [t]he aim here has not been to dismiss the dominant readings but to illustrate that they are, indeed, *readings* – that they can be read in different ways and that their status is derived not from any correspondence with an essential (real) meaning but from a discursive strategy intrinsically connected to a dominant form of (sociohistorical) knowledge and power.[22]

Poststructuralism does not seek to deny the relevance of the particular textual interpretations applied by neo-Realism, or anyone else for that matter. It merely seeks to draw attention to the fact that interpretive possibilities are open, that alternative interpretations are generally allowable in instances where they can be supported and that interpretation goes a long way towards shaping the sovereign terrain of the text, as object, and political realm, as subject. The elucidation of a practice of textual homogenisation cannot alone serve to destroy the foundations of a theoretical discourse, but it can serve to explicate the processes involved in practices of normalisation, particularly when the discourse in question is driven by the supposed force of an intellectual Tradition which is in complete internal agreement. To that end, George considers the textual reinterpretation of the defining moment of the Realist project, Thucydides's *History of the Peloponnesian War*, articulated in the work of Michael Doyle and Hayward Alker:

> [I]n *The History of the Peloponnesian War* Thucydides specifically rejects the notion of general (structuralist) laws capable of explaining international conflict.[23]

Doyle notes that, despite a certain reading of Thucydides's work which would espouse the structurally determined power-politics evident in neo-Realist thought, his overarching conclusions conflict with the very possibility of a structurally determined basis for international conduct.[24] Thus the 'wraithlike caricature' of Thucydides as the original structural realist is, claims poststructuralism, based on a particular reading of his work which, through processes of reductionism, homogenises the interpretive scope of the work to conform with the minimalist tenets of neo-Realism.

Kenneth Waltz, intertextuality and sovereignty in international relations

The above discussion has attempted to locate the origins of the poststructuralist critique of the categories traditionally used by International Relations theory in an attempt to contextualise and reanalyse the major works of the discipline and their foundational status in considering the logic of theorising about anarchy and structural determinacy. In particular, this strategy explicates the processes by which interpretive homogenisation serves to influence the categorisation of the epistemological reality received by IR theory, processes by which knowledge itself forms a crucial yet subtle part of the practices of *realpolitik*. The apparent existence of a linear monologue of traditional work aids this process by establishing and fixing the boundaries of authorised interpretation; as Walker notes, 'accounts of a tradition serve to legitimise and circumscribe what counts as proper scholarship'.[25] Clearly, an antecedent normative system is behind these practices, one that goes to the heart of the traditional configuration of IR theory, and serves to demarcate what is relevant and legitimate in both international theory and practice. This is the very normative system at work in the establishment of sovereign practices and the anchoring of those practices in a particular theoretical premise, or, even more fundamentally, in a particular conceptualisation of the categories of reality which exist. The crucial claim of the poststructuralist challenge to IR is that this normative system is itself contingent; that is, it is rooted in a particular cultural location and that it bears no universalisable justification. The means by which this system effectively 'hides' its own existence is part and parcel with the legitimisation of its particular brand of epistemological outlook.

The effects of this relationship between knowledge and power, and the establishment of a fixed sovereign space comprising both, are elucidated in Ashley's important consideration of Waltz's classic neo-Realist works *Man, the State and War* and *Theory of International Politics*.[26] This analysis represents not only an attempt to engage in an intertextual reading of a classic theorist in the tradition of neo-Realism, but moves further in considering the dichotomous and co-dependent nature of the nature of sovereign/non-sovereign practices in the vast cannon of IR thought. Waltz's discussions of the objective requirements of a system characterised by anarchy ('third-image' neo-Realism) provide prime examples of the means by which historicity and contingency are conceptualised as being in dichotomous contrast with the sovereign category of rationality and territorial certainty, yet each being co-dependent with the other. The title of the primary work, *Man, the State, and War*, indicates the subjects within which these sovereign conceptualisations manifest themselves:

> On the one side, at the beginning of the title, there is the sign of man: modern man, man as the ideal of a well-bounded rational identity, man who would assert his mastery over history and who would occupy the attentions of modern social science. On the other side, opposing the sign of man, there is the sign of war: an aleatory domain of history that escapes the controlling influence of man's reasoned narratives and that is known as dangerous, violent, and, therefore, anarchic. The thesis thus starts with a man/war hierarchical opposition, where the former term, man, is privileged over the latter term, war. Man is taken to be a prior rational identity – an originary presence – and the domain of anarchy and war is then known *only* in terms of its lack of rational identity, that is, as a recalcitrant domain of difference that is still to be subdued by the sovereign figure of reasoning man.[27]

Given this conceptualisation of sovereign reality, 'the state' occupies a position at the margins of this sovereign/non-sovereign dichotomy. The state may be aligned with the sovereign figure of rational man, as it is both legitimised by him/her, as well as providing the fixed, bounded space within which this rationality can be given territoriality. Domestic political space is thus rooted in the sovereign interpretation of rationality and transcendence, thus becoming a sovereign category in itself. The spaces between the boundaries of domestic politics, whose characteristics are synonymous with anarchy and war, form the flip-side to the construction of sovereign identity. These opposing categories are mutually co-dependent because, argues Ashley, it is only through the attempt to transcend the contingencies of history and anarchy that the sovereign nature of rationality is imbued with a purpose. In other words, rationality is made sovereign through those elements that constitute it which are in direct contrast to its counterpoint. Ashley's point is that understanding this knowledge practice is vital, because '[e]xplicitly or implicitly, the knowledgeable practice that structures *Man, the State and War* appears and reappears in all the far reaches of modern culture'.[28] It is the historicity of man which is invoked as the negative signifier, always juxtaposed against the transcendent, conquering characterisation of rationality and order. Ashley claims:

> Those events and limitations that can be assimilated to a figure of man can be recognised to be *of* the space of man, the identical space of domestic society subordinate to the state. And those events and limitations that resist assimilation – that threaten to transgress and put in doubt the limitations on knowing and doing that are taken to be essential to man – are *then* known, and known only, as the dangerous Other to man, to domestic society, and to the state whose reason is grounded in the reason of man. The logocentric procedure works, then, because it defers to the very end of this progression an encounter with the historicity of man and because, when it finally makes this encounter, it permits the historicity of man to be known only under the signs of anarchy and war, as a fearsome external field of contingency and chance that must be brought under control in the name of man.[29]

It is through this logocentric process that the domestic–international distinction, so crucial to the categorisation of world politics which traditional IR theory is so fundamentally based on, is invested with the extremes of meaning that characterise its function. The rational becomes sovereign through Walker's 'questions no longer taken seriously'; that is, through a self-perpetuating method whereby attempts to question rationality's sovereign status are associated with the anarchical negative, and thus treated with distrust:

> At the very moment one moves to question it, the procedure stifles questioning with its already prepared answer: You want to raise the question of the historicity of man, it says, but to do so you must be against man and therefore on the side of war and anarchy... You are why the state's means of violence are needed.[30]

Ashley's reanalysis of Waltz's later work *Theory of International Politics*, a work generally ascribed to the same monological tradition as *Man, the State and War*, is an attempt to identify the processes at work in neo-Realist/traditional claims of permanence, transcendence and ahistorical wisdom in the formulation of the reality of International Relations:

> Waltz, or anyone else imposing this framework, must suppose the ability to rely upon some generally recognised and unproblematic constitutive principle, some determinate rule of differentiation, that would allow one to decide, unambiguously, what shall count as the definite presence of a hierarchical centre of rational decision and what shall count as the absolute boundaries separating the 'within' of its domestic domain from the 'without' of the anarchy that escapes its sway.[31]

Thus, given the range of epistemological claims which could be invoked as an unproblematic (or post-problematic) foundational assertion concerning the nature of the reality received by International Relations theory, Waltz's incorporation of the inside/outside distinction necessarily relies on a sovereign principle which transcends epistemological contingency and produces meaning attributable to reality. This sovereign principle turns out to be the 'ambiguous place that modern culture reserves for a determinate figure of reasoning man whom, in all its variants, it is prepared to place at the centre of its narratives of history'.[32] This space is legitimated in the cultural practices that unanimously locate it as the foundational point of departure for the sovereign systems of knowledgeability that form the basis of 'serious' discourse about the social world. As such, it assumes the status of a 'norm', requiring no special justification or even an explicit reference towards the processes at work in the creation of these characterisations. Through his discussion of what he terms 'transversal struggles' (conflicts which cannot be characterised in terms of fixed, bounded sovereign spaces because they are intimately concerned with the relation of knowledge practices to power), Ashley outlines his crucial point concerning the means by which the dichotomous relationships traditionally categorise IR:

> [A] paradigm of sovereign man, far from being a pure and autonomous source of history's meaning, is never more than an *effect* of indeterminate practical struggles in history. It is to see the figure of man as an effect that is always resisted, always an effect that might not happen, and, therefore, always an effect in the process of being imposed, resisted, and reimposed, often in transformed form.[33]

In exposing the knowledge–power relationship and epistemological ordering inherent in Waltz's characterisation of the reality of world politics, Ashley's claim is that traditional IR theory has excluded from possible discourse any attempt to assert the historically contingent nature of the foundational practices relied on in asserting the sovereignty of any particular discourse. To imbue the inside–outside distinction and its corresponding categories with the meanings it must carry in order to create conformity of meaning enough to proceed with a transcendent discourse of international relations, foundationalist approaches which need, but lack, philosophical justification, are subconsciously adopted. Ashley identifies the aim of poststructuralism in IR as the identification and espousal of the contingent and historicised elements of these attempts to fix a definite, sovereign space for the theoretical viewpoint. Poststructuralist writings, he claims, 'far from pronouncing a stern no to this [logocentric] model, have in fact been content to exemplify a respect for the contingency, the historicity, the utter paradoxicality of every attempt to bend action and events to assertions of its absolute hegemony'.[34] Hence the 'post' in poststructuralism: the critique is conducted from within the processes of sovereignisation that it concerns, its role being to identify the historical and spatial nature of any such process in a world characterised by necessarily contingent epistemological debates.

Walker's *Inside/Outside* arrives at similar conclusions through a complex analysis of the traditional categories of International Relations. It is in the processes by which rationality becomes sovereign that Walker locates the importance of the principle of state sovereignty to traditional IR theory:

> I want to show how... [the] general sense of dissatisfaction must become especially acute when the historically specific

> understandings of space and time that inform the primary categories and traditions of international relations theory are challenged by speculations about the accelerative tendencies of contemporary political life. The most important expression of these understandings, indeed the crucial modern political articulation of all spatiotemporal relations, is the principle of state sovereignty.[35]

Here Walker is concerned to apply the intertextual approach to the principle of state sovereignty, and its central application in the theory of International Relations. Walker's claim is that sovereignty has assumed an unproblematic and crucial part of the analysis of world politics due to the desire to transcend the presence of spatial, temporal and epistemological uncertainties, and to order the world into clearly demarcated unitary systems which may affirm and maintain the inside–outside distinction. This is a continuation of the approach previously considered in relation to textual analysis; it is simply applied 'outwards' to consider the constructed nature of a category which has come to be reified and treated as unproblematic. The overarching problem with the reification of sovereignty is, claims Walker, that if one examines the intellectual processes by which the category developed, it may be identified as a normative response to a certain historical moment in political history:

> The primary resolution of this late-medieval and early modern struggle to free accounts of political life from the hierarchical incorporation of particularity into an overarching universalism – while also preserving the possibility that particularity might still be reconciled with a reconceptualisation of what universality entails – appears with the principle of state sovereignty. It embodies an historically specific account of ethical possibility in the form of an answer to questions about the nature and location of political community. Specifically, the principle of state sovereignty offers both a spatial and a temporal resolution to questions about what political community can be, given the priority of citizenship and particularity over all universalist claims to a common human identity.[36]

Thus the principle of state sovereignty perpetuates a distinction between internal 'politics', through which philosophical doctrines may be universalisable, and external 'relations', through which there may only be contingency but which offers the possibility for the existence of the universal. This, Walker considers, is the origin of the problematic relationship between questions of ethics and questions of international relations. The problematic is characterised by the politics–relations distinction which renders the latter susceptible to the contingencies of epistemological, and thus normative, disagreement, and provides a qualitative break between the two by which the latter is constituted as being fundamentally distinct and irresolvable with the former. Walker's claim is that state sovereignty is conceived by IR theory as both a question and an answer, that is, both as an originating source of questions of normativity in the international realm, and an answer, already expressed within its ontological categorisation, that ethical possibility is situated solely in the sovereign realm of politics. Thus, in affirming the transcendent nature of state sovereignty, International Relations affirms this normative break between politics and 'mere' relations. Put simply, '[i]nterpreted as an ethics of absolute exclusion, the theory of state sovereignty is an ethical principle that denies the applicability of ethical principles beyond a certain bounded space'.[37] The 'specified and reified' nature of the principle, while usually located within some combination of empirical assertion along with claims to normative transcendence and inevitability, coordinates with Ashley's claim that, given the vast evidence that the rigidity of the bounded view does not, in fact, accord with reality, it makes little sense to treat it as an unproblematic category. Walker asserts that the problem created by this reification has much to do with the equation of the problem of sovereignty in international relations with the particular form of sovereignty actualised in the principle of state sovereignty:

> [O]ne consequence, among many, of failures to make such an elementary distinction has been a pervasive discourse about the eternal presence or imminent absence of sovereign states: national or supranational, polis or cosmopolis, the need for multilevel governance, and so on. This discourse reproduces a specific framing of all questions about immanence/transcendence, universality/particularity, liberty/security and self/other expressed in the aporetic relationship between the claims of a sovereign state and the claims of the system of sovereign states that enables the claims of any sovereign state. This aporetic relationship... already assumes a distinction between the world of modernity and any other possible world, thereby rendering impossible any alternative to that specific structuring of norms and alternatives that might make claims to a 'world politics'. The limits expressed by claims to state/states-system sovereignty thus express both the limits of the political and the limits of the modern.[38]

It is this break between the limits and categories of that conception of sovereignty expressed in modern notions of *state*-sovereignty, and the systemic repercussions this entails, and alternative categorisations of sovereignty/politics that allows international relations theory to perpetuate as unproblematic the foundational discourse on which it relies. An attempt to intertextualise and deconstruct the isolation of the specific interpretation of sovereignty bound up with the principle of state sovereignty is, according to Walker, to reintroduce the possibility that ethical discourse may transcend the politics–relations distinction. The claim is that, traditionally, any analysis of the category of sovereignty could not transcend its association with the modern state, due to the processes of interpretive homogenisation already considered: 'the state came to be framed as an ahistorical category subject to the eternal laws of a political realism that was, some said, already perfectly understood by classical Greek historians like Thucydides'.[39] It is this privileging of the state as a transcendental presence in the spatiotemporal reality of politics that led to the establishment of an imaginatively fixed and closed category of state sovereignty, and with it the normatively crucial distinctions associated with international relations as a discipline distinct from politics. Walker's claim is that those contributions to the traditional field of International Relations that seek to highlight the historical processes at work behind the analysis of international relations, although containing much that is useful, necessarily serve to perpetuate the categorisations which stultify the possibility of ethics in the international realm because of their fundamental acceptance of the principle of state sovereignty. Specifically, attempts at normative IR theory which incorporate Hedley Bull's efforts to categorise the historical developments at work in the society of states which uncritically accept the principle of state sovereignty and the conceptual baggage accompanying such are constrained in the 'classification and typology' they must accept. These theories include, claims Walker, Terry Nardin's extension of Michael Oakeshott's practical form of political association to the creation of durable relations between states, Kratochwil's analysis of the development of those norms that constitute the 'rules of the game', and even elements of Ashley or Der Derian's poststructuralism which, allegedly, reinterpret elements of Bull's system of typology. Walker's claim is that these critical attempts to move beyond the 'Great Debate' mindset and characterisation of IR do some of the required work, but that they are limited in their acceptance of the categorisation of 'political' community as the limited space within which ethical possibility is established:

> [S]o much of the recent literature on the need for a more critical theory of international relations has emphasised the need to break with the discursive strategies that affirm a logic of same and different, inside and outside, pluralist and universalist, history and structure, theory/purpose and practice, friend and foe. But it is not enough to break with this logic in thinking about the principle of state sovereignty as a primary question or problematic that demands a resolution through some kind of international, or more accurately, inter-state society. It is also necessary to break with it in thinking about the more fundamental questions about political community to which the principle of state sovereignty has provided the conventional answer for so long.[40]

On this interpretation, the processes of reification bound up with the principle of state sovereignty extend far further than the principle itself, and begin to form the backdrop for the entire epistemological history of International Relations. Walker's crucial claim is that attempts to open up the political space which has been fundamentally closed by the reification of state sovereignty will be severely limited if they continue to affirm the authorising processes of spatiality/temporality which perpetuate the characterisation of the *political* (as a category in contrast to the *relational*) as the fixed arena within which ethical possibility may be maintained. On this reading, Walker's critique of sovereignty extends far further than simply a critique of neo-Realism. It has profound implications for those *normative* theories of international relations which, despite refuting some of the more structuralist claims of neo-Realism, still continue to affirm the categories of reality affirmed though the mantra of the 'Great Debate'. In other words, words most appropriate to the range of normative responses to the Realist–Idealist axis, refutations which perpetuate the distinctions between political–relational, inside–outside, or however else one wants to put it, serve to perpetuate the crucial processes of knowledge *as* power which have come to characterise and legitimise the dominant discourses of IR, and which form the bedrock of the poststructualist critique of sovereignty as a limiting category. Walker claims that

> [f]ar from being merely one of a series of debates that have characterised the history of the discipline, the distinction between political realism and political idealism has provided the broad, but severely restricted context within which other disputes about appropriate

> method or the priority of state-centred accounts of world politics could occur at all.[41]

Those accounts of world politics which follow Bull's method of typology serve to perpetuate this 'restricted context' by legitimating and demarcating the limits of political space through 'compromise positions' between the two. In affirming, however subconsciously, the reification of the epistemological outlook of the limiting-sovereign discourse of IR, theories which purport to critique the basis of traditional theory actually form legitimations of the parameters of international thought. By situating critique within the confines of the political–relational distinction, the distinction itself is placed beyond critique; the real business of critique is here seen as attempts to dispute the empirical or normative conclusions of 'Great Debate' theories.

Examples of the theories Walker has in mind in his critique of IR's use of the principle of state sovereignty include those attempts in the 1970s and 1980s to arrive at a normative analysis of world politics, generally framed in questions regarding the direction within which any change will take:

> With the claim to state sovereignty having been suitably externalised and naturalised, reified as the spatiotemporal ground of all political possibilities and impossibilities, the question of whether the sovereign-nation-state was here forever or about to depart this earth in a steady journey to some other kind of politics could also seem perfectly natural, and became a constant background to discussions of possible and impossible futures.[42]

Thus normative analysis proceeded from the firmly rooted spaces already established by the knowledgeable processes of the discipline and, while remaining important alternatives to the logic of the more traditional theory, necessarily conducted themselves from foundations which were unvindicated. In this vein, Stanley Hoffmann's *Duties Beyond Borders*[43] and Terry Nardin's *Law, Morality and the Relations of States*[44] remain classic examples of normative theoretical critiques of the stark claims of neo-Realism which affirmed the normalised practices of space and time as associated with the principle of state sovereignty. Thomas Pogge, in fact, picked up on just this sort of criticism of Hoffmann's work (in particular) in his claim that 'the differences Hoffmann sees between himself and the new global liberals are more apparent than real, that his recommendations can be accommodated almost entirely within the framework he attacks'.[45] Pogge is here referring to Hoffmann's claims that projects which attempt to construct principles of international justice are essentially meaningless given the constraining power of international anarchy in limiting the usefulness of ethical principles. Although not specifically referring to the poststructuralist challenge to IR, Pogge identifies a key problematic in the relationship between normative theory which asserts the spatial logic of the relational and those theories through which that logic became conceptualised as unproblematic. Pogge's assertion – that the limitations of the system as currently conceived necessitate attempts to construct principles of justice which transcend that system – does not explicitly contain elements of epistemological importance. However, I will want to argue that Pogge is (here) concerned with a form of international political theory which transcends the traditional IR attempts at prescription by rooting itself in foundations which take seriously, and contain the ability to answer, the poststructuralist critique of sovereign practices in IR, and which therefore attempt to locate grounds which do not perpetuate those practices. Such theoretical attempts do not legitimate the political–relational distinction associated with IR's incorporation of the specific form of state sovereignty constituted as the authoritative principle of world politics, but instead transcend that distinction by privileging grounds far more sophisticated in terms of the poststructuralist identification of the presence of contingency in any political analysis. Crucially, I will argue that those minimal foundations espoused by certain philosophical constructivists (chiefly John Rawls) contain the potential to provide an answer to the antifoundationalism required by critical poststructuralism – an antifoundationalism which requires that *any* process of legitimisation will be unvindicated, and any attempt to transcend spatiotemporal historicity provides a form of logocentric restriction on political imagination. It is to this antifoundational element of the poststructuralist critique that I now turn.

Non-foundations, anti-epistemology

In the special edition of *International Studies Quarterly* (Speaking the Language of Exile: Dissidence in International Studies, 34(3), September 1990) Ashley and Walker claim:

> The 'resolutions' to the problem of sovereignty proffered by texts or discourses can only be unstable and tentative. They are *unstable* because the texts or discourses that would enact such 'resolutions'

> cannot really be rid of the paradoxes of space, time, and identity that become visible in crisis and that the texts or discourses purport to solve. The margins of these texts or discourses always involve the arbitrary deployment of cultural resources in the performance of the paradoxical moves just mentioned – moves which, were they taken seriously, would undo the supposedly central logic by which a 'resolution' is made to seem certain and final. Such 'resolutions' are *tentative* because texts or discourses are able to postpone serious and unsettling attention to their marginal performance of these moves only so long as the moves themselves are received in an attitude of immediate and unquestioning familiarity, as that which goes without saying. With the unfolding of a crisis of representation – with time, change, the acceleration of activity, and the transgression of institutional limitations hitherto unquestioned – the themes, postures, words, and images that might once have elicited such a spontaneous and unquestioning reception are no longer able to do so. No longer self-evident, they become strange, of dubious validity, and subject to dispute in terms of their pretensions to truth. As this is so, the arbitrary marginal moves that a text or discourse undertakes through the development of these cultural resources take on a certain transparency, becoming immediately visible as the paradoxical moves they are. And when this happens, the supposed 'resolution' at the supposed centre of a text – always dependent upon the paradoxical moves at its margins – comes to be seen as no resolution at all. Paradox displaces the paradigmatic 'resolution'. Crisis surfaces. And wherever religious desire moves, the paradoxical problem of sovereignty announces itself anew.[46]

This lengthy passage is worth quoting due to what it reveals about Ashley and Walker's views regarding the *possibility* of authoritative knowledge in world politics. Only through an understanding of the radical scepticism embodied by these poststructuralist thinkers is it possible to unlock their claims to antifoundationalism (or, more precisely, non-foundationalism). These claims arise out of the critique I have examined above, and have profound implications for the entire history of international thought. The contention, shared with certain other proponents of antifoundationalism such as Richard Rorty,[47] that attempts to claim an authoritative status for any fixed space, time, discourse or grounding criterion are necessarily arbitrary serve to clear the way for the poststructuralist espousal of non-foundationalist contingency, but, unlike Richard Rorty, theorists such as Walker and Ashley do not locate the possibility of ethical discourse in either pragmatism or a 'hierarchy of sentiments'. Rather, it is located in an 'ethics of marginality', which, as we shall see, must profoundly change the way we conceptualise ethics if it is to be regarded as ethics at all. What I will want to argue in subsequent chapters is that, although the poststructuralist attack on sovereignty requires a radical reanalysis of the foundational categorisation of the discipline, it does not entail the radical antifoundationalism described in this section. Rather, it requires a constructivism which takes the poststructuralist critique seriously, which can accommodate the presence of contingency, and which can avoid those processes of normalisation and legitimisation which characterise traditional IR theory, but which may also form a point of departure for the possibility of considering more than questions of epistemology, the possibility of speaking about the issues of world politics, and the possibility of legitimate normative structure in international relations.

Molly Cochran locates what appears to be a paradox in the non-foundationalist method of the poststructuralist critique, the desire to engage with the issue of ethics in international relations alongside an assertion of the limitations of ethical theory as embodying processes of legitimisation of sovereign knowledge, characterised by

> the imposition and observance of limitations that can themselves be unambiguously defined and justified from the standpoint of a sovereign centre of judgement that commands a space, authenticates what is valuable and good within, defines alien and dangerous modes of thought and conduct to be excluded, and is itself beyond question.[48]

The paradox inherent in the presence of this dual aim requires a radical overhaul of the conceptualisation of what is required by ethics in the international realm, so that the foundationalist methodology whereby a particular set of considerations comes to be constituted as authoritative and legitimate may be avoided (the thrust of the poststructuralist project). Given the assertion in the extended quote above that the critique of sovereignty applies to *all* attempts to ground claims to knowledge in some sovereign spatiality, identifiable by its relationship with that which it is not, ethics must, according to Ashley and Walker, be located in 'marginality'. Given the illegitimacy inherent in all attempts to subvert contingency by characterising certain claims as sovereign-truth, moral claims must originate in a non-space, which explicitly avoids the claim that it represents some privileged ground from which to identify what is true, due to the fact that 'it is impossible to be blind to the active labour of marginalising paradoxes of space, time, and identity that threaten to undo every pretence that one might speak a sovereign voice of a discipline, a paradigm, a community, or a culture'.[49] Marginality is just such a non-space, a firm denial of the processes of reification which create sovereign discourses; indeed, it is a rejection of the very possibility of sovereign discourse, or sovereign truth. What it requires, as regards the possibility of ethical claims, is a 'celebratory register of freedom'. Ethics must be conducted from a non-place which 'affirms and exploits ambiguity, uncertainty, and the transgressability of institutional boundaries'[50] in which ethical claims may realise their own contingency and historicity, and from which objective epistemology is not only no longer possible; it is no longer needed. This non-foundation, claim Ashley and Walker, does not embody a denial of the possibility of ethical discourse, as it is only if one equates ethical claims with the objectively bounded, sovereign centre of judgement that one would render the celebratory register of freedom incapable of supporting just the kind of limited claims to moral discourse that the poststructuralists hope to challenge. What is needed is a liberation of the characterisation of ethical discourse that has stultified normative theory (particularly the category of international normative theory, so bound up with the politics–relations distinction). While open to the critique that this conception of ethical discourse excludes the possibility of truly authoritative moral claims, Ashley and Walker claim that the very paradoxicality of the traditional conception of morality necessitates this reconceptualisation:

> In the discipline of international studies and in general, to be practically effective any semblance of a sovereign centre to which ethical discourse might be referred depends upon the *forgetting* of the ongoing labour of marginalising those ambiguities, uncertainties, and contesting interpretations that would even now undo or disrupt the pretence of sovereign certitude. As this is so, any understanding of disciplined, ethical conduct that would aspire to cast all activities in the clarifying light of a sovereign centre of universal judgement – in the light of some given consensus, for example, or some cannon for the production of consensus – ironically depends upon the exemption of certain activities from the critical, juridical light to which it would refer.[51]

Ashley and Walker also attack the privileging of grounded ethical discourse as itself a form of sovereign reification, which necessarily conceptualises the celebratory register of freedom as the Other counterpoised against the sovereign space. The claim is that traditional conceptions of morality have always privileged those grounded truth claims which may assert their authority over other claims because of their situation within some sovereign territoriality, be it rationality or anything else. Ashley and Walker refute that claim, asserting that it necessarily carries with it epistemologically constructed meanings which cannot themselves be justified. In order to avoid these kinds of legitimation practices, ethical discourse must be conducted from that space which does not locate itself within some fixed sovereign territory, but which takes the challenge of contingency seriously and reflects that contingency in a celebration of freedom. Cochran's claim is that

> clearly, this is not an ethics in any comprehensive or *strong* foundationalist sense, yet it remains questionable whether it represents a non-universalised or a non-foundationalist ethics.[52]

The important point to extract from this assertion is that this form of poststructuralist non-foundationalist method represents a critique more than anything else. It attacks modernist/foundationalist notions of epistemology and ethics, but it appears as if the celebratory register of freedom has little to say of any substantive nature about ethical discourse. Of course, the celebration of freedom could itself feed into claims about democracy, perhaps, or pluralism. But then Ashley and Walker would be deriving substantive ethical claims from a standpoint which, apparently, refuses to privilege *any* ethical discourse as being grounded on predicates located in sovereign territoriality. The crucial questions to ask, when considering this critique, is are foundations located in contingency thus non-foundations, or is it possible to provide a privileged standpoint which arises from, and takes seriously, the presence of contingency?

In the subsequent chapters, I will be concerned with these epistemological questions. I wish to examine the claim that the poststructuralist challenge of IR necessarily requires a non-foundationalist methodology, or whether it is possible to assert the grounded status of ethical claims as privileged, distinct from the merely contingent. The poststructuralist critique demands a radical overhaul of how the connection between theory, epistemology and morality has been traditionally conceived in International Relations theory – the challenge now is to move beyond critique, to reach a place where constructive claims can be made about world politics.

2
Overcoming the Poststructuralist Critique?
Ontology and Epistemology in the Constructivist Theories of Wendt and Kratochwil

In the last chapter I provided an analysis of the poststructuralist challenge to the discipline of International Relations as propounded by Ashley and Walker. The fundamental point espoused by that critique is, I argued, that the discipline of IR is built on covert normative foundations which serve to construct and perpetuate dichotomised categories of rationality/anarchy and which exclude the philosophical space required to challenge the basis on which these processes of dichotomisation (through which rationality comes to form the dominant side of the coin) occur. This is achieved by a subconscious normalisation of both the symbiotic relations between the opposing categories and the alignment of attempts to question the legitimacy of ontological and epistemological privileging with that category which exists in opposition to the dominant norm. Within these knowledgeable processes of separation and exclusion, ontology and epistemology are to a large extent intertwined; certain ways of ordering the world will be aligned with a certain methodological approach and research agenda, which will itself serve to legitimise the ordering of world politics in a certain way, thus establishing the boundaries of acceptable scholarship and methodology. Epistemological debate will become a crucial variable, with a remit far exceeding its own academic area of study, as it becomes inextricably tied to the very processes which serve to shape power relations and thus define the form and content of world politics. Epistemology will come to be inextricably linked with ontology.

It is therefore extremely important to determine the limits of epistemology available to studies of international relations and world politics. Owing to the inherent nature of international relations, with its focus largely on conceptual rather than directly observable issues, methodological debate has often been particularly virulent, concerning to a large extent the polemic between those who privilege scientific method in the pursuit of knowledge, and those who advocate a wider approach to epistemology in dealing with conceptual phenomena. However, the rise of critical theories in the 1990s and 2000s (particularly the postmodernist challenge I explored in the last chapter) injected epistemological debates with a new sense of urgency. As we saw, methodological critique forms the driving force of the challenge and, in light of my claim that the critique must be taken seriously, a pragmatic solution to the problems of locating authoritative forms of political knowledge must be found. In effect, the postmodernists have gone to the very heart of IR methodology in confronting its distorting effects on the limits and possibilities characterising the discipline. The focus of this attack comes in the form of an assault on the presumption that scientific methodology, with its accompanying subject/object distinction and its emphasis on the observational nature of world politics, provides epistemologically privileged, legitimate knowledge, and that this knowledge forms the bedrock of a linear theoretical tradition, in other words, a 'positivist' epistemology. The prevalence of arguments that this form of methodology is authoritative is informed by the powerful claim that ontology is divorced from, and determines, epistemology. It is this claim, central to the vast majority of traditional approaches to IR, and its accompanying common-sense-like logic, that the postmodernists wish to challenge.

This chapter is concerned with an area of critical IR theory which, I believe, arose partially in response to, and partly alongside, the kind of problems introduced by Walker and Ashley.[1] *Constructivism* in IR is a fascinating theoretical approach, not least because of its ambition to introduce fundamental new concepts such as intersubjective sociality and agency into a discipline traditionally characterised by closed, structural logic. An examination of the central characteristics of different strands of constructivism will be an interesting and fruitful task in its own right, but it carries a special significance for my study. I want to consider constructivism in its role as an attempt by IR to come to terms with the full force of the poststructuralist challenge. The question I will be asking throughout is: does constructivism, on its own, contain the critical potential to overcome the charges laid at IR by poststructuralism? Or, more specifically, is constructivism able to avoid the un-vindicated foundationalism of realist methodology, and yet still anchor an authoritative analysis of world politics? To this end, I will examine whether the approach is able to avoid the unjustified normative processes of legitimisation identified by poststructuralism as being implicit in the traditional debates of International Relations. If constructivism can allow a theory of world politics to develop from normatively uncontentious foundations, through a methodology which neither illegitimately informs ontology nor ignores important work which considers the fundamental connections between ontology and epistemology, then it may be that the approach contains the tools necessary to overcome the challenge and engage in genuinely useful international theory.

Crucially, I have chosen to focus in particular on the work of two specific constructivist theorists: Alexander Wendt and Friedrich Kratochwil. This is not to dispute the fact that there are other important constructivist theorists working within IR with novel, important things to bring to the discipline, but by focusing on these theorists in particular, I will give myself an opportunity to examine the fundamental elements of two very different strands of constructivist approaches: conventional constructivism and critical (or holistic) constructivism.[2] The differences between the approaches of these two theorists can be seen as embodying a fundamental debate among constructivists concerning crucial epistemological and ontological issues; what is at stake is how much ontological and methodological issues are aligned with either the positivist, traditional elements of IR, or the post-positivism of critical theories. Fundamentally, the issue lies in how far positivism (informed by a distinct ontology) can support an accurate and above all *useful* theory of world politics, and how far a post-positivist methodology is needed to shape and develop a mind-dependent ontology, particularly given the fact that constructivists wish to introduce intersubjective elements into the constitutive processes of world politics. This will involve a close examination of the relationship between ontological claims and epistemology: the crucial claim when considering Wendt is that the socially constructed sphere of international politics presents itself to the individual as a distinct and separate entity. Particularly in his *Social Theory of International Politics*, and subsequent responses to critical reaction, Wendt develops a constructivist theory which explicitly incorporates a 'scientific realist' method: in other words, Wendt attempts 'to adopt an idealist and holist ontology while maintaining a commitment to science, or positivism broadly understood'.[3] The apparently contradictory elements of this approach are worked out at some length, but the practical upshot of Wendt's use of positivism is that his theory imports ontological conclusions from neo-Realism, for example, a focus on the structural level of international relations, a conceptualisation of states as unit-level participants in that structure and, crucially, a bracketing-out of internal politics and an antecedent approach to states' identities and interests.[4] These theoretical elements place Wendt very much within the 'conventional constructivist' camp; as Hopf claims,

> [t]o the degree that constructivism creates theoretical and epistemological distance between itself and its origins in critical theory, it becomes 'conventional' constructivism.[5]

Thus, by considering Wendt's constructivism and epistemology in relation to the poststructuralist challenge, I will also be in a good position to consider the forcefulness of the critique itself. If it turns out that a theory which embraces post-positivism only in terms of ontological categories contains enough critical potential to overcome the poststructuralist critique, it will be safe to assume that the critique is not particularly far-reaching, and that traditional IR contains all that is necessary to overcome it. As I will go on to argue, however, it is precisely this methodology which stultifies and confines Wendt's constructivism in ways which are unjustified and, crucially, which are still open to the charges laid before IR by Ashley and Walker[6] concerning methodological dogmatism. Wendt's insistence on the primacy and separability of ontology to epistemology leads to conclusions about state-centricity and antecedent interests which cedes much to Realism. This argument feeds nicely into an analysis of Kratochwil, as it is on this point that Kratochwil takes issue with Wendt's form of constructivism.[7] The constructivism developed by Kratochwil forms a much more holistic project, with many similarities to the critical project in IR. In particular, the use of a post-positivistic epistemology to open up processes of identity and norm creation, and an analysis of the methods by which these intersubjective processes serve to shape the rules of the 'game' of international politics, provides a truly constructivist approach which contains a great deal more critical potential with which to move beyond the methods spotlighted by the poststructuralist critique. I will argue that it is through Kratochwil's work that the critique can be overcome, and, crucially, the antifoundationalist conclusions of the poststructuralist theorists may be avoided. Holistic constructivism is unlikely to satisfy the poststructuralists and resolve the debate; foundationalism, ontology and epistemology will, as Stephan claims, always be an issue of contention between constructivists and poststructuralists.[8] But my central point here is that holistic constructivism, such as that of Kratochwil, contains the critical potential to begin to overcome the poststructuralist challenge to IR, and appears to reach a point from which meaningful ontological debate can take place. It is through these forms of theory which normative and political issues may begin to become a fundamental aspect of a multifaceted approach to the study of world politics, and thus these forms of theory may form a vital bridge between International Relations, political theory and philosophical constructivism. I will go on to claim in later chapters that Kratochwil's constructivism, and his complex and sophisticated account of the conditions of practical reasoning, get to the heart of the nature of international relations and, when combined with a Rawlsian conception of normative reason, can work to ground the most effective response to the poststructuralist critique.

(Conventional) constructivism as a response to structural realism

The most fruitful way of considering the central contentions of constructivist IR theory is to characterise it as a set of propositions which speak directly to the most fundamental commitments of the mainstream discipline. This characterisation reflects the approach in its most accurate reading as a response to those assumptions concerning the relationship between the structural nature of the international system, and the nature and identity of those actors whose interactions form the subject matter of IR. These assumptions, as is well known throughout the discipline, are most forcefully articulated in Kenneth Waltz's seminal work *Theory of International Politics*,[9] and it is no accident that Wendt's key work, and arguably the key work of conventional constructivism (whose relationship with neo-Realism is particularly fundamental), simply adds the word *social* to Waltz's classic title.[10] In that work, Waltz crucially distinguishes between 'systemic' and 'reductionist' theory, the latter of which constituting those factors which determine an agent's actions which are located below the level of structural determinacy. This category thus contains a large range of potential factors in explaining action and identity in world politics, most notably the vast ambit of domestic politics and foreign policy, and, more widely, the processes that inform an actor's identity and interests. In a very famous move, Waltz asserts the primacy of structural determinants over those of reductionism, arguing that a causal logic exists between the *fundamental* nature of world politics as anarchy[11] and the key Realist doctrines of state-centrism, self-help, and the power struggle engendered by war, empire and coercive diplomacy. Waltz does not dispel the relevance of reductionist studies to a complete picture of the nature of world politics,[12] but the claim is that these studies will constitute a separate area of study which will be dependent on the overarching causal logic of structural determinacy. For present purposes, the most crucial outcomes of this basic argument will be that actors will have no control over the constitution of their identities and interests, that structural continuity will inform a permanent character of international relations and that material analyses of power and interest will account for any changes in the relationships that exist between states as unitary actors.

This cursory look at the central tenets of Waltzian Realism serves as a satisfactory 'way in' to the constitutive fundamentals of constructivism, as it is with these conclusions concerning the role of structural determinacy in neo-Realism that constructivism is designed to take issue. Although examining the wide central tenets of constructivism in general, this analysis will focus in particular on Wendt's formulation of the social construction of international relations, for the dual reason that Wendt's primary theory embodies the most 'conventional' theory on offer (that is, the theory which is most fundamentally constituted through its relationship with neo-Realism) and thus the most widely accepted form of constructivism, and that Wendt presents the most comprehensive and (arguably) important statement of the constructivist project available. Focusing on Wendt's conventional constructivism will thus allow me a clear path into a consideration of the key claims of constructivism as per its relationship with structural Realism, while also refraining from doing theoretical injustice to the fundamentals of critical constructivism whose major departures from conventional constructivism have to do with methodological conflicts rather than substantive ones.[13]

Hopf's 1998 article is illuminating here.[14] He identifies a number of assertions which come to form the bedrock of any account of world politics purporting to be (at least conventionally) constructivist.[15] These assertions include the claim that 'actors and structures are mutually constituted'[16]; the characterisation of 'anarchy as having multiple meanings for different actors based on their own communities of intersubjective understandings and practices'[17]; the assertion that state identity forms 'an empirical question to be theorised within a historical context'[18]; the argument that 'both material and discursive power are necessary for any understanding of world affairs'[19] since '[t]he power of social practices lies in their capacity to reproduce the intersubjective meanings that constitute social structures and actors alike'[20]; and, finally, that '[c]onstructivism's conceptualisation of the relationship between agency and structure grounds its view that social change is both possible and difficult'.[21] Although these assertions are disparate, they flow from the same basic characterisation of world politics and so may be considered simultaneously.

Hopf's claim is that

> [c]onventional and critical constructivism do share theoretical fundamentals. Both aim to 'denaturalise' the social world, that is, to empirically discover and reveal how the institutions and practices and identities that people take as natural, given, or matter of fact, are, in fact, the product of human agency, of social construction.[22]

It is the relation of ideas to the construction of international relations which characterises the thrust of the constructivist project, and, in particular, the relationship of these *ideational* factors to the materialism of traditional approaches to the structural logic of international politics. The claim that '*normative* or *ideational* structures are just as important as material structures'[23] in analysing the make-up of world politics introduces all that is necessary for the wide-ranging claims made by constructivists; what is crucial is the idea that parties to the international system are able to constitute the nature of that system through intersubjective processes of identity and interest formation, that these processes determine the systemic nature of the international system, and that this system thus has a constitutive effect on the parties themselves. 'The assumption of real corporate agency enables states actively to participate in structural transformation'.[24] This assumption of agency has liberating effects on the constitution of the most crucial conceptualisations of international relations: state interests are no longer antecedent to structure ('[c]onstructivists think that state interests are in important part constructed by systemic structures, not exogenous to them'[25]); structures can no longer be conceptualised in terms of formal logic alone ('social structures are defined, in part, by shared understandings, expectations, or knowledge. These constitute the actors in a situation and the nature of their relationships, whether cooperative or conflictual'[26]); and material capabilities cannot be considered in isolation from the intersubjective structures they are embedded within:

> Insofar as power and interest are constituted by ideas, Wendt renders ineffective the tactic of neoliberals, rational choicers, and realists alike of treating power and interests, even institutions, 'as idea-free base-lines against which the role of ideas is judged'.[27]

Crucially, the introduction of ideational factors renders the neo-Realist argument concerning the causal logic of anarchy illegitimate. In a very famous phrase which is worth reconsidering, Wendt contends:

> There is no 'logic' of anarchy apart from the practices that create and instantiate one structure of identities and interests rather than another; structure has no existence or causal powers apart from process. Self-help and power politics are institutions, not essential features of anarchy. *Anarchy is what states make of it.*[28]

Since '[c]onstructivism does not ... make any particular claims about the content of social structures or the nature of agents at work in social life'[29] the claim here is not that Realist conclusions concerning self-help are an inaccurate analysis of the nature of the anarchy which actually features in international politics; it is simply that it need not necessarily follow from the mere existence of anarchy ('[a]narchies may contain dynamics that lead to competitive power politics, but they also may not, and we can argue about when particular structures of identity and interest will emerge'[30]). The nature of anarchy will not be determined by a single logic, but will rather be constituted through the interactions of the agents who operate within it:

> In using Kenneth Waltz's structural theory as a foil, Wendt argues that there is not one single logic of anarchy but rather several, depending on the nature of the actors who populate the international system, i.e., whether they approach the Hobbesian, Lockean or Kantian ideal-types.[31]

These approaches will be determined by intersubjective constructions of the meaning of anarchy; no one agent will possess a monopoly over the construction of meaning because discourse and identity formation are possible only through processes involving multiple agents. Power and national interests, so long the domain of materialism, retain their importance to the nature of international relations, but they become part of the same intersubjective processes of construction as anarchy and thus become active concepts:

> [T]he meaning of power and the content of interests are largely a function of ideas. As such only after the ideational conditions of possibility for power and interest explanations have been exposed and stripped out can we assess the effects of materiality *as such.*[32]

This is an important point, as it emphasises Wendt's commitment to a place for materialism at some level of an analysis of international relations. The defence of a 'rump materialism' leads him to the conclusion that world politics is not constituted by 'ideas all the way down', but the crucial point is that through intersubjective interest formation states can construct the meaning of distributions of power. Thus, for example, a superpower is constituted as such through intersubjective constructions of identity and interests; and these processes in turn require that the power in question acts as a 'superpower'. Thus transformative phenomena such as the end of the Cold War can be explained through an analysis of the identity and interest formation which occurred through the discursive processes by which a relationship characterised by conflict and self-help was adapted into reciprocity. So profound was this adaptation for the nature of international relations that discursive analysis becomes crucial to a true understanding of the way world politics changed throughout this period, and constructivism becomes a response to what seems to be lacking in explanations which are limited to objective power quantification (which presumably did not change much through the period), and fixed interests. Of course, it is possible to offer an explanation of the end of the Cold War through the medium of structural determinacy (as I have noted earlier, Waltz attempts just that), but the emphasis on intersubjective process has a special significance in accounts of a conflict of perception:

> The international system was transformed by the rapid succession of mostly non-violent revolutions that replaced Eastern European communist governments in 1989 and by the lack of any action by the Soviet Union to stop these changes.[33]

As Price and Reus-Smit assert, the non-materially driven nature of this monumental change in the nature of international relations constitutes a 'failed test' for the relevance of Realism:

> Not only did a substantial systemic change occur without any significant shift in the distribution of capabilities, that change resulted, in large measure, from transformations within domestic political systems.[34]

Thus an emphasis solely on strategic elements, or rational calculations of actors, will only provide part of the true picture of international relations because calculations must form part of a larger intersubjective process which constitutes the meaning of any structure in world politics. 'Ideas always matter, since power and interest do not have effects apart from the shared knowledge that constitutes them as such'.[35] Thus, it is the claim that 'social reality is constituted by intersubjective consciousness based on language and that human beings are free to change their world by a collective act of will'[36] that constitutes the driving force behind the constructivist approach to world politics.

Wendt, ontology and 'Scientific Realism'

As well as cataloguing the central tenets of the constructivist approach, Hopf provides an illuminating discussion into the relationship between the different forms of constructivism on offer.[37] An insightful passage:

> Conventional constructivism, while expecting to uncover differences, identities, and multiple understandings, still assumes that it can specify a set of conditions under which one can expect to see one identity or another.... In contrast, critical theory rejects either the possibility or the desirability of a minimal or contingent foundationalism.... To reach an intellectually satisfying point of closure, constructivism adopts positivist conventions about sample characteristics, methods of difference, process tracing, and spuriousness checks. In making this choice, critical theorists argue, constructivism can offer an understanding of social reality but cannot criticise the boundaries of its own understanding, and this is precisely what critical theory is all about.[38]

The crucial issue uncovered by Hopf here is the key source of dispute between conventional constructivism, which shares methodological characteristics with the positivism of mainstream theory, and critical theory which informs holistic constructivist epistemology, and from which constructivism as an approach first emerged.[39] As we shall see, conventional constructivism as propounded by Wendt in *Social Theory of International Relations* attempts to incorporate a post-positivist ontology (social constructivism) with a positivistic methodology ('scientific realism'), and it thus no great surprise, and no coincidence, that Wendt's conventional brand of constructivism was the most accepted and assimilated form of the approach within mainstream IR theory.

A further debate exists within IR theory as to the relative importance of metatheoretical argument. The argument here is that constant debate over epistemology and methodology is obstructing the actual point of any theory of international relations; the useful study of politics in the global arena. This argument is particularly virulent when directed at postmodernism, which appears to find it harder to reach a point from which to engage in substantive theorising since it purports to exclude the possibility of any form of authoritative theoretical knowledge, but the charge is also equally effective when directed at the debate between different forms of constructivism, for which epistemological questions seem to have a particularly tenacious quality (and for which postmodernism plays a major role). Wendt himself claims that 'IR scholars have been too worried about epistemology and have not sufficiently let the nature of their problems and questions dictate their methods'.[40] I shall consider Wendt's claims to a 'question-driven approach' below, but I wish to make a wider point concerning this argument. My belief is that epistemological debate is an important *precursor* to the substantive study of international relations. Granted, one cannot engage in a useful and illuminating study of international political phenomena if debates over the inadequacies of certain forms of knowledgeable processes stultify the research agenda. But, equally, as I have attempted to demonstrate in the last chapter, and will (hopefully) continue to demonstrate in this chapter, it is impossible to get at the truth of world politics if the methodology adopted proceeds from arbitrary starting points or follows unjustified processes of knowledge legitimisation. The major thrust of the postmodernist critique is a simple attempt to show that the apparently innocuous methods of traditional approaches are not as innocuous as they themselves believe they are. There is, of course, no point in problematising concepts and categories for problem's sake (as postmodernism is sometimes accused of doing[41]), but if genuinely unjustifiable elements are included in an overarching theory of international politics then it is crucial, in usefully analysing the subject matter of IR, to draw these elements out and find alternative means to engage in the analysis. Thus, in finding a solution to the problems identified by Walker and Ashley, epistemological enquiry will form a crucial element, and it therefore becomes essential to engage in it before moving on to the more substantive elements of theorising which will, in the long run, be of more practical use.

Wendt, of course, can be seen as *the* archetypical attempt to reach Hopf's 'intellectually satisfying point of closure'. His adoption of a scientific approach to method appears intuitively to conflict with a constructivist approach to ontology – as Wendt himself points out, *if* social structures are primarily made up of ideas, then the fundamental separation of subject and object which forms a crucial part of positivist epistemology seems redundant.[42] Furthermore, adopting this conception of ontology must have profound effects on appropriate methodology, since causal logic would not seem to tell us much about the intersubjective processes of constitution identified by constructivism. It is in Wendt's lengthy rejoinder to these challenges, and the justification of his epistemology which is entailed by such, that the limitations and compromises of Wendt's methodology to the critical nature of his theory can be identified.[43]

Wendt characterises his 'scientific realism' as an 'opposition to the view, held in various forms by its sceptical critics, that what there is in the world is somehow dependent on what we know or believe'.[44] He lays out its principal claims thus:

1. the world is independent of the mind and language of individual observers;
2. mature scientific theories typically refer to this world;
3. even when it is not directly observable.[45]

The purported aim of this method is to place ontology firmly before epistemology (the former thus determining the latter), and to provide a rejoinder to the 'relational theory of reference' favoured by postmodernists, according to which theory no longer refers to an independently existing world but informs that world through discourse processes. Wendt views this 'abandonment of epistemology' (as the postmodernists would have it) as fundamentally flawed in that, by rendering ontology dependent on epistemology, it cannot account for 'representational failures or *mis*interpretations'.[46] Representational failures can occur as regards socially constructed structures, argues Wendt, because, despite what the postmodernists claim, social structures *do* have an existence as observable social facts. This is a crucial claim for the justification of Wendt's scientific realism, and his vindication of it can be discerned from two crucial passages:

> The international system confronts the IR theorist as an objective social fact that is independent of his or her beliefs, and resists an arbitrary interpretation of it. While it is true that individuals can represent the world any way they want to, that does not mean those representations will be correct or help them succeed. Individuals do not constitute social kinds, collectives do, and as such social kinds confront the individual as objective social facts,

and,

> [t]o varying degrees, social kinds are materially grounded, self-organising phenomena with intrinsic powers and dispositions that exist independent of the minds and/or discourses of those who would know them. These phenomena should regulate social scientific theorising, even though they cannot determine it.[47]

These processes of reification form the crucial justification behind Wendt's claim that ontology ought to determine epistemology. Crucial for his scientific realism, and its accompanying 'causal theory of reference' (the theory that 'beliefs are determined by discourse *and* nature'[48]), is the claim that social structures can be seen as facts existing independently of the representation of the individual, through processes of reification and an important assertion that 'rump materialism', to varying extents, still plays a part in determining the nature of ideational relations. Wendt specifically incorporates the claim that 'all observation is theory laden' into his scientific realism, and claims that this fact must play a significant part in our methodological outlooks concerning the extent to which an objective social reality exists. However, he argues, notwithstanding this allowance, ontological independence exists in a significant enough proportion to allow an ontologically driven, scientific methodology to yield meaningful results – 'all observation is theory-laden, but this does not mean that it is theory determined'.[49] In additional support for his preferred epistemological outlook, Wendt's claim is that many important postmodernists in IR tacitly accept the assertion that it is possible to gain meaningful knowledge through ontological observation (the passage is lengthy, but, I believe, justifiably reproduced):

> I don't want to tar postmodernists with the brush of ridiculous views: I want to know why they hold such conventional ones. Thus, in her own empirical work on representations of subordinate peoples in imperial discourses, Doty proceeds more or less as any positivist would – amassing data and developing the best narrative she can to make sense of them. The same could be said about the empirical work of other IR scholars who are identified with postmodernism, like David Campbell or Cynthia Weber. Yet, if in practice postmodernists do not deny the existence, and even knowability, of a world outside of discourse, then what exactly are they saying? That all observation is theory-laden? That theories cannot be tested directly against the

> world but only against other theories? That as a result knowledge can never have perfectly secure foundations? These are all positions held by sophisticated positivists today. The straw man here in fact tends to be naïve versions of positivism, which even if still believed by some are hardly a challenging target for post-positivist ire.[50]

The passage attempts to do two things: firstly, it asserts that scientific realism is more widely adhered to by apparently critical theories than is generally accepted; and, secondly, Wendt is here trying to downplay the importance of Third Debate epistemological argument by showing that less extreme versions of postmodernism have far more in common with 'sophisticated' versions of positivism than that which exists in debates about the general philosophy of science. Wendt's central claim is that it is the preoccupation with 'epistemological prejudices' which causes methodological stalemate, and that ontology ought to inform what is appropriate in a methodological sense. Given his adherence to the view that social structures (such as those which exist in international relations) can be seen as objectively existing social facts through processes of reification, and the core role which materialist factors play in their constitution, Wendt's view is that a 'method driven' approach necessitates scientific realism which is able to accommodate empirical observation, as well as the realisation that all observation is theory laden. This in turn informs his attempt to provide a new reading of the well-documented distinction between causal and constitutive theory, and it is to this aspect of Wendt's methodology that I now turn.

Causation and constitution in International Relations

Wendt claims:

> It is a mistake to think that reasons must be *either* causal *or* constitutive. The belief that we must choose one or the other stems from conflating acting 'for' a reason (cause) with acting 'with' a reason (constitutive). Human beings do both. As such, trying to say that only one or the other is an appropriate way of talking about reasons will serve no purpose except to limit our inquiries and reduce our knowledge. The kinds of knowledge that ensue from studying these two senses of reason-giving are different, revealing things about the motivations of actors on the one hand and about the cultural context that gives those motivations meaning on the other. Our field needs both kinds of knowledge.[51]

Wendt's approach to the debate concerning causal *versus* constitutive theory is to attempt to resolve the two approaches through a 'question-driven' approach; that is, the attempt to unite the two characterisations of reasons by highlighting their *mutual* relevance for social enquiry. This debate, generally identified around the phrase 'explanation *versus* understanding',[52] is understood by Wendt as a polemic between those who advocate the primacy of causal questions in a true account of international relations (and thus adopt a scientific, 'causal' methodology), and those who argue that social structures cannot be treated in the same way as natural objects, and to truly understand international politics we must ask questions about the 'constitution' of the deep structures which motivate action. This debate is taken seriously by Wendt, since the polemical arguments inform the methodological commitments of their respective proponents which in turn have profound effects on the conceptions of ontology and epistemology adopted by each.[53] The important issue here is the claim that the 'zero-sum' conceptualisation of explanation and understanding, according to which the assertion of explanatory primacy informs the strictly positivistic methodology employed by the mainstream of IR theory, at the exclusion of constitutive questions; this, in turn, has led to a backlash, not only against the positivist tradition, but more generally against *causal questions* themselves by post-positivists. What is left is an argument whose proponents tend to exclude the respective research agendas of the other as a methodological approach which is purportedly 'irrelevant' to the study of world politics.

Wendt's 'via media' is an attempt to resolve this polemic. He claims:

> The 'via media' seeks a path between these positions by arguing that while the ideational aspect of human social life has important implications for international politics, these do not include a rejection of science.[54]

Thus the argument is that scientific realism incorporates *both* approaches to theorising by reconceptualising the methodological importance of both explanation and understanding. Wendt's argument is that 'the Third Debate has tended to conflate two distinct issues – what things are made of (ontology) and what questions we should ask (part of epistemology)', and by divorcing these concepts from one another the theorist will identify the importance of accommodating both approaches within a comprehensive account of social reality.[55] By divorcing ontology from epistemology we will be able to see its true nature, and thus know what questions we should ask and what methods we should employ to ask them. Given the way that 'social kinds' present themselves to the individual (as discrete social facts), and given Wendt's emphasis on the retention of a 'rump materialism', a similar order of question can be embodied in social scientific enquiry as that of natural science:

> [D]espite this important ontological difference between the objects of natural and social inquiry, there is no fundamental epistemological difference between the natural and social sciences. The intellectual activities associated with Explanation and Understanding *both*, are, and should be, practised in *both* domains. To the extent that 'Explanation and Understanding' is equated with 'science and non-science', therefore, it is misleading and encourages unnecessarily zero-sum arguments about epistemology. These arguments can only lead to the impoverishment of our collective efforts to make sense of international politics and, given the disciplinary dominance in IR of Explainers, to the professional marginalisation of Understanders. In my view, the essence of the insider's story is not a focus on actors' understandings, but an interest in a particular kind of *question*. That question, speaking broadly for the moment, is 'how are things in the world put together so that they have the properties that they do?'[56]

Thus, although causal questions ('why?') and constitutive questions ('how possible?') 'have different truth conditions, this does not mean that causal and constitutive theories imply different "epistemologies" ', since '[b]oth kinds of theory are true or false in virtue of how well they correspond to states of the world'.[57] Scientific realism can, claims Wendt, incorporate both these types of questions into its methodology, even going so far as to accommodate the claim that all observation is in some respect theory laden, since it is the *relative* success of scientific methodology as it stands in relation to different theoretical methods in conforming to the world which underpin the realist claim. Given the fact that post-positivists tacitly incorporate realist assumptions into their observational work, the argument is that consensus does exist around the fact that both causal and constitutive questions in world politics require methodologies which relate to the state of the world as it exists as a distinct social entity – the 'scientific solution'. Ideational phenomena require both causal and constitutive questions, as do natural phenomena (even if substantively these questions will be different). Scientific realism can accommodate both types of approach, and can therefore accommodate the epistemological requirements of international relations as conceptualised by constructivists.

It is crucial to understand Wendt's argument relating to this issue. Steve Smith's claim that, for Wendt,

> Explanation rather than Understanding is the appropriate way of analysing the social world. In short, Wendt accepts naturalism,[58]

is fundamentally misleading as it ignores the fact that Wendt is attempting to reconceptualise the categories by incorporating both causal and constitutive questions within explanation. He is attempting to move past what he terms 'epistemological prejudice' to allow ontology to guide the methodology employed in theorising about the former. Thus it is crucial that we divorce explanation from its association with purely causal theory if we are to understand Wendt's argument; his claim is that scientific realist methodology is able to accommodate both causation and constitution in international relations, which is necessitated by the ontology of social kinds which present themselves to individuals as distinct social facts. In doing so, it dispenses with stultifying epistemological debate, since its conceptualisation of social reality allows ontology to lead theory:

> The central point of IR scholarship is to increase our knowledge of how the world works, not to worry about how (or whether) we can know how the world works. What matters for IR is ontology, not epistemology.[59]

Wendt continues:

> It is simply not the case that we have to undertake an epistemological analysis of how we can know something before we can know it, a fact amply attested to by the success of the natural sciences, whose practitioners are only rarely forced by the results of their inquiries to consider epistemological questions.[60]

These claims, although surely an appealing sentiment to any scholar of international relations who simply wants to 'get on' with the study of international phenomena, will only be acceptable *if* Wendt's methodology does what it sets out to do; that is, provide a relevant means of considering both causal and constitutive questions. The success of scientific realism depends for its legitimacy on Wendt's crucial claim that social kinds represent a distinct, scientific entity whose ontology can be divorced from epistemology. Smith represents a sizable group of post-positivist scholars who doubt whether this is, in fact, the case:

> Ultimately I think that social phenomena are indeed intersubjective and therefore cannot stand in relation to human subjects *As Objects*; without this relationship scientific realism cannot operate.[61]

Smith's claim is that Wendt presents 'a confusing and ambiguous picture of the relationship between the material and the ideational, sometimes the material is an independent causal variable, at other times it is a dependent variable whose power depends on the ideational, at still other times it is an intervening variable'.[62] This confusion leads, according to Smith, to the unjustified reification of social kinds without adequate appreciation of the fact that their perceived bases – intersubjective understandings – cannot be divorced from discourse because they '*are* discourse'.[63] This problem is exacerbated by Wendt's insistence that scientific realism can accommodate constitutive theory just as adequately as causal theory:

> The problem ... is that this distinction between causal and constitutive theory involves treating constitutive theory in a social scientific way, rather than seeing it as something that requires a different form of social theory, such as those forms commonly found under the label of Understanding (or Verstehen) .... I read Wendt as seeing constitutive theory as a form of causal theory, or at least as a form of theorising that leads to, or is prior to, causal explanation. In this light my worry is that Wendt seems to be avoiding the issue of how relevant is causal analysis to the social world by proposing an additional form of theory that turns out to be more an adjunct than an alternative to causal theorising.[64]

This is a crucial point. Smith's claim is that the fundamental nature of constitutive theory is such that it cannot be reconciled with a scientific approach without adapting it into a form of causal theory. The attempt to assimilate it into a naturalistic or scientific realist methodology would then lead to the reification of social reality because constitutive theory would in effect be ignored in favour of a purely causal analysis – in effect, the essential qualities of the *ideational* constituents of social kinds would need to be overlooked in order to facilitate this adaptation. The justification for this argument is the assertion that Wendt has confused the fundamental nature of constitutive theory in his claim that social reality presents itself as a distinct entity to the individual. Given the fact that Wendt wants to assert the ideational nature of social structures, if it turns out that he fundamentally misconceives the epistemological nature of ideational constructions then the 'via media' will not adequately incorporate all that is relevant for a study of world politics but will instead exclude that theory which is inconsistent with the claim that social structures constitute a distinct reality. Crucial here is the issue of foundations: Kratochwil's claim is that 'because Wendt's *Social Theory* is based on a particular version of "scientific realism", it relies on some problematic foundationalist notions'.[65] This claim relates to Wendt's belief that because we can come to know social constructions as they are 'in themselves' (i.e. distinct from our perception of them), then scientific realism can offer an adequate, and above all, responsive, method by which we can usefully study the arena of world politics: 'the foundational idea that "truth" is a property of the world'.[66] The charge made by Smith, Kratochwil and others is that this foundational claim ignores the way in which constitutive theory becomes knowledge of the world, and this in turn leads to the importation of those assumptions of structural Realism that I emphasised in Chapter 1.[67]

Wendt himself claims that his scientific realism, and its accompanying 'causal theory of reference' is in actuality antifoundationalist:

> Realism entails a correspondence theory of truth, which means that theories are true or false in virtue of their relationship to states of the world. Still, realists agree with Quine, Kuhn, and Lakatos that all observation is theory-laden. Theory to some extent constructs its own facts. This means that *realism is antifoundationalist*. Thus, although it is common to conflate the two, the correspondence theory of truth does not entail epistemological foundationalism. What makes a theory true is the extent to which it reflects the causal structure of the world, but theories are always tested against other theories, not against some pre-theoretical 'foundation' for correspondence.[68]

Thus, scientific realism does not entail a verification of theory against a foundational notion of truth; instead the relevance of a particular theory is tested against its relative level of 'maturity' implied by its observed conformity to the state of the world:

> This raises the question of how we can know for certain that a claim of reference is true. The answer is that we cannot, and so we should

> have confidence only in the referents of 'mature' theories that have proven successful in the world. Even then we can speak only of 'approximate' truth, but this does not matter. A key virtue of the causal theory is that it separates truth from reference.[69]

The significance of this claim is twofold. Firstly, Wendt is privileging the claims of those 'mature' theories which seem to best conform to the realities they seek to explain; these are tested against other theories rather than a distinct criterion of truth. This would seem to explain the procedures whereby Wendt comes to reify exactly those features of neo-Realism which the poststructuralists seek to critique. Neo-Realism has, according to Ashley and Walker, *become* a 'mature' theory of International Relations by adopting precisely those methods of logocentric discourse-privileging that the poststructuralist challenge (as explored in Chapter 1) was so concerned to identify and critique. Ashley and Walker have drawn attention to the fact that the methods used by neo-Realism to establish itself as the dominant discourse in IR rely on unvindicated foundations, and therefore it makes little sense to privilege its characterisations of reality simply because it has been established as a 'mature' theory of IR. Wendt will be engaging in exactly the same reification processes as traditional IR theory. Secondly, Wendt is arguing that his methodology is antifoundationalist because it is not tested against a base criterion of truth, but only against other forms of theory. But this claim does entail an epistemological foundation in the sense that it relies for its validity on an ontology completely divorced from, and knowable to, the theorist or individual to whom it will form the subject matter of enquiry. In other words, Wendt's method requires that social kinds present themselves to the individual as distinct and knowable facts, despite their constitution through intersubjective discursive processes, in order to support his claim that mature scientific methodology can accommodate both causal and constitutive questions. It makes little sense to talk about a realist approach to mature theories unless there is an objective world, conformity with which renders theory 'mature' in the first place.

This is the nucleus of the 'question-driven' approach. The claim that the ontological nature of international relations necessitates a scientific method will make sense only if Wendt's characterisation of social reality is accepted. It is *not* accepted by Kratochwil:

> [H]ardly anyone – even among the most ardent constructivists or pragmatists – doubts that the 'world' exists 'independent' from our

> minds. The question is rather whether we can recognise it in a pure and direct fashion, i.e., without any 'description', or whether what we recognise is always already organised and formed by certain categorical and theoretical elements.[70]

Kratochwil's claim is that this conceptualisation of epistemology misinterprets the means by which social reality presents itself to the individual:

> Contrary to Wendt, and without necessarily embracing the postmodern position, the problem constructivism raises in a big way *is not* the one of *existence* but of recognising *what* the existing thing is. In other words, we cannot talk about 'things in themselves', but need descriptions; these descriptions are not neutral and somehow objective but embrace all types of social practices and interests that then make the things into what they are called or referred to.[71]

This is fundamentally a question of *epistemology*, since it concerns not the order of existence but the way that individuals (most crucially, theorists) can come to know social reality. The question relates to methodology since, if it turns out that Wendt's insistence on the relevance of scientific realism to the realm of social science does not do justice to the nature of social reality as a realm of *representation*, then the 'question driven', unified approach to method espoused by Wendt will no longer be capable of doing justice to the study of international relations. 'Understanding' will be intrinsically connected with issues of constitution since it is only through a fundamental connection between social reality and its representation through discourse that social constitution can come to be known. If this is the case then the *foundational* assumption employed by Wendt in claiming that the international realm is an arena of distinct social facts will be contentious, and serve to reify the categories of existence imported from structural Realism. This assumption works to inform Wendt's understanding of both causation and constitution, since it in effect posits the view that there is no fundamental distinction between constitutive and causal questions because they both rely for their content on the subject matter of social reality.

Given Wendt's insistence on the fact that 'all observation is theory-laden',[72] the justification for his foundational assertion about the distinction between mind and social reality consists in highlighting the existence of an essential material base in international politics,[73] and then asserting the reifying nature of the constitutive processes which give rise to the 'causal theory of reference'. Wendt is explicitly arguing against the assertion by many constructivists that the ideational basis of social construction necessitates a methodology rooted in hermeneutics:

> The dependence of social kinds on ideas has led post-positivists to argue that we cannot study society in the mechanistic way we study nature, and should instead seek a hermeneutical understanding of actors' subjective interpretations and the social rules which constitute them.[74]

This kind of analysis is fundamentally linked with the holistic constructivism of Kratochwil (particularly his work on the constitution of the social rules which regulate actors' understandings), and I want to argue that this kind of hermeneutical understanding is crucial in order to provide a theory with enough critical potential to transcend the poststructuralist critique. Wendt's insistence on the primacy of a naturalistic methodology in reconciling epistemology with ontology creates the conditions for the reification of the conclusions of neo-Realism regarding the politics/relations and inside/outside dichotomies; it relies for its reconciliatory potential on a conceptualisation of constitutive theory which misconceives the relationship between social reality and the individual, as well as a particularly narrow conception of causation.

Naturalism, hermeneutics and Kratochwil's critique of Wendt

The hermeneutical approach to epistemology regarding international relations theory is neatly summarised by Dixon and Dogan:

> *Hermeneutics* assumes that the social world is subjective and ideational... The truth about it should, thus, rest on interpretations embedded in day-to-day expressions derived from practice, discourse, and language... Human knowledge is, therefore, generated by acts of *Ideation* (personal reflections and ruminations) that rest on intersubjectively shared symbols, or typifications, that allow for the sharing (reciprocity) of perspectives.[75]

This is contrasted with naturalism (evident in Wendt's methodology), which 'assumes that the social world is objective and material' and whose truth claims are thus 'grounded in the observation and analysis of material phenomena'.[76] It is Wendt's claim that, despite the differences between natural and social kinds, the methodological approaches required to theorise about them need not be distinct that allows him to espouse a largely naturalist position concerning social theory. But the hermeneutical approach, or, as Guzzini terms it, 'epistemological constructivism',[77] and the approach that I want to adopt here, contends that the ideational nature of social kinds is such that it cannot be sufficiently equated with natural enquiry to adopt a naturalist theoretical approach. This is not because social reality does not exist outside of interpretation (as Osterud's caricatured postmodernist would want to argue), but because it cannot be *known* to us as a field distinct from the intersubjective processes by which it is constituted. As Guzzini claims:

> [Epistemological] Constructivism does not deny the existence of a phenomenal world, external to thought. This is the world of brute (mainly natural) facts. It does oppose, and this is something different, that phenomena can constitute themselves as objects of knowledge independently of discursive practices. It does not challenge the possible thought-independent existence of (in particular natural) phenomena, but it challenges their language-independent observation. What counts as a socially meaningful object or event is always the result of an interpretive construction of the world out there.[78]

This 'interpretive construction' cannot be theorised about via a naturalistic methodology because it is 'based on a shared system of codes and symbols, of languages, life-worlds, social practices'. In this sense, 'the knowledge of reality is socially constructed'.[79]

It is the intersubjective nature of social construction which necessitates these processes of interpretive construction. Social reality depends for its constitution on discursive processes of rule formation. It is only through an analysis of these intersubjective processes that we can understand questions of constitution and identify the attribution of meaning to social kinds. Thus, we can only come to know the meaning or significance of a social kind through knowledge of the discursive practices which constitute the norms that necessitate or legitimise certain kinds of action. This flows from the basic constructivist premise that ideas form a key constituent in the make-up of social structures. Simply put, ideational constituents require a hermeneutical understanding because they cannot be divorced from the discourse processes by which they come to constitute social kinds, and thus the only way to understand the social kind is to understand the discourse process through which it became constituted. This applies to epistemology because the meaning of a social construction will always be derived through social norms which develop from intersubjective interpretation. Guzzini, borrowing a phrase from Anthony Giddens,[80] asserts the 'double hermeneutical' character of understanding social action:

> We have to think about the two levels of action involved in a scientific explanation – the level of action proper and the level of observation. In both instances we interpret, at one time making sense within the life-world of the actor, and at another time making sense within the language shared by the community of observers.[81]

So methodology will need to reflect the fact that the act of theorising will always require an interpretation of the intersubjective processes by which legitimate theoretical parameters will be constructed. This interpretive process is then linked to the interpretation of the discourse by which social norms are constituted. Only by understanding these processes will we be able to understand the constitution of social structures in a meaningful way.

Wendt's denial of the necessity of epistemological constructivism in the face of social constructivism forms the crucial link between his scientific realism, and his reification of the central characteristics of structural Realism concerning the inside–outside dichotomy. The claim that a naturalistic methodology can unite both causal and constitutive theory ignores the intersubjective processes by which the meaning of social reality is constituted through ideas. Moreover, the claim that observation will get at 'deep structure' in international relations also ignores the discourse processes through which knowledge is constituted. Wendt's claim is that only those claims of 'mature theories' which have proven themselves successful in their analysis of the world can form the bedrock of knowledge claims, but this is to gloss over the means by which social scientific theories come to be 'mature' in the first place. The 'question-driven' approach cannot, therefore, get at the 'deep structure' of constitutive theory.

Wendt's conceptualisation of the processes by which social structures are meaningfully constructed is the core of Kratochwil's critique of Wendtian constructivism. While sharing Wendt's claims regarding the ideational constitution of international relations, Kratochwil's constructivism takes seriously the role of norms or rules in the construction of meaningful social structures:

> [R]ules and norms constitute a practice within which certain acts or utterances 'count' as something.[82]

This simple allowance alone contains vast potential for theoretical transformation, since it fundamentally alters the location of sources of change in world politics (away from simple causal mechanisms, and into discourse practices), and thus requires a radical overhaul of the methodological requirements needed in the understanding of international relations. The claim is that positivistic methodology will prove inadequate in its ability to account for the emergence of meaningful social structures once the constitutive role of norms is treated with due importance. This is due to the fact that any adequate conceptualisation of international relations will need to take seriously the normative component involved in the construction of structures; normativity is rooted in intersubjective discourse processes; and positivism does not contain the tools necessary to incorporate discursive processes into the ambit of explanation:

> Before it does anything else, positivism posits a radical separation of subject and object. It then focuses on the 'objective' forces that move actors in their social interactions. Finally, intersubjective meaning, where it is considered at all, is inferred from behaviours.... epistemology fundamentally contradicts ontology![83]

Here epistemology fundamentally contradicts ontology since the common definition of 'international regimes' generally involves convergent expectations. The positivist assertion that actors' behaviour will infer intersubjective meaning cannot account for the fact that intersubjective meaning influences an actor's behaviour. This occurs through the discursive processes by which social norms are constituted. An account of international relations rooted in a causal theory of reference will be inadequate to consider these processes of norm creation: 'a positivist epistemology simply cannot accommodate itself to so intersubjective an ontology'.[84] This is rooted in the fact that, rather than 'causing' behaviour, norms express convergent justifications or legitimations for action. It will therefore make little sense to consider norm creation from a causal theory of reference. This is intrinsically linked with the intersubjective nature of the discourse processes through which constitutive norms are created and developed:

> Precisely because state behaviour within regimes *is* interpreted by other states, the rationales and justifications for behaviour which are proffered, together with pleas for understanding or admissions of guilt, as well as the responsiveness to such reasoning on the part of other states, are all absolutely critical component parts of any explanation involving the efficacy of norms.[85]

A true understanding of normative structural constitution will thus require an understanding of the discursive processes through which agent's actions are legitimated and confined. Intersubjective phenomena such as discourse practices cannot constitute an ontology distinct from epistemology because their ideational basis is rooted in the understandings of the parties involved, as well as the interpretations of the theorist in assessing these understandings. Wendt will be mistaken, therefore, in his claim that ontology can be divorced from epistemology in the realm of constitutive theory.

The holistic element of Kratochwil's theory plays a hugely significant part in this assertion. One element of his critique of Wendt is his assertion that Wendt has missed the holistic processes by which agents come to constitute the structures by which their actions are constituted:

> Wendt is certainly right in holding that many decisions (or rather non-decisions) do not result from explicit cost/benefit analyses. But in order to show the 'mechanisms' at work here, one needs something like 'hidden faces of power' or the 'disciplinary' understandings of Michel Foucault, in which the limits of sense are not neutral description of the things, but are recognised as being part of a disciplinary program according to which actors fashion themselves.[86]

This programme posits the mutual reliability of the actions of agents and the normative structures which accommodate them. For Kratochwil (and Ruggie),

> [a]ctors not only reproduce normative structures, they also change them by their very practice, as underlying conditions change, as new

> constraints or possibilities emerge, or as new claimants make their presence felt.[87]

This holism relates to epistemology in the sense that what counts as epistemologically privileged knowledge will not be based on a Wendtian notion of theoretical potential to explain the observational phenomena it conforms to, but will be intrinsically connected to the processes whereby the actions and reactions of agents determine the normative basis of meaning in international relations: '[t]ruth is...not only contingent on some theoretical framework and some taken-for-granted or background knowledge (measurement), but is also derived from argumentative procedures'.[88] Truth and knowledge here become constructed concepts, just as 'deep structure' in international relations is itself socially constructed, and the two are crucially linked through the ideational processes of meaning construction involved in the procedure of 'doing' international relations. These constructions will delimit the ambit of legitimate action in the international arena, with the emphasis less on counterfactual rule analysis than with this process of legitimisation (as Frost notes,[89] a norm conditions a form of behaviour which requires no special justification). Constructed norms then play a crucial constitutive role in the construction of meaning within the context of social structures. Kratochwil asserts, contrary to Wendt, that norms are fundamentally associated with the categories of reasons and intention, rather than a form of causation, and the two cannot be equivalencies. The former rely for their parameters on conventions (similar in kind to norms) and as such are constructed concepts, knowable through a study of discourse practices:

> Common understandings can be arrived at through the stabilisation and evocation of certain generally shared expectations among actors in a specific situation. The medium of understanding is then neither logical cogency nor semantic truth, but rather *Claims to the Validity of Norms* on the basis of which actors can communicate, coordinate their actions, and adjust their preferences.[90]

The fact that Wendt ignores the role of normative convention in the construction of agents' intentions (and the reasons for having them) is directly linked to his claim that explanation can accommodate both causal and constitutive theory, which in turn informs his distinct ontology and 'question-driven' approach, leading ultimately to the reification of the inside/outside distinction imported from structural Realism (thus leaving Wendt open to the poststructuralist challenge). Part of the problem is the fact that Wendt relies on a particularly narrow conception of causation. By positing an essential link between the observed world and epistemologically privileged science which posits causal theories in conformity with that world, Wendt is in effect provoking a situation in which constitutive theory will necessarily need to conform to a scientific realist conception of causation if the via media is to function in the way that Wendt wants it to. Since the emphasis is on scientific method, a form of causation rooted in empirical observation will need to be espoused; this will have its basis in a Humean conception of causation which, as Kurki notes, posits that 'based on one's systematic observations of the world one can infer causal relations between events'.[91] This is ultimately why Wendt asserts the equivalence of causes and reasons, and why he therefore believes that constitutive theory can be accommodated in a positivist methodology. But this ignores the fundamental link between convention, discourse and ideational constitution, as the hermeneutical approach highlights. Collingwood's philosophy of history demonstrates the connection between the individual and the conceptualisation of causation when considering ideational phenomena. By identifying three distinct notions of causation[92] Collingwood moves beyond the narrow conception of causation employed by Wendt, and by introducing a claim to manipulation of causes by individuals, Collingwood fundamentally denies that causal relations can be inferred from the principles of mature theories which correspond well with observed phenomena:

> [T]he word 'cause'... expresses an idea relative to human conduct, because that which causes is something under human control, and this control serves as means whereby human beings can control that which is caused.[93]

This conceptualisation of causation in human relations serves to deny a distinction between ontology and intention, and is crucially linked with the assertion that intersubjective processes inform both ontology and epistemology in international relations:

> Thinking coherently about the social world might have less to do with our ability to produce theories that satisfy the criterion of correspondence between our concepts and the world, than with

> our capacity to develop a critical awareness that choosing certain descriptions of our practices over others has consequences for our understandings and actions.[94]

Collingwood's conception of causation informs Kratochwil's claim. Kratochwil wants to posit an account of motivations for actions which is *not* based on a scientific conceptualisation of causation, but is instead grounded in an account based on holistically constructed norms (as he himself claims, 'causal explanations via antecedent conditions and motivational accounts are two *different* ways in which we understand reality'[95]). Social science is, for Kratochwil, fundamentally distinct from natural science *precisely* because of the intersubjective construction of social reality: '*causal explanations within the action-perspective are fundamentally different from the causes of nature*'.[96] Therefore, in order to conceptualise causation in a manner appropriate to Kratochwil's constructivist ontology, Collingwood's theory which takes seriously the role of convention in any account of causation in social theory will be imperative, as will Kratochwil's claim that epistemology and ontology are fundamentally connected. The conceptualisation of causes as intentions in the social realm renders any claim that there is no fundamental difference, in terms of epistemology, between natural and social science, extremely difficult to maintain. As Skinner noted in 1975, '[i]t is coming to be widely accepted that Quine, Kuhn, and Feyerebend, in their different but converging ways, have all succeeded in undermining any attempt to build up a structure of empirical knowledge on a basis purporting to be independent of our judgments'.[97] Kuhn's *The Structure of Scientific Revolutions*[98] highlights the connection between what is regarded as legitimate scholarship within a scientific community, and the paradigm (intersubjective practice) that that community is working within. Crucially, counterfactual data will not negate the paradigm but rather adapt it in a revolutionary sense (a similar concept to Kratochwil's study of the adaptation of norms). This conceptualisation of social science relies on the connection between knowledge and human practice. Skinner's own work[99] on the connection between convention, understanding and discourse practices (following J.L. Austin's *How to do Things With Words*[100]), as well as Strawson's focus on Austin's theory[101] are designed to highlight the role of convention in the development of the illocutory force of utterances, and thus ultimately substantiate the basis of the understanding of intentions. This informs Kratochwil's claim that 'there is a crucial difference between causal explanations in the world of observational facts and that of intentions'.[102] Wendt's analogy between the realms of natural and social kinds will break down. Convention will be fundamentally linked with human intention, and will be present in any adequate theory of motivation for action in any holistic constructivism.

Kratochwil, political theory and the poststructuralist challenge superseded?

In the preceding section I have attempted to show that Kratochwil's constructivism takes epistemological questions seriously and, crucially, recognises the fundamental connection between ontological and epistemological constructivism. He therefore takes seriously the proposition that '[w]hat is at issue in most theoretical debates is ... the plausibility of choosing one description over another and the consequences of this choice'.[103] Traditionally, the denial of a distinct social ontology has been seen as inviting charges of epistemological relativism or nihilism since, it is argued, without a distinct ontology there can be no corresponding criterion of truth by which to assess knowledge claims. Kratochwil disagrees:

> I reject both the notion that the world has to be 'out there', for otherwise we could not make knowledge claims, and that, conversely, the denial of a 'world out there' inevitably results in nihilism.[104]

This is possible, claims Kratochwil, because truth claims are associated with discourse practices rather than an objectively existing world: ' "truth" is not a property of the "world", but of *assertions about the world*'.[105] Knowledge claims always take place from within a situated discourse and, in the context of social science, will refer to a constructed and therefore unfixed entity. These two claims are always connected 'because our concepts and vocabularies ... always involve us in the making of this world, in a political project'.[106] Kratochwil's conception of the relationship between epistemology and ontology will have profound effects on his theoretical methodology:

> [W]hen we accept the thought that we cannot get in between the 'things' and our description of them, but that in true constructivist fashion, their 'ontology' depends on the purposes and practices embedded in our concepts, then we no longer need to hold on to the 'thing in itself' as an anchor. We are finally free to address the question of how to go about our inquiries.[107]

By taking the role of epistemology in determining social reality seriously, Kratochwil's constructivism will contain the tools required to overcome the ungrounded processes of reification evident in Wendt. The assertion that social constructions rely for their substantive form on intersubjective processes intrinsically linked to discourse, norms and convention will open up huge amounts of theoretical space, and by making the connection between these discursive processes and theory explicit, Kratochwil will be able to proceed via a methodology which is self-reflective. Kratochwil's constructivism is therefore able to take the poststructuralist challenge to IR seriously, but is able to *supersede* the anitfoundationalist assertions of Walker and Ashley by locating the foundations of meaningful constructions in the processes whereby social norms come to influence (and, in turn, be influenced by) action. Antifoundationalist relativism will be avoided:

> Perhaps the metaphor of a game of Scrabble provides a better image. We begin with a concept that makes certain combinations possible. In criss-crossing we can 'go on', and our additions are justified by the mutual support with other words and concepts. Sometimes, we cannot proceed as our attempts at continuing get stymied. Then we begin somewhere else, and might, by circuitous routes, reach again some known terrain. Potentially there are innumerable moves, and no two games are identical since moves at different times will have different consequences. On the other hand, no move of them is free in the sense that 'anything goes'. But nor could they have been predicted by the 'view from nowhere'.[108]

Thus, contrary to Walker and Ashley, knowledge claims will be constructed via *justifiable* and *identifiable* processes, and contrary to Wendt, will not rely on a reification of the tenets of 'mature' theories dependent on a claim to distinct ontology which is untenable.

As I have attempted to highlight, Kratochwil's assertion of the importance of 'constructivism as a metatheoretical commitment'[109] has been largely informed by debates within philosophy and political theory. Specifically, he has relied on a Wittgensteinian connection between interpretation and understanding, with a conception of causation rooted in convention which is informed by Collingwood. This results in a hermeneutical methodology with a specifically holistic focus on the role agents play in determining the normative parameters of the motivation and justification of their actions. Kratochwil combines these measures by focusing specifically on the role of norms in the construction of social structures and the construction of knowledge. The theorist as a situated individual is a point to take seriously:

> In addition to the usual semantic distinction between object and observer we have to realise that the point from where observations are made matters. In other words we have to deal with the problem of 'observing' the observation, that is we also have to move to an observation of a higher order.[110]

Thus the double hermeneutical emphasis. What Kratochwil has succeeded in doing is providing an approach firmly rooted in the discipline of International Relations, but which opens up the possibility of transcending the poststructuralist challenge by positing a self-reflective methodology which takes the role of epistemology in shaping theory seriously. In opening up the space for a critical methodology, Kratochwil has built a bridge between IR theory (and its traditionally closed methodological commitments), and political theory whose purpose is to build normative structures based on secure foundations and legitimate means of proceeding. It is this form of theory which contains the critical potential to supersede the poststructuralist critique and construct a characterisation of world politics which can move beyond the stultifying presence of the inside–outside dichotomy in terms of theoretical possibility. This is not to say that all attempts to do this will be both legitimate and useful, but at least the possibility is there. The object of the second part of my book will be to consider those forms of international political theory which can take seriously and accommodate the elements that Kratochwil has brought to IR, whose purpose it is to transcend the distinction between politics and relations and bring a genuinely grounded normative theory of international relations to the debates concerning the nature of contemporary world politics.

3

Constitutive Political Theory: Mervyn Frost and the Role of Norms in International Political Theory

In the last chapter I provided a critical analysis of the IR constructivist methods of Wendt and Kratochwil, and, in particular, the distinction between the ways in which they treat the relationship between agency and structure. I argued that, in order to overcome the poststructuralist critique of the foundations and sovereign processes of (particularly) neo-Realism, a holistic constructivism which takes seriously the symbiotic link between the discourse practices that constitute justifications for action, and the structures within which that action takes place, is necessary. Kratochwil's emphasis on the evolution and constitutive role of norms in the formation of international social structures amounts to such a constructivism; it does not proceed from a foundational conception of a distinct realm of social fact, but asserts a truly constructive process whereby action and its justification come to form the discourse which informs those norms required in the constitution of any form of social practice. Crucially, this form of constructivism allows IR to move beyond the poststructuralist challenge since, in asserting the centrality of agency to the constitution of the subject matter of international politics, a self-reflective methodology may be advanced which does not perpetuate those either/or distinctions which have worked to exclude the viability of international political theory. Kratochwil has thus opened up the space required for the merging of debates in IR and political theory concerning the fundamental nature of international politics.

We have therefore reached a point from which to attempt to construct a theory of international relations which does *not* rely on unvindicated foundations or sovereign processes, but which may reach definite conclusions regarding the nature of world politics, and which contains enough critical potential to avoid slipping back into the poststructuralist net. These criteria, being philosophical in nature, are sources of great contention in themselves, and I want to engage with those political theories of international relations which attempt to do all these things, namely, philosophical constructivism. Although the range of these types of theories is broad, they generally share as a common goal the aim of constructing strongly critical theories of international relations which avoid foundationalism. It is this hope which distinguishes these theories from the antifoundationalism of theorists such as Walker and Ashley, since, in the case of the latter, the abandonment of any legitimate form of authoritative knowledge necessitates an entirely open, groundless conception of morality. International political theory which engages in political constructivism, by contrast, claims that an account of the nature of international relations can be grounded on entirely *legitimate* predicates. Moreover, the type of theory that I wish to engage with is optimistic in the ability of constructivism to reach *strong* conclusions about world politics from essentially *minimal* starting points, so as to exclude those assumptions which are irrelevant or illegitimate in understanding the nature of international relations, and hence remains both critical and legitimate theory. The key to the debate lies in identifying what this exclusion entails, an enquiry fundamentally linked to the various means by which theories are anchored. This, in turn, is rooted in the various conceptions of the requirements of normativity on offer. Kratochwil's constructivism represents a theory whose conception of normativity is fundamentally bound up with the concept of constitutive norms,[1] and it is this equivalence that I wish to examine in this chapter.

I chose to examine Kratochwil's constructivism in the last chapter since I perceive it as being one of the most critical, far-reaching forms of theory currently on offer in the discipline of International Relations. Given my aim in this book to locate a theory of international politics with enough critical potential to overcome the poststructuralist critique of traditional IR, but which can also ground a strong understanding of the nature of international ethics through legitimate means, Kratochwil has provided an inroad into that theory which moves beyond the dichotomies which require a severing of the link between IR and political theory. But conceived of as a form of political theory, Kratochwil's constructivism taken alone represents but one attempt to understand the normative processes inherent in the structure of international relations. In fact, Kratochwil's constructivism could be conceived of as being (at least superficially) one of the more conservative forms of international political theory currently on offer. The reason for this is that it incorporates a conception of normativity rooted in the constitutive norms of social practices. This is what Kratochwil believes grounds an understanding of the nature of international social structures. Despite the role of agency in determining these norms, their constraint on the limits of justifiable action are accorded ethical importance through the fundamental link between the constitution of social structures and the constitution of meaning.

This conception of the ethical significance of the constitutive norms of social structures is the subject matter of this section. It provides a perfect means through which to begin a consideration of attempts to formulate the normative heart of international relations through the lens of political theory, since it forms a mid-point between the necessarily closed concepts of ethical exclusion and the more far-reaching forms of philosophical constructivism which argue that a basis for the legitimate construction of principles of political justice can exist independently of the normative social structures of contemporary IR.[2] What I want to ask in this chapter is: does an account of international relations based on a conception of normativity located purely in the constitutive norms of international social structures contain the critical potential to transcend the poststructuralist critique of IR, and ground a strong theory through legitimate means? I choose to do this through an analysis of a particularly successful attempt to provide an understanding of international relations based on the concept of constitutive norms: the 'secular Hegelianism' of Mervyn Frost.[3] Frost provides a useful 'way in' to the international political theory debates about the nature of normativity in international relations since his theory takes as centrally important the place of the constitutive norms of international social structures in the ethical development of the individual. The crucial claim is that

> we could not be the individuals we are, were we not members of a specific set of social arrangements which are based upon specified sets of norms.[4]

This indicates the essence of Frost's assertion that the constitutive norms (or 'settled norms' as he calls them) of international social structures must feature in any legitimate understanding of international relations: the claim that individuality is constituted in ethically important ways through participation in such social structures, and thus that any account of international relations must afford them a central place if it is to be legitimate. It becomes immediately apparent why an analysis of Frost's broadly Hegelian constructivism should follow an analysis of Wendt and Kratochwil. Kratochwil, in particular, shares the affording of norms a central place in an understanding of international politics with Frost, through their relationship with the development of individuality and the construction of meaning.[5] Moving from an analysis of Wendt, to Kratochwil, and then to Frost will bridge the gap between debates which have mutually existed for a long time, but which have only recently, through the work of theorists like Kratochwil, been brought together: the debates of contemporary IR theory and those of contemporary international political theory.

This ordering of analysis will also allow me the opportunity to consider Frost's work in the light of the arguments in Chapter 2 concerning the relationship between ontology and epistemology – it will be important for Frost to overcome the pitfalls experienced by Wendt in understanding the crucial link between agency and structure. Frost claims that, despite the fact that grounding individuality on the settled norms of social structures is open to a charge of conservatism (the norms reflect the moral conditions of those social structures which are currently in existence), he is able to ground a sufficiently critical theory to overcome these charges. This is achieved through a process of reflective equilibrium which derives a background justificatory theory from 'what everyone knows' about the character of the 'settled norms' which characterise them.[6] The claim is that internal critique provides enough critical potential to transcend poststructuralist (and other) charges of illegitimate processes designed to perpetuate the status quo:

> Intra-practice argument is *not* inevitably an endorsement of the status-quo. Argument and reasoning within the practice can lead to the practice changing in specific ways over time.[7]

If this is indeed the case, and Frost's arguments as to the legitimacy of an account of international relations which accords the constitutive norms of international social structures a central place in the understanding of normative IR theory are accepted, then what we have in Frost is a truly far-reaching, strongly grounded theory. The settled norms of the 'modern state domain of discourse' do indeed provide a strong grounding for an understanding of the fundamentals of international relations. However, questions about the legitimacy and critical potential of a theory which relies solely on constitutive norms are more contentious.

In particular, Frost's reliance on the concept of *coherence* in justifying his preferred background theory (the 'constitutive theory of individuality') is unlikely, on its own, to transcend the charge of illegitimacy. It does not provide a strong justification of the centrality of the settled norms, or the background theory which is derived from them. Moreover, it is questionable whether coherence between norms and background theory could, on its own, provide enough critical potential to overcome the poststructuralist critique: in effect, Frost has relied on the device of *narrow* reflective equilibrium (a concept originally developed by Rawls in his earlier work) here. Given his belief in the constitutive importance of the overarching structure of international relations to the ethical constitution of the individual,[8] it is questionable whether the process could be widened to provide a stronger potential for internal critique (by allowing norms to be tested against a wider range of theories than simply the background justificatory theory). It is thus crucial to consider whether Frost's theory can accommodate a wide enough conception of reflective equilibrium – and a strong enough critical potential to allow internal critique to transcend simple coherence. If it cannot, then it may be that grounding normativity in the constitutive norms of international social structures cannot transcend the poststructuralist challenge by itself, or, if it can, it cannot compete with other, more far-reaching conceptions of the requirements of normativity. Much will depend on the strength of Frost's claim that constitutive norms are of crucial importance to any attempt to understand international relations. These are questions I want to explore in what follows.

Constitutive norms as starting points

Frost's most basic claim concerning the nature of normativity is summarised thus:

> A problem cannot be formulated as a normative issue except within the context of a given practice of normative argument. Normative issues only arise as such within the context of certain shared understandings.[9]

This formulation reflects the stated aim of his study of international relations: to solve the 'hard questions' or pressing normative issues of world politics where there is no 'established rule' or norm covering the dilemma. Frost asserts that this is only possible from inside those convergences of agreement on the meaning of normative issues which constitute a social practice or structure. In other words, solving hard cases in international ethics is only viable where the language inherent to the relevant practice, and incorporated in the formulation of the dilemma itself, is properly understood by the enquirer. Since practices are constituted by norms or rules which shape their nature, functions and limitations, it is only through an exposition and understanding of those constitutive rules that the IR theorist can hope to gain a true understanding of the nature of the subject matter of international relations. Frost believes the form and purpose of normative theory is to critically understand those settled norms that constitute the arena within which debates in international relations take place: the 'modern state domain of discourse'[10]:

> [P]articipating in a practice (be it a game or a political arrangement) requires that the participants recognise themselves as bound by a set of rules; that is, as bound by certain norms. The argument is that no coherent account of the structure of the state can be given without referring to this practice of mutual recognition: the set of ideas and rules constituting the civil and political relationship between them. If the argument is sound then the evaluation of these rules – which activity I have called normative theory – is clearly of cardinal importance.[11]

Moreover, this conception of the nature of normative theory requires that it is present in any social scientific inquiry. To be constituted as individuals, or social structures, is necessarily to hold *some* kind of understanding of the constitutive rules of the practices within which we are engaged. '[I]ndividuals and states must have *some* moral position, for having such a position is partially constitutive of what being a person or being a state is'.[12] Thus, Frost believes, there is necessarily a normative component required of any self-reflective understanding, including a true understanding of the structures of international relations. That normative component comes to the fore when moral problems arise, since arguments about moral issues necessarily involve a reflective testing of those interpretations of the character and coherence of constitutive norms held by the participants in the practice in question:

> Disputes about the proper understanding of a practice involve we who are participants in it referring one another to different features of our common practice – such disputes involve our putting forward rival accounts of how the components of the practice hang together or cohere.[13]

So discussion about particular aspects of the inclusive practices of international relations necessarily involves recourse to language developed and conditioned by the constitutive norms of those practices. Thus Frost believes that all issues in international relations must contain a normative element, and that element must necessarily refer to the 'modern state domain of discourse':

> I contend that all normative issues in world politics today refer, either directly or indirectly, to the state, inter-state relations and the role of individuals as citizens of states.[14]

A further claim is that the language of rights has come to be of constitutive importance to the ethical make-up of the individual, and thus the modern state domain of discourse is supplemented by the language of 'global civil society'.[15] A true understanding of the structures of international relations will therefore need to engage with the language of rights and the context in which individuals claim them:

> [A] focus on human rights is not a secondary activity for scholars interested in world politics, but . . . , on the contrary, in the contemporary world, it is difficult to make any sense of international relations without giving proper attention to human rights.[16]

Much of Frost's project is thus devoted to showing how the language of modern state discourse and global civil society gives rise to the constitutive norms which define these global practices, and how these norms might best be justified. Norms are identified in a similar manner as Kratochwil; they condition action which requires no special justification.[17] Thus action which states feel needs no justification, or the converse of action which is carried out clandestinely, provides a way of identifying those areas of normative consensus on the good from the points of view of the global practices of international relations. Frost's list of settled norms is relatively uncontentious: it includes sovereignty norms; norms of international law; 'modernisation' norms; and norms of democracy/human rights (which form the core of the norms that constitute global civil society).[18] These culminate in one overarching justificatory question, which precedes all other normative questions since they all ultimately rely on its conclusion:

> Combining the first two items, it appears that the preservation of a system of sovereign states is the primary good. The majority of the other goods mentioned imply a prior acceptance of this good. Thus

> any satisfactory background theory will have to justify the settled belief that the preservation of a system of sovereign states is such a good... 'What is the best justification for the preservation of a system of sovereign states?'[19]

Since Frost accords ethical significance to the system of sovereign states in the moral constitution of the individual, this underlying question coheres with later questions he asks, which have a more individualistic basis, that is, 'In what set of foundational practices are we constituted as valued individuals?'[20] The theory which Frost espouses as the best justificatory background theory on offer – the 'constitutive theory of individuality'[21] – is arrived at through Dworkin's jurisprudential procedure whereby the theory which best coheres with 'what everyone knows' the settled norms are designed to achieve is adopted as a background justification for the institution as a whole.[22] This procedure is not only designed to avoid foundational claims about the nature of international relations, but also to take seriously the fact that any issues in IR must be debated from within the framework supplied by the constitutive norms of the society of states and global civil society. Thus Frost's claim is that the settled norms of international relations are the only point from which to begin attempting to solve hard ethical questions that arise in IR, and that from them a theory can be derived which is capable of generating answers to those gaps in the corpus of settled norms which exist. This involves reconciling those norms which appear to conflict with one another – the reconciliation of sovereignty norms with human rights norms, since 'we cannot simultaneously participate in foundational practices the requirements of which contradict one another'.[23] This indicates Frost's belief in the justificatory link between the constitutive norms of the modern state domain and global civil society, and the constitution of the individual as an ethical being. The constitutive theory of individuality claims that, in order to achieve an identity as an ethical being, we must be constituted as a holder of particular rights through recognition as a rights-holder within a specified practice:

> Rights talk always presupposes the existence of a speaker and an audience who between them recognise one another as being able to make certain kinds of claims on one another. Another way of putting this point is to say that rights always presupposes a practice of rights: a practice, that is, within which people make claims of right upon one another.[24]

This recognition is of constitutive importance to the individual, as recognising oneself as a rights-holder is fundamental to the ethical development of individuality:

> Considering myself to be the holder of certain fundamental human rights is not something which I, at some point, chose to do and which I could stop doing at will. Understanding myself in this way is part of my self-conception – it is, if you like, a component of my identity.[25]

Following Hegel, Frost's claim is that we can only be fully constituted as an ethical human being within the practices of the family, civil society, the state and the states-system,[26] since each of these social structures provides a context within which individuals can recognise each other as such in ever more 'complete' ethical ways (culminating in the argument that 'for... citizenship to be fully actualised their state needs to be recognised by other states as autonomous'[27]). The emergence of global civil society allows for a reconciliation of 'citizenship' and 'civilian' rights, since we can only be ethically 'complete' individuals through the recognition allowed by both practices, in a mutually coherent way: 'we realise, through our participation in them, certain values that could not be realised any other way'.[28]

However, unlike Hegel, the significance of Frost's argument is his claim that no strong metaphysical foundation is needed in support of the claim that moral individuality requires a successive series of practices within which to develop:

> Constitutive theory does not require of us that we understand or accept Hegel's metaphysical system.[29]

This is a bold claim, and one that is fundamentally linked to Frost's basic contention that normative argument entails argument both within and concerning the social structures inherent to international relations. Thus the constitutive theory of individuality is arrived at through a consideration of the 'point or character' of the practices of the states-system and global civil society, identified through analysis of the settled norms which characterise those practices and the key questions they reveal. Its justification lies in the fact that it reconciles those norms of sovereignty and rights which appear, superficially, to conflict with one another (leading to a logical incomprehension within the practices that are foundational to individuality), since the theory offers an account of the fundamental link between norms of sovereignty and the realisation of rights. Once established, the theory can then be applied to hard cases where no prior normative consensus exists: that norm which best coheres with the background justification which itself best coheres with the body of settled norms will itself become part of the corpus. Frost, following Dworkin, claims that, if more than one background justificatory theory appears to cohere with the body of constitutive norms, the theorist 'must decide which gives the deepest and most satisfying account of the concept'.[30] In doing this the theorist may make a philosophical enquiry into the 'basic commitments of the participants in the practice',[31] but these are only relevant as an indicator of that background theory which gets to the heart of the settled norms and, therefore, should be incorporated as justification. The claim is thus that the constitutive norms of those international social structures which accommodate the ethical development of individuality are the only place to begin the development of a true understanding of international relations, and that, due to their central importance in constituting us as the kind of ethical beings we value ourselves to be, they assume an inherent importance to human nature itself. Frost believes that these assertions flow from the domain of discourse which normative debate must necessarily take place within, and does not rely on strong, foundational claims about the realisation of spirit in order to be both vindicated and strong enough to form a critical theory of international relations.

The strength of a norms-based theory of International Relations

Cochran identifies a major charge against Frost's form of secular Hegelianism:

> Hegel's means for demonstrating that internal critique is indeed effective critique – that the measure of things lives up to its rational structure – is compromised by the secularisation of his philosophical system. This means that there is a new problem for those who make this move, the problem of how one justifies the now qualified ground from which dialectical method and ethical critique must follow, since recourse to the *strong* foundation of Geist is at an end.[32]

The point here is that Frost's claim that the constitutive norms of modern state discourse and global civil society are both necessary and strong enough to ground a critical theory of international politics appears to be compromised by the fact that the norms themselves constitute a contingent set of moral principles from which to derive the background theory. Since Frost has claimed that normative argument must necessarily be conducted within, and regarding, the overarching practices of international relations, internal critique presents itself as the only available form of critique on offer: thus the background justificatory theory forms the only available place from which to conduct normative critique. Hegel's metaphysical system allowed him to make claims such as 'the history of the world presents us with a rational process'[33] and allowed him a strong foundation from which to conduct normative debate concerning the development of those norms inherent to the social practices of the world. But Frost has explicitly stated that he does not want to rely on such a foundation: his claim is that a critical theory can be derived from the settled norms which condition the domain of discourse within which normative debate must necessarily take place. But the problem becomes justifying the motor behind normative critique, which is derived solely from the constitutive norms themselves and thus may have no strong vindication on offer:

> Given that Frost is not claiming that there is a Hercules to make judgements in international relations, we must be aware that the thought experiment he offers us is certainly subject to the charge of partiality (i.e. that the moral judgements used are not universally shared and stem from one dominant tradition).[34]

If this is indeed the case, then the 'critical' theory that Frost offers us would be no more than an exercise in hegemony; it would conduct normative critique from the viewpoint of a dominant tradition which has asserted its own normative consensus on the social structures of international relations. As is immediately clear, this would not transcend the poststructuralist critique of IR: the constitutive norms would not form a legitimate grounding from which to conduct normative critique. In the attempt to avoid relying on metaphysical foundations, Frost would have sacrificed the strength of his theory.

Frost's rejoinder to these charges provides an insight into the way he believes the constitutive norms of international relations can ground internal critique, and which, coupled with his argument that normative debate is debate about the interpretation of the settled norms conducive to overall coherence, allows him to claim that constitutive theory in fact allows for a strong and legitimate form of critique. He claims:

> The task for political ethics is to construct a theory which shows how the values, which we have created for ourselves in the diverse practices within which we are constituted, cohere or fail to cohere. This task of theory construction might bring us to question (and in the long run, abandon) some of our settled norms. The background theory itself cannot be given some deeper justification.[35]

Thus the claim is that coherence forms the only available means through which strong internal critique can occur. Part and parcel with the claim that normative debate is crucially linked to the discourse of world politics, the background justificatory theory can be used not only to solve the hard cases of international relations by conditioning the development of norms but can also filter those settled norms which do not cohere with the corpus as a whole. Through this process of maintaining a *reflective equilibrium* between the corpus of norms and the background justificatory theory, Frost believes that a norm-based conception of normativity can transcend conservatism and ground a strong critical edge:

> Asserting the primacy of the modern state domain of discourse for my purposes does *not* commit me to holding that people will always live in states as we know them or that life in states, as we know them, is the only proper life for human beings... I simply contend that any discussion about what ought to be done in world politics (be the proposed action a small one or a large one such as, for example, the wholesale reorganisation of the global political system) must be conducted in the language of the modern state system. No other suitable language is available.[36]

So through the constant application of reflection in maintaining between the background justificatory theory and the norms which initially gave rise to it, the social structures of international relations can be altered through internal critique. The claim is that no other method for conducting normative critique is available: there is no further justification of the background theory, other than that of coherence with the settled norms of international relations. And since those norms are of foundational importance to our development as ethical individuals, we cannot but afford them a central place in our conception of what is required for normative reflection about the nature of international relations.

Thus the challenge to Frost's arguments concerning the centrality of the settled norms in any normative debate is that of avoiding resort to foundationalist claims, while still grounding a truly critical theory. As charged by Cochran, Frost works 'procedurally from a background theory that takes as *given* the ethical status of the state',[37] and 'proceeds as if the modern state domain of discourse was a *strong* foundation that is not up for question or negotiation'.[38] Since Frost wants to avoid metaphysical, or 'mid-air reasoning', it is crucial to the integrity of his argument to justify his assertions about the nature of normativity and its relationship with the structures of international relations.

Part of the challenge faced by Frost in achieving this is the failure to distinguish between two crucial claims. On the one hand, Frost argues that normative debate is bound up with, and must take place from within, the social structures of international relations characterised by the constitutive norms of those practices by which structure is constituted. This is his chosen starting point, and he attempts to justify the claim through sustained argument concerning the nature of normativity as a debate between competing interpretations of the settled norms and what such norms imply for the nature of international politics. On the other hand, Frost also wants to claim that the modern state domain of discourse and global civil society are of foundational importance to the ethical constitution of the individual (through the recognition made possible by these structures). This is a wholly separate claim, which itself requires justification to avoid becoming an illegitimate foundation from which the constitutive theory of individuality may be constructed. The first claim does not entail the second: asserting the necessity of affording the settled norms a central place in any normative debate does not, in itself, justify the claim that individuality requires membership of these 'authoritative and ethically foundational'[39] practices. The justification for the adoption of the constitutive theory of individuality is that it affords the best theoretical 'fit' between the character of the settled norms of the social structures of international relations and a background theory which reconciles those apparently competing principles and allows us to formulate new norms when required in the face of morally difficult cases. But this does not justify the foundational importance of these social structures on the development of the ethical individual. To avoid recourse to unjustified foundational claims, an endeavour explicitly stated as an aim of his study, Frost must properly distinguish between these two wholly separate arguments.

Coherence forms the core of the solution to these challenges which are fundamental to Frost's theory. To avoid relying on foundational claims concerning the necessity of the state or civil society to the development of human nature in general, his claim is that, in order to be the kinds of individuals we value ourselves in being, we must necessarily be constituted as such from within *these* institutions in particular. In the passage quoted in the introduction to this chapter, Frost claims that 'we could not be the individuals we are, were we not members of a specific set of social arrangements which are based on specified sets of norms'. The first section of this sentence assumes importance here. Frost cannot claim that individuality must necessarily be constituted through the institutions of the system of states and global civil society: to do so would constitute reliance on a foundational claim which, since Frost believes no external justification is available, would necessarily be illegitimate. Rather, the claim must be that, if we want to be the individuals we are (i.e. those who possess the rights associated with citizenship and membership of civil society), we need to be members of those structures which allow us to be constituted in this way. It is a claim Frost makes elsewhere:

> Were we not given the recognition we enjoy through our participation in these practices, we would consider ourselves to be fundamentally ethically deprived.[40]

Thus it is the coherence between our conception of ourselves as rights holders and our understanding of the practices within which we may become rights holders that forms the bedrock of Frost's espousal of the constitutive theory of individuality. Given his basic contention that normative debate about the nature of international relations must be framed in the discourse of the contemporary institutions of IR, it is only through a background theory which is derived from the constitutive norms of this discourse that we can ever get at the 'deep structure' of the practices that constitute us as rights holders. To be constituted as the ethically complete rights holders we value ourselves as, those authoritative practices foundational to the development of ethical individuality as such will need to cohere since, if they did not, 'my participation in one of them is not, at the end of the day, crucial to my standing as who I value myself to be'.[41] Thus the background theory which provides for the best coherence of the constitutive norms of the practices foundational to the development of self-reflective individuality will become the theory which best unites our need to be constituted as rights-holders with the means through which we may become so: an understanding of the authoritative structures of international relations. Through this, the constitution of individuality comes to be crucially linked with the settled norms of the state and civil society, and the process of reflective equilibrium allows us to filter those norms which do not cohere with the corpus and are thus detrimental to the constitution of the ethical individual.

Is coherence enough?

Frost outlines the role of reflective equilibrium as forming a crucial part of the critical edge to his theory:

> The technique of reflective equilibrium is designed to overcome an incompatibility (a lack of fit) between the body of settled rules and the background theory which might arise at this point. In seeking to construct a coherent background theory to justify the whole body of settled rules, the judge finds that it challenges (calls into question) some bits of the settled corpus of law. He now faces a dilemma: either he must modify the background theory as to encompass awkward law, or accept that the settled body of law is not fully coherent. Thus it is possible that in any piece of legal reasoning the judge will end up with some bits and pieces of the settled law which do not fit the proposed justificatory background theory. In this way bits of settled law will become suspect and may well with time fall into disuse.[42]

Given that Frost's normative theory is designed to apply to the overcoming of difficult ethical dilemmas in IR, the usefulness of this process lies in its ability to critique and discard those norms which do not cohere with the background theory as a whole and which are thus not justified by it. As has been discussed above, Frost must be extremely careful not to fall into the trap of relying on foundational claims about the dependence of any form of individuality on the modern institutions of international relations. Thus the equilibrium must be designed to allow us to align our ethical constitution as citizens and civilians (a phenomenon Frost is claiming is central to a true understanding of the nature of international relations) and the 'perfect' corpus of norms which coheres both with itself and this constitution of individuality. The crucial question becomes: given that Frost believes there is no deeper justification for constitutive theory than what is derived from the constitutive norms of contemporary international relations, is coherence between the settled norms and the background theory enough to ground the critical potential necessary to avoid an illegitimate and unvindicated conservatism, which would serve to perpetuate the characteristics of IR challenged by poststructuralism? Frost's position here is open to attacks such as:

> [A] constructivist account of political ethics must do more than cohere with the settled norms of the international system[43];

or:

> From the non-metaphysical perspective adopted here, this interpretation of the state can only be an 'interpretation'; it cannot be the only possible interpretation.[44]

The problem here is that Frost's use of the technique of reflective equilibrium as a motor for internal critique is an example of a form of *narrow* reflective equilibrium – simply, 'the best fit of principles with judgements'.[45] The driving force behind normative criticism becomes a back-and-forth procedure designed to achieve the best possible coherence between norms and background theory at any given moment. But there is no other criterion by which the settled norms, or indeed the background justificatory theory, may be tested, leading to a rather weak form of internal social critique (based solely on coherence). This is exacerbated by the fact that, if the background theory were to cause a seismic shift in those norms which cohered and were thus legitimate, the background theory itself would then presumably need to be altered in the light of this new corpus of constitutive rules, and thus the background theory itself is on particularly thin ground. This may be unlikely given that the aim of the procedure is to achieve equilibrium, but it highlights the fact that, if the motor for normative critique is derived solely from that set of norms which exists in international relations, it is weak, and open to the charge of illegitimacy and unjustified conservatism. Frost's claim that the background theory cannot be given a deeper justification will limit the critical potential of this form of constructivism, since the theory is ultimately derived from the principles it seeks to criticise. Narrow reflective equilibrium does not have the potential to move beyond a coherence based form of critique: it takes its standards solely from the same set of normative principles from which the background theory itself is derived. It cannot provide a normative justification of the settled norms in particular, or, more generally, the constitution of the individual as rights-holder. Constitutive theory is justified by Frost as the theory which best accords with the multiple practices we are all embedded in: but he cannot avoid the fact that his is but one interpretation of the constitutive norms of international relations, and thus that other theories which reconcile the settled norms of the different practices of contemporary international relations may be equally as viable here.

Moreover, given Frost's claim that global civil society and the society of states constitute 'foundational' authoritative practices in the development of the individual as rights-holder, it is unclear whether the process of reflective equilibrium at the heart of his theory could ever be adapted into its wider form. Frost's justification for the derivation of the background theory from the settled norms of the structures of international relations is that we cannot but engage with these practices to be constituted as the ethical individuals we are: in other words, these practices have foundational importance to the development of the individual as holder of civilian and citizenship rights, for without them these rights would be impossible. All normative debate must proceed from within the language of these practices, since there is no other means by which to make sense of international relations. Thus the constitutive norms themselves form a discrete set of principles which must dictate our theorising about IR. It does not appear, therefore, as if other considerations may be introduced into the process of reflective equilibrium at the core of Frost's theory. To do so would be to imbue constitutive theory with a greater degree of critical potential (since it would allow a wider form of reflective equilibrium which would consider the coherence of norms in relation to other theories accepted by the practitioners in question). But it would require that these considerations were also foundational to the constitution of the ethical individual, a claim which Frost would not want to accept since it would detract from the importance of the settled norms of international relations as foundational practices. If normative debate is necessarily debate about competing interpretations of the constitutive norms of IR, then only coherence between those norms may feature in any normative consideration. Thus reflective equilibrium must necessarily be in its narrow form here, and the problem of justification remains. Models for the coherence of a set of laws do not justify or legitimise those laws. This form of coherence theory is useful for solving the hard normative questions in IR, so long as the principles themselves are not open to charges of illegitimacy, which will persist so long as the theory does not possess the tools required to critically examine those principles. Frost's conception of normativity does not appear to allow such a potential, without relying on foundational assumptions about the requirements of individuality which Frost will not want to import.

Frost's problems regarding critical potential are rooted in the way that he uses the settled norms to ground his theory. He treats them in a similar manner to Wendt. The norms are seen as distinct social entities which present themselves to the participants in the practices they characterise as a set of facts which must form the backbone of any theorising about the nature of international relations. But this is to ignore the way that norms come to evolve and develop as intrinsically linked to the actions and legitimisations which constitute them as discrete principles. As I have attempted to show in relation to Wendt and Kratochwil, an understanding of the role of norms in the context of social structure, and the ways in which norms are constituted, is vital as a basis for a theory which can transcend the sovereign processes at the heart of the poststructuralist critique of IR. Through this kind of understanding, constitutive norms can form an important part of any theory of international relations, but their historical nature will be properly realised. Thus they will come to be seen as historically conditioned principles which *can* be given a deeper justification than a theory designed to facilitate coherence between them, a justification based on the way norms come to develop and the way in which they are linked with the agents who create them. Frost limits the true potential of this form of normative theory through his belief that coherence is the only form of legitimacy open to a theory of international relations which does not want to rely on foundationalism or unvindicated claims to sovereign status. The conception of normativity on offer here has much to bring to IR theory and as a way of avoiding the antifoundationalist underpinnings of poststructuralism it has the potential to ground a truly constructivist theory. The key question becomes whether Frost's use of norms, and his claims concerning the justifications on offer and the reliant critical potential, are indeed correct, or whether the constitutive norms of IR are capable of a stronger, more justified and hence more critical normative theory of international relations. I will argue in the next chapter that Kratochwil's sophisticated conception of practical reasoning with norms can, when situated within the philosophical framework of Rawlsian constructivism and combined with Rawls' account of public reason, ground a strong, critical and, ultimately, *legitimate* understanding of international relations.

Part II

The Solution – Constructing Normative Reason

4
Beyond Coherence: Rawls' Conception of Public Reason

By exploring and analysing certain concepts which underpin Rawls' international theory I wish to begin identifying the means of offering a robust theory of international relations underpinned by an account of the authority of public reason and, crucially, the ability of public reason to ground normative principles appropriate for international relations. Such a theory must, I will argue, be able to accommodate Kratochwil's holistic understanding of the link between epistemology and ontology (as well as his sophisticated consideration of practical reason, which I will consider in detail below) and contain the tools needed to transcend the inside/outside dichotomy identified by Walker. The latter is crucial to the argument in this and subsequent chapters. I wish to take seriously Walker's contention that

> the term 'international' permits an understanding of modern politics as nothing more than a collection of those states enabling properly political (and sometimes democratic) communities of self-determination and citizenship to thrive or as an expression of that humanity that is expressed as the collective condition within which mere states and their communities of citizenship can thrive.[1]

For Walker, 'international' is traditionally conceptualised as being dichotomously opposed to the term 'political', the latter being imbued with rationality and the applicability of practical reason, the former being invested with neither. This is not to deny distinct and fundamental differences between the realm of the domestic and that of the international, and a proper account of the role of public reason in international relations will need to consider in detail the subtle and distinct ways in which political constructivism must be formatted to take account of the unique conditions inherent in international relations. But the point I wish to assert (in agreement with Walker but contra his insistence that, because the idea of practical reason cannot be divorced from its own spatiotemporal contingency and the logocentric traditions of thought that have rendered it authoritative in the mainstream of modern political theory, it will not be possible to identify a stable and robust constructivist underpinning for the development of principles of international ethics) is that a sophisticated understanding of the role of public reason in international relations allows for a form of political constructivism which does not rely on acceptance of 'a conception of a well-ordered constitutional democratic society' for its normative force. There is no need, in my contention, for the idea of public reason to be thought of as being incapable of transcending political liberalism. While this is at odds with Rawls' own conception of the nature of political constructivism in international relations (as an extension of political liberalism), my claim is that it is both possible and desirable (the latter insofar as it allows a true synthesis of political theory and International Relations, thus overcoming Walker's concerns regarding the inside/outside dichotomy) to divorce political constructivism from political liberalism. However, such a claim will require a deep and sophisticated understanding of (1) the potential for public reason to move beyond reliance on liberal conceptions of morality and justice, (2) the manner in which a conception of public reason arises out of a more fundamental conception of reasonableness, which is properly formatted to take account of the conditions of international relations, and (3) the complex and sophisticated ways in which public reason can interact with and accommodate a Kratochwilian conception of normative reasoning (which is intimately bound up with the fundamental emphasis he places on the role of norms in international relations).

My claim in this and subsequent chapters is that the Rawlsian conception of public reason may be divorced from Rawls' political liberalism and can be effectively conjoined with Kratochwil's conception of practical reasoning to form a viable and robust response to the challenge of poststructuralism in international relations.

In this and the following two chapters I will highlight certain competing conceptions of the role of reason in grounding an international political theory, including constructivist (both critical and philosophical) and non-constructivist positions. Such a consideration will set up what follows in two distinct ways: (1) It will allow me a 'way in' to contemporary debates between constructivists and non-constructivists and will indicate that the question of the form and role of reason in international relations is far from being settled (thus justifying my reanalysis of the claims made by Rawls in *The Law of Peoples*); and (2) It will allow me to consider the conceptions of the role of reason employed by those who espouse alternative forms of constructivism to the one worked out by Rawls and, in particular, will allow a consideration of the ability of a theory of international relations underpinned by a constructivist account of normative reason to accommodate the key elements of the alternative theories which I have considered (and which I have claimed are normatively significant and thus vital to a true understanding of global politics). I will thus set out in detail the conceptions of reasonableness and public reason laid out by Rawls in *Political Liberalism* and *The Law of Peoples* before looking at Buchanan's critique of the methodology and conclusions reached by Rawls therein in the next chapter. In the subsequent chapter I will give consideration to how Rawls' ideas concerning public reason might be properly adapted to form an authoritative and objective standard by which to ground principles of justice applicable and appropriate to international relations (through a consideration of Kratochwil's conception of normative reasoning and the potential for a mutual augmentation between the different conceptions of normative reasoning developed by Rawls and Kratochwil).

Rawls' conception of public reason

Public reason in *Political Liberalism*

In *Political Liberalism*, Rawls fleshes out in great detail the idea of political liberalism and its fundamental characteristics; crucially, the idea that a 'freestanding' political conception of justice can be divorced from the wider questions of moral or philosophical disagreement and can come to form the grounding for an 'overlapping consensus' between 'reasonable but incompatible' comprehensive doctrines (which Rawls crucially conceives of as a *permanent* feature of liberal constitutional democracies):

> The general problems of moral philosophy are not the concern of political liberalism, except insofar as they affect how the background culture and its comprehensive doctrines tend to support a constitutional regime. Political liberalism sees its form of political philosophy as having its own subject matter: how is a just and free society possible under conditions of deep doctrinal conflict with no prospect of resolution?[2]

Thus Rawls conceives of political liberalism as addressing 'two fundamental questions': 'what is the most appropriate conception of justice for specifying the fair terms of social cooperation between citizens regarded as free and equal?' (in other words, citizens of liberal democratic states); and 'what are the grounds of toleration understood in a general way, given the fact of reasonable pluralism as the inevitable result of the powers of human reason at work within enduring free institutions?' These questions combine to form: 'how is it possible for there to exist over time a just and stable society of free and equal citizens who still remain profoundly divided by reasonable religious, philosophical, and moral doctrines?'[3]

A freestanding political conception of justice, properly worked out to take into account the crucial presence of divergent yet reasonable comprehensive doctrines, should provide answers to this question and can when properly worked out come to regulate the 'relation of citizens within the basic structure of society, a structure we enter only by birth and exit only by death'.[4] Rawls argues that *Political Liberalism* intends to build on three fundamental ideas which, he claims, had been left generally unconsidered in his earlier accounts of constructivism:

1. The idea of justice as fairness as a freestanding view and that of an overlapping consensus as belonging to its account of stability[5];
2. The distinction between simple pluralism and reasonable pluralism, together with the idea of a reasonable comprehensive doctrine; and
3. A fuller account of the reasonable and the rational worked into the conception of political (as opposed to moral) constructivism, so as to bring out the bases of the principles of right and justice in practical reason.[6]

Political liberalism, therefore, looks for 'a political conception of justice that we hope can gain the support of an overlapping consensus of reasonable religious, philosophical, and moral doctrines in a society regulated by it'.[7] Crucially, such an overlapping consensus will only be possible if we identify a conception of the citizen which incorporates accounts of the reasonable and rational which are properly worked out to be suitable to a *political* idea of constructivism. It is the idea of the *reasonable*, specifically, which needs to be fleshed out in such a way as to be appropriate for application to political, as opposed to moral, questions (such as the one formulated above). Rawls claims:

> Gaining [the] support of reasonable doctrines lays the basis for answering our second fundamental question as to how citizens, who

> remain deeply divided on religious, philosophical, and moral doctrines, can still maintain a just and stable democratic society. To this end, it is normally desirable that the comprehensive philosophical and moral views we are wont to use in debating fundamental political issues should give way in public life. Public reason – citizens' reasoning in the public forum about constitutional essentials and basic questions of justice – is now best guided by a political conception the principles and values of which all citizens can endorse;

And:

> Political liberalism, then, aims for a political conception of justice as a freestanding view. It offers no specific metaphysical or epistemological doctrine beyond what is implied by the political conception itself.[8]

Thus the idea of a reasonable agent, at least in regards to a political conception of justice, incorporates the idea of public reason.

The ideas of the reasonable and the rational, which are inherent in Rawls' conception of the person, are the basis on which an overlapping consensus may be reached between those who affirm reasonable, yet incompatible, comprehensive doctrines. They are introduced as part of Rawls' consideration of how citizens ought to be constituted in the original position, in order that they might accurately represent democratic citizens entering into justificatory debate over matters of basic justice. Crucially, the ideas are complementary yet distinct; 'there is no thought of deriving the reasonable from the rational',[9] although it appears that the rational precedes the reasonable in Rawls' consideration of the powers of the citizen.[10] When applied to an agent seeking ends and interests of its own, the rational 'applies to how these ends and interests are adopted and affirmed, as well as to how they are given priority'.[11] Rawls ascribes more to the idea of the rational than the ability to invoke means-ends reasoning; rational agents 'may balance final ends by their significance for their plan of life as a whole, and by how well these ends cohere with and complement one another'[12]; and may also carry a wide variety of types of interests, not all of them interests 'in benefit to themselves'.

The crucial point about rationality, however, and the reason that it cannot by itself ground an overlapping consensus on a political conception of justice, is that purely rational agents lack 'the particular form of moral sensibility that underlies the desire to engage in fair cooperation as such, and to do so on terms that others as equals might reasonably be expected to endorse'[13]; essentially, they lack the motivation to locate an overlapping consensus and fundamentally lack a capacity for a sense of justice. The reasonable, in contrast, contains the part of moral sensibility 'that connects with the idea of fair social cooperation'.[14] While rationality is essentially a *private* characteristic of citizens (necessary for a complete conception of an agent in that it specifies the ends they will 'want to advance by fair cooperation'[15]), reasonableness is a *public* characteristic and is identified in the way agents are willing to approach relations with others and begin to answer questions concerning how they are to justly coexist with those others:

> [I]t is by the reasonable that we enter as equals the public world of others and stand ready to propose, or to accept, as the case may be, fair terms of cooperation with them. These terms, set out as principles, specify the reasons we are to share and publicly recognise before one another as grounding our social relations. Insofar as we are reasonable, we are ready to work out the framework for the public social world, a framework it is reasonable to expect everyone to endorse and act on, provided others can be relied on to do the same. If we cannot rely on them, then it may be irrational or self-sacrificial to act from those principles.[16]

Rawls does not conceive of the reasonable as being overtly altruistic; it simply 'underlines the capacity to propose, or to endorse, and then to be moved to act from fair terms of cooperation for their own sake', which Rawls considers an 'essential social virtue'.[17] It is essentially to be understood as a *capacity* for a sense of justice and a *willingness* to discover a political conception that can form the basis of a public form of justification.

Alongside this first aspect of the reasonable (i.e. 'the willingness to propose fair terms of cooperation and to abide by them provided others do'[18]), which constitutes the fundamentally public and normative nature of the concept, a second crucial aspect is what Rawls calls 'a willingness to recognise the burdens of judgment and accept their consequences for the use of public reason in directing the legitimate exercise of political power in a constitutional regime'.[19] The 'burdens of judgment', the 'sources, or causes, of disagreement between reasonable persons so defined', are identified by Rawls as 'the many hazards involved in the correct (and conscientious) exercise of our powers of reason and judgment in the ordinary course of political life'.[20] Rawls fleshes out in broad terms some of the more obvious sources of reasonable disagreement (or disagreement among reasonable persons):

a. The evidence – empirical and scientific – bearing on the case is conflicting and complex, and thus hard to assess and evaluate.
b. Even where we agree fully about the kinds of considerations that are relevant, we may disagree about their weight, and so arrive at different judgements.
c. To some extent all our concepts, and not only our moral and political concepts, are vague and subject to hard cases; and this indeterminacy means that we must rely on judgement and interpretation (and on judgements about interpretations) within some range (not sharply specifiable) where reasonable persons may differ.
d. To some extent (how great we cannot tell) the way we assess evidence and weigh moral and political values is shaped by our total experience, our whole course of life up to now; and our total experiences must always differ. Thus, in a modern society with its numerous offices and positions, its various divisions of labour, its many social groups and their ethnic variety, citizens' total experiences are disparate enough for their judgements to diverge, at least to some degree, on many if not most cases of any significant complexity.
e. Often there are different kinds of normative considerations of different force on both sides of an issue and it is difficult to make an overall assessment.
f. Finally . . . any system of social institutions is limited in the values it can admit so that some selection must be made from the full range of moral and political values that might be realised. This is because any system of institutions has, as it were, a limited social space. In being forced to select among cherished values, or when we hold to several and must restrict each in view of the requirements of the others, we face great difficulties in setting priorities and making adjustments. Many hard decisions may seem to have no clear answer.[21]

Thus, contends Rawls, any exercise of reason will necessarily be 'imperfect' and susceptible to outside influences and competing considerations. Crucially, however, the burdens of judgement do not require that disagreement be *un*reasonable: 'many of our most important judgments are made under conditions where it is not to be expected that conscientious persons with full powers of reason, even after free discussion, will all arrive at the same conclusion'.[22] This point is vital as, if it were the case that 'perfected' tracts of reasoning would always yield the same conclusion, it would be incumbent on Rawls to attempt to reconstruct such tracts in the representative device of the original position and, ultimately, to insist on one single formulation of the most reasonable political conception of justice. This, however, is not the case, and crucial for a proper recognition of the burdens of judgement is a recognition of how the fact of reasonable disagreement 'limits the scope of what reasonable persons think can be justified to others', a fact which Rawls believes 'leads to a form of toleration' and 'supports the idea of public reason'.[23]

In order to truly understand the role of the reasonable, and the burdens of judgement, in leading us to and ultimately grounding the authority of *public* reason in Rawls' political constructivism, it is necessary to understand Rawls' idea of a reasonable comprehensive doctrine:

> Assume first that reasonable persons affirm only reasonable comprehensive doctrines. Now we need a definition of such doctrines. They have three main features. One is that a reasonable doctrine is an exercise of theoretical reason: it covers the major religious, philosophical, and moral aspects of human life in a more or less consistent and coherent manner. It organizes and characterizes recognized values so that they are compatible with one another and express an intelligible view of the world. Each doctrine will do this in ways that distinguish it from other doctrines, for example, by giving certain values a particular primacy and weight. In singling out which values to count as especially significant and how to balance them when they conflict, a reasonable comprehensive doctrine is also an exercise of practical reason. Both theoretical reason and practical reason (including as appropriate the rational) are used together in its formulation. Finally, a third feature is that while a reasonable comprehensive view is not necessarily fixed and unchanging, it normally belongs to, or draws on, a tradition of thought and doctrine. Although stable over time, and not subject to sudden and unexplained changes, it tends to evolve slowly in the light of what, from its point of view, it sees as good and sufficient reasons.[24]

Rawls intentionally keeps this formulation of a reasonable doctrine fairly 'loose' as, he claims, he is keen to avoid excluding doctrines as unreasonable 'without strong grounds based on the reasonable itself'[25];

but he claims that a minimal conception of a reasonable doctrine is sufficient for the purposes of working out a political conception of justice.

Because reasonable agents will understand and, crucially, *respect* the burdens of judgement (and thus the fact of reasonable pluralism), they will think it unreasonable to try and use force to subvert a comprehensive doctrine which, while different from their own, is reasonable (in the sense that it itself incorporates the two fundamental ideas of reasonableness as listed above):

> [R]easonable persons will think it unreasonable to use political power, should they possess it, to repress comprehensive views that are not unreasonable, though different from their own. This is because, given the fact of reasonable pluralism, a public and shared basis of justification that applies to comprehensive doctrines is lacking in the public culture of a democratic society. But such a basis is needed to mark the difference, in ways acceptable to a reasonable public, between comprehensive beliefs as such and true comprehensive beliefs.
>
> Since many doctrines are seen to be reasonable, those who insist, when fundamental political questions are at stake, on what they take as true but others do not, seem to others simply to insist on their own beliefs when they have the political power to do so. Of course, those who do insist on their beliefs also insist that their beliefs alone are true; they impose their beliefs because, they say, their beliefs are true and not because they are their beliefs. But this is a claim that all equally could make; it is also a claim that cannot be made good by anyone to citizens generally. So, when we make such claims others, who are themselves reasonable, must count us unreasonable. And indeed we are, as we want to use state power, the collective power of equal citizens, to prevent the rest from affirming their not unreasonable views.[26]

This is the essence of the need to work out the content and limits of a fully *public* form of reasoning, from within the general conception of reasonableness set out above, in order to ground an overlapping consensus regarding a political conception of justice for the regulation of relations among citizens. To be reasonable we must *not* rely on reasons grounded in our particular beliefs, even if those beliefs are reasonable.[27] To be reasonable, to be 'ready to propose principles and standards as fair terms of cooperation' and to understand and respect the burdens of judgement, when considering questions of political justice we must invoke reasons which we expect agents who also affirm reasonable (but incompatible from a comprehensive point of view) comprehensive doctrines to understand, and to accept. Public reason is reasoning which is informed by, and which is appropriate in fulfilling, what Rawls calls the 'publicity condition' of a public political form of justification which, according to Rawls, has three 'levels':

> The first...is achieved when society is effectively regulated by public principles of justice: citizens accept and know that others likewise accept those principles, and this knowledge in turn is publicly recognized. Further, the institutions of the basic structure of society are just (as defined by those principles) and everyone with reason recognises this. They do so on the basis of commonly shared beliefs confirmed by methods of inquiry and ways of reasoning generally accepted as appropriate for questions of political justice.
>
> The second level of publicity concerns the general beliefs in the light of which first principles of justice themselves can be accepted, that is, the general beliefs about human nature and the way political and social institutions generally work, and indeed all such beliefs relevant to political justice. Citizens in a well-ordered society roughly agree on these beliefs because they can be supported (as at the first level) by publicly shared methods of inquiry and forms of reasoning....I assume these methods to be familiar from common sense and to include the procedures and conclusions of science and social thought, when these are well established and not controversial....
>
> The third and last level of publicity has to do with the full justification of the public conception of justice as it would be presented in its own terms. This justification includes everything that we would say – you and I – when we set up justice as fairness and reflect why we proceed in one way rather than another.[28]

For Rawls, a 'well-ordered society', a crucial hallmark of a reasonable society (i.e. a society regulated by principles which are justifiable from within the limits of public reason) will satisfy all three of these publicity conditions (i.e. satisfaction of what he calls 'the full publicity condition').

So we see that a political conception of justice rests on a public form of justification, itself grounded in public reason:

> Given the fact of the reasonable pluralism of democratic culture, the aim of political liberalism is to uncover the conditions of the possibility of a reasonable public basis of justification on fundamental political questions. It should, if possible, set forth the content of such a basis and why it is acceptable. In doing this, it has to distinguish the public point of view from the many nonpublic (not private) points of view. Or, alternatively, it has to characterize the distinction between public reason and the many nonpublic reasons and to explain why public reason takes the form it does. Moreover, it has to be impartial (in ways that need to be explained) between the points of view of reasonable comprehensive doctrines.[29]

Public reason is the companion idea to the idea of political justice; whereas the latter fleshes out Rawls' account of what a substantive liberal conception of justice looks like, the former is intended as a procedural conception and therefore the limits and content of the former will wholly define the limits and content of the latter:

[L]iberal political values are . . . of two kinds:

> a. The first kind – the values of political justice – fall under the principles of justice for the basic structure: the values of equal political and civil liberty; equality of opportunity; the values of social equality and economic reciprocity; and let us add also values of the common good as well as the various necessary conditions for all these values.
>
> b. The second kind of political values – the values of public reason – fall under the guidelines for public inquiry [i.e. 'principles of reasoning and rules of evidence in the light of which citizens are to decide whether substantive principles properly apply and to identify laws and policies that best satisfy them'], which make that inquiry free and public. Also included here are such political virtues as reasonableness and a readiness to honour the (moral) duty of civility, which as virtues of citizens help to make possible reasoned public discussion of political questions.[30]

Public reason draws its content from 'well-established' ideas already available to citizens from within the background culture of their society and about which, owing to the existence of publicly accessible 'methods of inquiry' and 'processes of reasoning', citizens can generally agree. Rawls is clear that, in order to ensure that the basis of justification for the political conception of justice can properly be thought of as being publicly available, public reason may *only* appeal to methods of inquiry and beliefs which are *presently* generally accepted, owing to what he calls the 'liberal principle of legitimacy':

> [I]n discussing constitutional essentials and matters of basic justice we are not to appeal to comprehensive religious and philosophical doctrines – to what we as individuals or members of associations see as the whole truth – nor to elaborate economic theories of general equilibrium, say, if these are in dispute. As far as possible, the knowledge and ways of reasoning that ground our affirming the principles of justice and their application to constitutional essentials and basic justice are to rest on the plain truths now widely accepted, or available, to citizens generally. Otherwise, the political conception would not provide a public basis of justification.[31]

Rawls conceives of the *basis* of the values underpinning the willingness of agents to respect the constraints of public reason as being, at least in his idea of justice as fairness and 'in many other liberal views',[32] the same as that underpinning the values of political justice (the heuristic device of the 'original position' as a means of representation is brought into play here) – the idea of a principle of *legitimacy*:

> [T]he parties in the original position, in adopting principles of justice for the basic structure, must also adopt guidelines and criteria of public reason for applying those norms. The argument for those guidelines, and for the principle of legitimacy, is much the same as, and as strong as, the argument for the principles of justice themselves. In securing the interests of the persons they represent, the parties insist that the application of substantive principles be guided by judgment and inference, reasons and evidence that the persons they represent can reasonably be expected to endorse. Should the parties fail to insist on this, they would not act responsibly as trustees. Thus we have the principle of legitimacy.[33]

It is crucial to note that, for Rawls, the idea of public reason does not *necessarily* lead us to the idea of the original position, and the values which would be chosen by representatives of citizens therein, as the 'criterion' by which to judge the public acceptability of the principles we propose. The crucial point is that the requirements of public reason necessitate that reasoning agents must have *some* criterion for determining the public justifiability of principles and that this criterion must *itself* be publicly justifiable:

> The point of the ideal of public reason is that citizens are to conduct their fundamental discussions within the framework of what each regards as a political conception of justice based on values that the others can reasonably be expected to endorse and each is, in good faith, prepared to defend that conception so understood. This means that each of us must have, and be ready to explain, a criterion of what principles and guidelines we think other citizens (who are also free and equal) may reasonably be expected to endorse along with us. We must have some test we are ready to state as to when this condition is met. I have elsewhere suggested as a criterion the values expressed by the principles and guidelines that would be agreed to in the original position. Many will prefer another criterion.[34]

A variety of different ideas about which reasonable conception of political justice a society should affirm is, according to Rawls, inevitable given the fact of reasonable pluralism, and lends itself to a dialectic convergence of ideas which ultimately deepens the richness of the public political culture. The point is that the requirement that a public justifiability criterion is present is the active, constraining factor which provides limitations on the reasons agents are able to invoke when justifying the proposal of a particular principle of justice:

> Of course, we may find that actually others fail to endorse the principles and guidelines our criterion selects. That is to be expected. The idea is that we must have such a criterion and this alone already imposes very considerable discipline on public discussion. Not any value is reasonably said to meet this test, or to be a political value; and not any balance of political values is reasonable. It is inevitable and often desirable that citizens have different views as to the most appropriate political conception; for the public political culture is bound to contain different fundamental ideas that can be developed in different ways. An orderly contest between them over time is a reliable way to find which one, if any, is most reasonable.[35]

The limits of public reason will determine the limits of public justification. Such limits do not preclude agents from invoking reasons derived from their own comprehensive doctrines, so long as this is done in a manner consistent with 'ways that strengthen the ideal of public reason itself' (Rawls calls this the 'inclusive view'[36]) – although Rawls believes that in a well-ordered society, given the high level of convergence and agreement on the constitutional essentials which will be present (notwithstanding reasonable debate about their exact form), citizens will generally have recourse to the political values inherent in the public political culture itself (the 'exclusive view').[37] This view accords with Rawls' general contention, crucial to his political constructivism, that 'citizens themselves, within the exercise of their liberty of thought and conscience, and looking to their comprehensive doctrines, view the political conception as derived from, or congruent with, or at least not in conflict with, their other values'[38] (chief among them, the values dictated by their comprehensive doctrine). So long as the reasons invoked by citizens accord with the limits of public reason, their origins are unimportant and will be informed by citizens' general affirmation of a particular comprehensive doctrine (to claim otherwise would be to claim that we are *solely* political beings; a contention which Rawls has no interest in making). The manner in which a freestanding political conception of justice is attained by citizens from the starting point of their own comprehensive doctrine is not of chief importance; what is of chief importance is the fact that, owing to a concern to propose fair terms of cooperation, citizens are motivated to locate such a freestanding conception and that in doing so they respect the limits of public reason.

Thus the content of public reason is informed by publicly accessible ideas inherent in the background culture of a democratic society, and its requirement that reasoning invoked in the justification of principles of justice be confined to that which agents reasonably expect others to endorse. It is essential to a proper understanding of Rawls' conception of public reason to understand its unique place at the heart of his political constructivism. The passage from *The Idea of Public Reason Revisited* cited above explicitly reveals the double-conditional nature of its formulation as envisaged by Rawls – I reproduce it here for ease of reference:

> A citizen engages in public reason ... when he or she deliberates within a framework of what he or she sincerely regards as the most reasonable political conception of justice, a conception that expresses political values that others, as free and equal citizens might also reasonably be expected reasonably to endorse.[39]

Thus the exact formulation of the idea of public reason is as follows:

1. Citizens will draw on publicly available ideas, methods of inquiry and forms of reasoning and, having considered these, will arrive at a political conception of justice which they consider the most reasonable. This way they will understand and accept the burdens of judgement;
2. A political conception of justice will express purely political values;
3. Political values should themselves be grounded in a manner consistent with the limits of public reason (whether or not these originate within or outside of a comprehensive conception). They must be reasons which the citizen reasonably expects other free and equal citizens reasonably to endorse;
4. Reasonably expecting other citizens to reasonably endorse one's principles (and the reasons underlying them) means that the principles one proposes must be *capable* of endorsement by other free and equal citizens (that is, capable of cohering with the principles found in all alternative reasonable comprehensive doctrines); but also must be principles that we would reasonably expect other free and equal citizens to *actually* endorse.

The double 'reasonable' condition is essential in point 3 (at this point it is easy to think that the discussion employs the words 'reasonable' or 'reasonably' too much, but not so). The first 'reasonably' denotes the point that citizens must not *un*reasonably expect others to endorse the reasons grounding their proposed principles of justice. The second 'reasonably' denotes the point that *if* citizens can expect that others could reasonably accept the reasons grounding their proposed principles of justice, such reasons cannot be rejected on the argument that others might reject them anyway (i.e. *un*reasonably). Both uses of 'reasonably' are fundamental to the constitution of public reason and reflect the fact that, in acting in accordance with the ideal of public reason, citizens who propose principles of justice are entitled to assume that others will accept or reject such principles in a manner which is *itself* in-keeping with the ideal. This reflects the *reciprocal* nature of Rawls' ideal of public reason.[40]

Crucial to my understanding of Rawls' conception of public reason is the idea that its limits are applicable to the proposer of principles *in him/herself*. Consider the formulation of public reason as set out above. It is applied solely to the proposer – the proposer must propose reasons which he/she reasonably believes others might reasonably be expected reasonably to endorse (all uses of 'reasonable' in this sentence are necessary). The formulation is not dependent on others *actually* endorsing the proposed reasons (or, indeed, the principles they ground). Actual endorsement (meaning, on my understanding, an acceptance of a citizen's proposed principles as reasonable and, accordingly, an affording of proper respect to them and a consideration of them in debates between reasonable conceptions of justice) will, of course, occur if the proposer has remained within the limits of public reason, since, if he/she has, the principles proposed/reasons invoked *will* be reasons which others can reasonably be expected reasonably to endorse (note that the second 'reasonably' here prevents proposees from *un*reasonably rejecting reasonably proposed principles). On my understanding, *actual* endorsement is a natural consequence of citizens adhering to the limits of public reason; but it is *not* a constituent part of public reason itself, which is effectively designed by Rawls to ensure that principles reasonably proposed cannot be reasonably rejected. Again, my understanding is that, by 'endorsement', Rawls means that the principles proposed will be acknowledged as reasonable by other free and equal citizens, and will thus be taken into consideration in debates among reasonable political conceptions of justice. 'Endorsement' does not mean, on my understanding, that every principle reasonably proposed by a citizen must immediately and necessarily be *adopted* by all reasonable peoples. But a reasonable principle which is reasonably proposed by recourse to publicly accepted, publicly available ideas could not reasonably be rejected (i.e. dismissed out of hand) by other citizens.

This interpretation of Rawls' conception of public reason appears at odds with the meaning ascribed to it by Onora O'Neill in her paper 'Political Liberalism and Public Reason: A Critical Notice of John Rawls, Political Liberalism'.[41] In this paper O'Neill considers Rawls' grounding of political liberalism in the idea of public reason which, she claims, is developed out of a conception of reasonableness which is identified 'very closely with a commitment to a form of second-order reciprocity, or rather reciprocity about second order principles'.[42] She claims:

> [B]eing reasonable is clearly not a matter of being impartial: reasonable persons remain motivated by their own ends, rather than by any conception of the general good. Equally, it is not a matter of pursuit of mutual advantage: persons may be reasonable even when their desires preclude the identification of any mutually advantageous outcome. Reasonableness is in the first place a second-order, procedural notion, a matter of being prepared to propose, to listen to, and to

abide by proposals that constrain the pursuit of ends *if others will accept the same constraints*.[43]

For O'Neill, this 'convergence of wills' is insufficient to ground a truly *normative* overlapping consensus concerning a political conception of justice:

> A conditional willingness to agree *if there are terms that will (or would) be agreed on by all* binds nobody when the condition does not obtain. Yet we would often think that certain standards and principles were reasonable even without such assurance – and others unreasonable even with that assurance. In short we would often think that willingness to agree on standards or principles *if others will agree on them too* is neither necessary nor sufficient for reasonableness.[44]

For O'Neill, there are two fundamental issues with Rawls' conception of public reason which, she claims, are not easily resolvable from within Rawls' own theory:

1. O'Neill claims that Rawls' account of public reason is fundamentally *motivational* in nature – that is, that Rawls needs a proper account of *why* citizens would be motivated to reason and act within the limits of public reason.[45] This, she claims, lies in Rawls' account of *citizenship*; more specifically, *citizenship within a closed society*:

> The power of Rawls's conception of public reason is drawn from its connection to his account of *citizens*. Being a citizen with a sense of political identity is much more than being one of a plurality of beings capable of rational and reasonable justification, and cognizant of the limits placed on reasonableness by the burdens of judgment: it is constitutive of reasonableness. Citizens conceive of themselves and one another as able to hold and to revise, and entitled to advance, their comprehensive conceptions of the good, and they acknowledge that although they may hold different comprehensive conceptions of the good, they cannot resolve disagreements about them. They also conceive of themselves as the citizens of a certain society with abilities 'to be normal and cooperating members of society over a complete life'. Even more strikingly, Rawls assumes that the society of which citizens are members is conceived of as 'self-contained and as having no relations with other societies. Its members enter it only by birth and leave it only by death'.[46]

This, claims O'Neill, means that Rawls can conflate the modal and the motivational with relative impunity; citizens of a well-ordered constitutional democracy will naturally enjoy a robust 'shared sense of political identity'.[47] If one removes the bonds of citizenship which exist in the context of a closed constitutional democracy, O'Neill's claim is that the authority of Rawls' motivation-based account of public reason falls away:

> If we did not assume that the context of reason is a closed society of democratic citizens, we might well have doubts about a conception of reasonableness that is conditional on an assurance that others will agree on the principles and standards we propose. Looked at from the perspective of outsiders, others' agreement might be thought to reflect matters quite other than their reasonableness.[48]

2. Related to this charge, O'Neill contends that Rawls' reliance on a conception of a closed society in grounding his claims regarding the authority of public reason constitutes more than reliance on abstraction; for O'Neill, Rawls relies on an *idealisation*:

> [T]he assumption that political justification presupposes a closed society is, as Rawls acknowledges, 'a considerable abstraction'. To be more precise it is no mere abstraction, since abstractions (taken strictly) omit or bracket certain predicates true of the matter from which they abstract. Rather the idea of a closed society is an *idealisation* that assumes predicates which are false of all existing human societies. Idealisations can of course be of great help in theory building. But they have to be handled with care. In particular, they have to be handled with care in practical reasoning, whose aspiration is to fit the world (to some degree) to certain conceptions or principles. In theoretical reasoning an appeal to idealized conceptions (ideal gases, perfect vacuum) is disciplined by the fact that we seek to fit theory to the world: an idealisation that is wide of the mark will reveal its failings. In practical reasoning an inappropriate idealisation is not exposed to the same stringent test, and it is easy to conclude that the world rather than the idealisation is at fault.[49]

Thus there are essentially three charges made by O'Neill regarding Rawls' conception of public reason:

1. That it oscillates between a modal and a motivational account of practical reasoning;
2. That it relies on an idea of a closed society which constitutes an illegitimate idealisation when compared with actual societies; and
3. That the motivational power behind the limits of public reason falls away once Rawls' conception of citizenship in a constitutional democracy (and its correspondingly high degree of shared political identity) falls away.

These are all serious charges and could have the following effects on the integrity of Rawls' account of public reason:

1. Its authority could be limited to grounding principles of justice relevant to the domestic society found in a constitutional democracy *only*;
2. Even then, it could be relevant only in an idealised conception of a closed society rather than actual societies which exist today.

I shall explore elements of these specific charges later on and in subsequent chapters, as they are crucial to a consideration of the authority and appropriateness of public reason in grounding a political conception of justice to regulate *international relations*.[50] However, I want now to focus on O'Neill's interpretation of Rawls' account of public reason and, specifically, the distinction she draws between motivation and modal accounts of practical reason.

O'Neill charges Rawls with shifting between *modal* and *motivational* conceptions of reasonableness. She claims (p. 416):

> in a variant formulation of his conception of reasonableness Rawls relaxes the condition that others be willing to agree to standards and principles proposed, and construes reasonableness as a matter of willingness to accept terms 'which all can accept' or 'to govern their conduct by a principle from which they and others can reason in common'. The significant difference here is the reference to willingness to abide by principles and standards which all *can* rather than *would* or *will* accept. This conception of reasonableness is apparently *modal* rather than *motivational*: reasonableness is a matter of proposing and accepting only principles that others too can accept, but is not conditional on an assurance or expectations that they will do so.

In my understanding, Rawls' conception of public reason incorporates both modal and motivational elements. The first claim which this assertion rests on is that public reason arises out of, but is not equivalent to, Rawls' general account of reasonableness. Reasonableness, the willingness 'to propose principles and standards as fair terms of cooperation and to abide by them willingly, given the assurance that others will likewise do so',[51] combined with an understanding of and respect for the burdens of judgement, provides the motivation for a concern to find publicly justifiable principles of political justice from within the limits of public reason. But it does not describe the limits themselves, which are consequences of a deep consideration of how these abstract motivational ideas would best be adapted into a *practical* form of reasoning which essentially represents the procedural element of a commitment to political justification (with its many companion ideas). Rather, the limits of public reason developed through the five-stage process I outlined above *begin* from Rawls' account of reasonableness as set out at stage 1, but are subsequently refined, honed and applied to the specific issue of choosing what kinds of principles, supported by what kinds of reasons, are appropriate to propose in relation to questions of basic justice and constitutional essentials.

It is crucial to note that my formulation of Rawls' conception of public reason does *not* include the requirement that citizens only be willing to abide by political principles of justice if others are also willing to do the same. This condition is located in Rawls' general account of reasonableness and, as we have seen, is present because Rawls believes that it would be nonsensical to agree to abide by principles of justice if we were *not* convinced that others would do the same (what O'Neill calls a 'contractarian' understanding of justice). However, in public reason the requirement is only that agents propose principles which others might reasonably be expected reasonably to endorse. *Actual* agreement is not an element of public reason; agents must propose only those principles which they genuinely believe other agents *can*, and *will*, accept. The *fact* of agreement will flow from the use of public reason.

My argument is that, rather than presenting alternative conceptions of public reason, as O'Neill claims Rawls does at various points in *Political Liberalism*, there is no great distinction between the motivational and the modal in Rawls' account. As stated above, an *actual* convergence of wills is extrinsic to the constitution of public reason – it is the natural consequence that would flow if citizens confined their reasoning to the limits of public reason. It is not, as O'Neill claims, a necessary part of public reason itself, and is therefore not a condition on which the authority of a political conception of justice is grounded (although it is a condition of reasonableness more generally, it is not a condition implicit *within* the definition of public reason). O'Neill's error, therefore, is to conflate Rawls' account of reasonableness and Rawls' account of public reason. On my understanding, the motivational element of public reason is *antecedently* established as part of Rawls' general conception of reasonableness, and actual agreement on political principles of justice is not built in to the formulation of public reason. Thus the modal and the motivational are *both* present in Rawls' conception of public reason without issue.

Public reason in *The Law of Peoples*

I now proceed to consider Rawls' claims about the form and role of public reason in working out the content of principles for the regulation of *international relations* (i.e. a reasonable Law of Peoples). This is a long citation, but worth reproducing:

> What can be the basis for a Society of People given the reasonable and expected differences of peoples from one another, with their distinctive institutions and languages, religions and cultures, as well as their different histories, variously situated as they are in different regions and territories of the world and experiencing different events? (These differences parallel the fact of reasonable pluralism in a domestic regime.)
>
> To see how to obtain a basis... it is important to understand that the Law of Peoples is developed within political liberalism. This beginning point means that the Law of Peoples is an extension of a liberal conception of justice for a *domestic* regime to a *Society of Peoples*. Developing the Law of Peoples within a liberal conception of justice, we work out the ideals and principles of the foreign policy of a reasonably just liberal people. I distinguish between the public reason of liberal peoples and the public reason of the Society of Peoples. The first is the public reason of equal citizens of domestic society debating the constitutional essentials and matters of basic justice concerning their own government; the second is the public reason of free and equal liberal peoples debating their mutual relations as peoples. The Law of Peoples with its political concepts and principles, ideals and criteria, is the content of this latter public reason. Although these two public reasons do not have the same content, the role of public reason among free and equal peoples is analogous

> to its role in a constitutional democratic regime among free and equal citizens.
>
> Political liberalism proposes that, in a constitutional democratic regime, comprehensive doctrines of truth or of right are to be replaced in public reason by an idea of the politically reasonable addressed to citizens as citizens. Here note the parallel: public reason is invoked by members of the Society of Peoples, and its principles are addressed to peoples as peoples. They are not expressed in terms of comprehensive doctrines of truth or of right, which may hold sway in this or that society, but in terms that can be shared by different peoples.[52]

Rawls distinguishes the *idea* of public reason (above) with the *ideal* of public reason:

> Distinct from the idea of public reason is the *ideal* of public reason. In domestic society this ideal is realized, or satisfied, whenever judges, legislators, chief executives, and other government officials, as well as candidates for public office, act from and follow the idea of public reason and explain to other citizens their reasons for supporting fundamental political questions in terms of the political conception of justice that they regard as the most reasonable. In this way they fulfill what I shall call their duty of civility to one another and to other citizens. Hence whether judges, legislators, and chief executives act from and follow public reason is continually shown in their speech and conduct.
>
> How is the ideal of public reason realised by citizens who are not government officials?... [t]o answer this question, we say that, ideally, citizens are to think of themselves *as if* they were legislators and ask themselves what statutes, supported by what reasons satisfying the criterion of reciprocity, they would think it most reasonable to enact. When firm and widespread, the disposition of citizens to view themselves as ideal legislators, and to repudiate government officials and candidates for public office who violate public reason, forms part of the political and social basis of liberal democracy and is vital for its enduring strength and vigor. Thus in domestic society citizens fulfill their duty of civility and support the idea of public reason, while doing what they can to hold government officials to it. This duty, like other political rights and duties, is an intrinsically moral duty. I emphasise that it is not a legal duty, for in that case it would be incompatible with freedom of speech.

> Similarly, the ideal of public reason is realised, or satisfied, whenever chief executives and legislators, and other government officials, as well as candidates for public office, act from and follow the principles of the Law of Peoples and explain to other peoples their reasons for pursuing or revising a people's foreign policy and affairs of state that involve other societies. As for private citizens, we say... that ideally citizens are to think of themselves *as if* they were executives and legislators and ask themselves what foreign policy supported by what considerations they would think it most reasonable to advance. Once again, when firm and widespread, the disposition of citizens to view themselves as ideal executives and legislators, and to repudiate government officials and candidates for public office who violate the public reason of free and equal peoples, is part of the political and social basis of peace and understanding among peoples.[53]

Through these extended citations about the role of public reason in determining the content of the Law of Peoples, Rawls reveals much about his thinking regarding the nature of international relations. In summary, the essential points are as follows:

1. As has already been noted, the fact of reasonable pluralism is present in the international realm as it is within a constitutional democracy;
2. The Law of Peoples is worked out from within a liberal conception of justice, and extends such a conception to considerations of how liberal peoples should govern their relations with other liberal, and non-liberal but reasonable (what Rawls calls 'decent'[54]), peoples;
3. The content of the Law of Peoples is worked out by 'free and equal liberal peoples debating their mutual relations as peoples' through the use of public reason; Rawls claims that 'the meaning of the idea of decency is given in the same way' as the idea of liberal reasonableness; the basic point that '[i]t is simply politically reasonable to offer fair terms of cooperation to other free and equal citizens, and it is simply politically unreasonable to refuse to do so'.[55] Reasonable liberal and 'decent' non-liberal peoples will understand this basic constituent of reasonableness; and therefore the Law of Peoples will satisfy the liberal principle of toleration because it will be acceptable to decent non-liberal peoples;
4. Analogous with the role of public reason within a constitutional democracy (where 'principles are addressed to citizens as citizens'), the use of public reason in the international involves addressing principles to 'peoples as peoples'. Thus reasonableness involves addressing only those principles which do not rely on recourse to arguments

arising from within a comprehensive moral doctrine (i.e. only principles 'in terms that can be shared among peoples'). Peoples must be addressed in their political capacities as peoples, rather than their more comprehensive capacity as a moral collective which subscribes to a comprehensive moral doctrine;

5. The *ideal* of public reason is realised in international relations when public officials (or other spokespeople for the actions of a people) act from, and justify their action through recourse to, the Law of Peoples as an expression of the use of public reason. A 'realistic utopia', or 'peace and understanding among peoples', is achievable through citizens holding their officials and governments (and, presumably, peoples holding other peoples) to the standards and requirements of public reason.

In *The Law of Peoples,* Rawls' conception of the reasonable, and ultimately of public reason, is implicit within the idea of a *utopian* society, with its companion principle of reciprocity. He claims:

> There is a family of reasonable liberal conceptions of justice, each of which has the following three characteristic principles:
>
> The first enumerates basic rights and liberties of the kind familiar from a constitutional regime;
>
> The second assigns these rights, liberties, and opportunities a special priority, especially with respect to the claims of the general good and perfectionism values; and
>
> The third assures for all citizens the requisite primary goods to enable them to make intelligent and effective use of their freedoms.
>
> The principles of these conceptions of justice must also satisfy the criterion of reciprocity. This criterion requires that, when terms are proposed as the most reasonable terms of fair cooperation, those proposing them must think it at least reasonable for others to accept them, as free and equal citizens, and not as dominated or manipulated or under pressure caused by an inferior political or social position. Citizens will differ as to which of these conceptions they think the most reasonable, but they should be able to agree that all are reasonable, even if barely so. Each of these liberalisms endorses the underlying ideas of citizens as free and equal persons and of society as a fair system of cooperation over time. Yet since these ideas can be interpreted in various ways, we get different formulations of the

> principle of justice and different contents of public reason. Political conceptions differ also in how they order or balance, political principles and values even when they specify the same principles and values as significant.[56]

We can see in the above the clear parallels between Rawls' conception of public reason, and the origins of such – Rawls' conception of reasonableness – in *The Law of Peoples* and that of *Political Liberalism*. Indeed, in *The Law of Peoples* Rawls essentially restates the requirements of reasonableness as developed in such detail in *Political Liberalism*:

> [R]easonable citizens are characterised by their willingness to offer fair terms of social cooperation among equals and by their recognition of the burdens of judgment. In addition, they are said to affirm only reasonable comprehensive doctrines. In turn, such doctrines are reasonable provided they recognise the essentials of a liberal democratic regime [this appears to mean an acceptance of reasonable pluralism and a respect for the burdens of judgement] and exhibit a reasoned ordering of the many values of life (whether religious or nonreligious) in a coherent and consistent manner. Though these doctrines should be relatively stable, they may evolve in the light of what, given the development of their tradition, are accepted as good and sufficient reasons.[57]

5
Contemporary Moral Foundationalism: Buchanan's Conception of Normative Reasoning and the Role of Institutions in Political Justification

Buchanan, one of Rawls' most notable contemporary scholars – as well as one of his fiercest critics – is one of the main proponents of what could be described as an 'institutional cosmopolitan' approach to international relations (specifically human rights). The central tenet of his voluminous work regarding human rights is the belief that the institutions which have developed as a response to human rights concerns contain at their 'normative core' the idea that moral claims to human rights can be justified through universalist, ahistorical forms of philosophical argument – or, in other words, the belief that philosophical work which attempts to locate a universalist underpinning for moral claims to human rights must take seriously the need for the contextualisation and realisation of those rights (and the need for them) through appropriate and *legitimate* institutional forms:

> [S]urely at least part of what makes the concept of HR [Human Rights (i.e. a concept of human rights that can be understood without reference to the global legal/institutional phenomenon of human rights)] of philosophical interest is that it seems to be the normative core of the IHR [International Human Rights (i.e. a theory of the existing global legal/institutional phenomenon of human rights, not a theory of the history of the idea of human rights, nor a theory of individual rights that can be characterized without reference to their role as constraining sovereignty in a state system)][1];

And:

> human rights are institutional in the sense that their formulation recognises the role of institutions, both in standard threats to well-being and in countering those threats.[2]

In his more recent work[3] we see the development of Buchanan's conception of the moral and institutional underpinnings of human rights norms through an extended critique of the concept of reasonableness employed by Rawls, the list of human rights he endorses, the idea of 'decency' as a minimal concept and the exclusion of representatives of individuals in *The Law of Peoples*.[4]

The importance of Buchanan's work in the context of my book is as follows: Buchanan's status as a contemporary scholar of Rawls' means that his political justification arises out of the critique of Rawls' conception of reasonableness as referred to above but, crucially, Buchanan's own conception of political justification is itself *not* Rawlsian, nor constructivism. An analysis of Buchanan immediately after an analysis of Rawls' conceptions of political reasonableness and public reason will, therefore, allow me to consider the relative strengths and weaknesses of a contemporary form of *foundational* political justification in the international context as compared with the constructivist concepts I wish to extrapolate from Rawls. To this end, I will consider Buchanan's work in detail in order to ascertain the nature of his preferred form of political justification and, ultimately, to consider its potential viability as a legitimate answer to the poststructuralist critique (a detailed consideration of Buchanan's critique of Rawls' conception of reasonableness as developed in his international work will also afford me an opportunity to augment my analysis of Rawls' conception of public reason as applied to a consideration of international justice). I will then critically compare his most fundamental claims about the nature of international relations with Rawls' conception of the role of public reason. After that, and in order to complete my analysis of the most fundamental tenets of the debates concerning the nature of practical reasoning in international relations, I will in the next chapter critically compare Kratochwil's account of the role of reason as part of a constructivist theory of international relations with the respective forms of justification developed by Rawls and Buchanan. Ultimately, I will argue that, in my contention, a constructivist account of the nature and conditions of public practical reason will provide for a more robust form of political justification than the contemporary foundationalism espoused by Buchanan, but that nevertheless Buchanan's sophisticated work in highlighting the centrality of an account of the role of institutions, and institutional reasoning, as a crucial component of political justification should be taken seriously by constructivist political theorists in providing a response to the challenge of poststructuralism.

Buchanan's critique of Rawls

I turn first to Buchanan's consideration, and ultimate critique of, the conception of public reason employed by Rawls in *The Law of Peoples*, before moving on to consider Buchanan's own theory of justification in international relations.

Buchanan's stated aim in 'Justice, Legitimacy and Human Rights' is to reconstruct the arguments set out in 'The Law of Peoples' so as to consider the tenacity of the criticisms levelled at Rawls' international thinking by certain liberal human rights' theorists (he cites Teson[5]; Moellendorf[6]; Tan[7]) – chiefly, the objection to Rawls'

> conclusion that a reasonable law of peoples would require only that societies respect a proper subset of what liberals usually regard as human rights, that societies should be regarded as fully legitimate even if they lack democratic institutions, make no provisions for distributive justice beyond the guarantee of subsistence, do not recognise freedom of expression or of association, and include serious institutionally sanctioned inequalities between men and women or even between castes or races.[8]

A reconstruction of Rawls' arguments in 'The Law of Peoples' will, claims Buchanan, 'make clearer the basis for his claim that a reasonable law of peoples would require only [Rawls'] truncated list of rights'.[9]

As part of his reconstruction of the basis of Rawls' putatively 'truncated' list of human rights which, claims Rawls, are necessary for a people to observe in order for it to be considered 'well ordered' by a 'reasonable conception of the good', Buchanan characterises Rawls' conception of reasonableness as a grounding criterion in the search for political legitimacy thus (note that he appears to be addressing only the 1993 version of 'The Law of Peoples'):

> In 'The Law of Peoples', Rawls says little explicitly about how the notion of reasonableness is to be applied to the comprehensive conceptions of the good that order hierarchical societies. In *Political Liberalism*, in contrast, Rawls explicitly first characterises reasonableness

> as applied to persons: 'Rather than define the reasonable directly, I specify two of its basic aspects as virtues of persons. Persons are reasonable in one basic aspect when, [(a)] among equals, say, they are ready to propose principles and standards as far terms of cooperation and to abide by them willingly, given the assurance that others will likewise do so... and [(b)] they are willing to recognise the burdens of judgment'. To recognise the burdens of judgment is to appreciate that there are a number of factors that can lead to reasonable disagreements among persons on matters of value, including questions of justice. Rawls says little about what this appreciation amounts to practically speaking, that is, in efforts to determine whether a conception of the good is reasonable. He does not articulate a set of minimal epistemic conditions – standards of minimal rationality that any acceptable argument for organising a society according to a conception of the good must satisfy – and then argue that appreciation of the burdens of judgment entails that one not attempt to impose on others any principles of social order that one cannot support by arguments that satisfy those standards.
>
> After characterising reasonableness as applied to persons, Rawls goes on to connect the idea of the reasonable as applied to persons with that of a society organised by reasonable principles: 'The reasonable is an element of the idea of society as a system of fair cooperation and that its fair terms be reasonable for all to accept is part of the idea of reciprocity'. It would seem to follow that a society organised according to a comprehensive conception of the good would meet the criterion of reasonableness if, and only if, that comprehensive conception could be consistently held by a reasonable person, one who is willing to propose and accept fair terms of cooperation with others as equals, assuming they are so willing, and who properly acknowledges the burdens of judgment.[10]

The issue, for Buchanan, is that the inclusion of what are clearly *liberal* predicates as part of Rawls' conception of reasonableness – specifically, the inclusion of 'as among equals' – renders the idea illegitimate when applied to the Society of Peoples:

> [T]he difficulty is that if the notion of reasonableness (as including aspects [a] and [b] previously) is only applicable to liberal societies, then that notion cannot be used by Rawls in 'The Law of Peoples' to determine which societies are entitled to be regarded as members in good standing of the society of peoples, and hence to non-interference.[11]

Hence, claims Buchanan, reasonableness cannot ground Rawls' 'two criteria' which are required for a society to be conceived of as 'well-ordered' (the requirement that the society be non-expansionist; and the requirement that the society respect 'human rights proper' (i.e. Rawls' 'truncated' list)).

Buchanan claims:

> In 'The Law of Peoples', Rawls does offer a reason why these particular rights, and only these, must be respected by a society if that society is to be well ordered and, hence, entitled to non-interference. He asserts that hierarchical societies that are well ordered are those that are organised according to a 'common good conception of justice'. A common good conception of justice includes three elements: (1) 'the system of laws imposes moral duties and obligations on all members of society'; (2) the conception of the good according to which the society is organised 'takes impartially into account what it seems not unreasonably as the fundamental interests of all members of society'; and (3) 'there is a sincere and not unreasonable belief on the part of judges and other officials who administer the legal order' that the law is indeed guided by a common good conception of justice.[12]

Thus, claims Buchanan, if we assume that the 'institutional embodiment' of the idea of a common good conception of justice includes Rawls' list of human rights, then observance of Rawls' list qualifies a society to be properly conceived of as well ordered. However, asks Buchanan, '[w]hy should we assume that a society is entitled to non-interference (assuming it is non-expansionist) if and only if it is organised according to a common good conception of justice?'.[13]

The argument that Buchanan favours which, conveniently for present purposes (given that Rawls explicitly seeks to do this in *The Law of Peoples*) connects Rawls' international thought with the central ideas of *Political Liberalism*, is reconstructed as follows:

1. A society is entitled to non-interference (and to be regarded as a member in good standing in the society of peoples) if and only if it is organised by reasonable principles.
2. Principles for organising a society are reasonable if and only if they could be accepted by reasonable persons, that is, by those who (a) acknowledge the burdens of judgement and (b) are willing to propose and accept fair terms of cooperation.

3. Those who acknowledge the burdens of judgement will not attempt to impose their conception of the good on other societies (i.e. are nonexpansionist).
4. A society is organised on the basis of fair terms of cooperation if and only if it is organised by a common good conception of justice.
5. If a society is organised by a common good conception of justice, it will respect the human rights proper.
6. Therefore, a society is entitled to non-interference (and to be recognised as a member in good standing in the society of peoples) if and only if it is nonexpansionist and respects the human rights proper.[14]

Buchanan prefers this interpretation of the justifying arguments behind Rawls' two principles because, he claims, the interpretation 'provides an argument for the conclusion that there can be reasonable, though illiberal, societies and that reasonable persons will tolerate such societies'.[15] He conceives of this notion of reasonableness as being 'a more general sense of reasonableness' than the one proposed by Rawls in *Political Liberalism* – one which omits the 'among persons considered as free and equal' qualification – and hence this conception may be legitimate when applied to both liberal and reasonable non-liberal peoples as a justificatory argument.

Therefore, Buchanan conceptualises the distinction between Rawls' domestic and international theory as a two-tier system of legitimacy which applies different forms of justification – and hence legitimacy – grounded by distinct conceptions of reasonableness (in the case of the domestic, reasonableness among free and equal citizens which is rooted in a liberal conception of justice and hence is legitimate in determining principles for the regulation of a constitutional democracy; in the case of the international, an idea of reasonableness acceptable to reasonable peoples who are organised by common good conceptions of justice, on the basis of their willingness to propose and accept fair terms of social cooperation). Buchanan labels this the 'duality of justice' thesis:

> According to the duality of justice thesis, to require hierarchical societies to comply with the liberal egalitarian principles of justice that Rawls's theory of justice as fairness advocates would be to act illegitimately. The proper standard of justice for the international system is far less demanding: Instead of the full list of civil and political rights set out in Rawls's 'Equal Liberty Principle' (which includes rights to participate in democratic government and rights to freedom of expression and freedom of religion), 'the Principle of Fair Equality of

> Opportunity' and 'the Difference Principle', all that a legitimate international order can require of any state is that it be nonaggressive in its foreign relations and that it respect the human rights proper.[16]

It is here that Buchanan's critique of what he conceives as the 'conservative' (or 'regressive') nature of Rawls' 'view of international law'[17] (essentially his conception of what should count as human rights) kicks in. It is clear from the outset that Buchanan's issue is with the types of regime which Rawls' international theory of justification would determine was reasonable, and hence legitimate:

> In 'The Law of Peoples', Rawls concludes that a proper application of the notion of legitimacy yields the result that it would be wrong to try to use international legal institutions or unilateral action to compel any state to do more than respect the human rights proper in its dealings with its own citizens. This means that even states that prevent women or members of a particular racial or ethnic minority from getting an education, from voting, or from holding public office are to be regarded as fully legitimate so long as they do not threaten the physical security of such persons, provide them with a minimal of material means for subsistence, do not persecute them for their religion, and allow them to voice their views at some 'appropriate' level of consultation hierarchy (and are nonexpansionist).[18]

Although Buchanan agrees with certain more traditional liberal critiques of Rawls which attack the apparently permissive standards of international toleration (those theorists he labels the 'liberal critics of "The Law of Peoples" ', again citing Teson, Moellendorf and Tan), his stated aim is to 'take Rawls's distinction between justice and legitimacy seriously but to argue that Rawls is mistaken as to the implications of this distinction for a morally defensible international legal order'.[19] Buchanan claims:

> I argue that Rawls's view on the primacy of legitimacy as well as his particular principle of legitimacy (the general reasonableness criterion) can be preserved without the regressive implications concerning human rights that critics of 'The Law of Peoples' find so disturbing. To do this, I will have to show that at least the more inegalitarian of what Rawls regards as well-ordered hierarchical societies do *not* pass the test prescribed by his legitimacy principle – or at least I will have to show that it is unwarranted to assume, as Rawls does, that such societies fall within the domain of the reasonable.[20]

In order to undertake this project, Buchanan focuses on Rawls' 'general conception of reasonableness', as outlined in stages 1–6 above. For Buchanan, Rawls' claim that reasonableness at the international level requires a common good conception of justice is solid since, he claims, to regard this element as unnecessary for an international conception of reasonableness would mean that at least some agents (whether the subject or object of considerations of justice) would be excluded from the scope of moral deliberations:

> A system of law that exempted some persons from having any moral duties or obligations would not treat those individuals as being minimally equal in the sense required for even the most austere notion of fair cooperation: They would either be above others, occupying a position of godlike privilege, or they would be beneath others (as when slaves are said to be 'morally dead' – beings who are not understood to have moral obligations because they are assumed to lack moral personality). Similarly, a comprehensive conception of the good that did not impartially take into account everyone's essential interests would not be a fair basis for cooperation in even the most minimal sense; in such a system the good of some would not count at all, and hence to require their cooperation would not be fair.[21]

In considering Rawls' arguments for stage 5 – the necessity of the link between a common good conception of justice and a respect for the 'human rights proper', and in reconstructing the argument he suggests that Rawls must rely on in making this connective step, Buchanan's own thinking on the moral underpinnings of human rights begins to be revealed:

> What Rawls calls human rights appear to be institutional embodiments of the conviction that everyone's essential interest are to count in the organisation of society where this, in turn, is understood to be required by the idea of fair terms of cooperation. It would be difficult to argue that a society which did not honour these basic rights could be described as being organised according to a comprehensive conception of the good that is reasonable in the sense of being acceptable to persons who are willing to accept fair terms of cooperation, even according to the least robust interpretation of fair cooperation. The question, then, is not whether respect for Rawls' truncated list of human rights (along with nonexpansionism) is necessary for a hierarchical society to be justified in enforcing its principles of social order,

> and to be free from interference by other societies, but whether it is *sufficient*.[22]

Thus, claims Buchanan, the underpinnings of human rights are located in the minimal moral claim that 'everyone's interests are to count', which he claims Rawls must argue is a necessary element of the idea of fair terms of cooperation. This idea then informs Buchanan's analysis of Rawls' claim that a respect for the burdens of judgement necessitates a suitably minimal list of norms which are to count as human rights. For Buchanan, it does not follow that a respect for the burdens of judgement requires toleration of those societies who, while respecting their subjects' minimal rights to physical integrity, foster gross inequalities on the basis of 'dubious assumptions' about the inferior status of the subset in question (whether it be women, a certain racial group, a certain social group etc). Rawls, claims Buchanan, cannot support his assumption that all societies who respect his list of basic human rights (and are non-expansionist) must be considered reasonable because he has not developed a rigorous account of what is entailed by respecting the burdens of judgement – which Buchanan claims would reveal the inherent *unreasonableness* of many societies which *actually* justify gross inequalities on the basis of flawed empirical claims or unstable epistemological standards and which apparently, on Rawls' account, would have to be considered reasonable members of the Society of Peoples:

> Rawls supplies no account of what a proper recognition of the burdens of judgment requires when it comes to assessing the reasonableness of comprehensive conceptions of the good. He provides no set of epistemic standards for empirical claims used in arguments to justify inequalities nor any minimal standards for reasonable inferences. However, reflections on the sorts of justifications actually given for extremely inegalitarian regimes suggest that any plausible account of the burdens of judgment is likely to rule out much more than Rawls assumes.[23]

In contrast, Buchanan argues that Rawls *must* accept that a true recognition of the burdens of judgement necessitates the requirement that significant inequalities (i.e. anything beyond what Buchanan calls 'minimum inequalities') themselves be supported by justificatory arguments which are *not* based on spurious empirical claims or flawed epistemological standards. This, he claims, is required by Rawls' commitment to a comprehensive conception of the good as part of the minimal requirements for a reasonable society, and itself necessitates a justificatory argument which is grounded in a morally significant concern for the fundamental interests of human beings:

> Properly recognising the burdens of judgment, in a world containing not only different religious conceptions of the good but secular ones as well, requires that argumentation concerning what counts as 'fair terms of cooperation' *among human beings* be framed primarily in terms of the interests of *human beings*, considered in their own right. By asserting that reasonableness requires at least that a comprehensive conception of the good that is to serve as the basis for organising society must recognise the minimal freedom and equality of persons captured by the idea of a common good conception of justice, Rawls himself admits as much. But once we go this far, the burden of justification lies on those who support inequalities beyond this minimum, and that burden cannot be born simply by making religious claims that are not accessible to those who hold reasonable secular views. Given that what is at issue is fair terms of cooperation among human beings, defenders of ethnic, racial, caste, or gender inequalities must support their views with reasons that engage directly with the interests of those who are expected to participate in such a cooperative scheme.[24]

This is a very significant early insight into the heart of Buchanan's thinking on international justice. Essentially, Buchanan is arguing that societies wishing to organise themselves in such a way that promotes systematic inequalities *must*, in order to be considered reasonable by the Society of Peoples (and thus in order to qualify for non-intervention), justify their internal arrangements in argumentative terms that are grounded in reasonably abstract claims which refer to the general interests of human beings and that, moreover, *such justificatory argument must be kept within the limits of public reason*. This latter element can be discerned from the fact that he explicitly excludes argument which relies on acceptance of a comprehensive religious doctrine (we can assume he would also include non-religious comprehensive doctrines), and also from the assertions he makes regarding the necessary engagement of this required justificatory argument with the interests of the human beings who are to participate in the society in question. These two elements combined lead to the conclusion that the justificatory claims which Buchanan has in mind are necessarily reasonably abstract. They must also, presumably, be *accessible*, both to the reasonable Society of Peoples, and the subjects/citizens of the particular society in question.

Given Buchanan's claim that justificatory arguments must be couched in terms which do not rely on recourse to the language of a comprehensive doctrine, and given Buchanan's professed agreement with Rawls' commitment to *legitimacy* in any proper justificatory account of human rights, it is clear that the justificatory arguments he has in mind will need to be abstract enough to be accessible both by its own citizens/subjects and the reasonable Society of Peoples. Thus it appears that they will need to be based on Rawls' idea of 'publicly available ideas, forms of enquiry and methods of reasoning' which, as we saw in my analysis of *Political Liberalism*, informed the content of public reason. By drawing on only these elements of the 'background culture' of international relations, Buchanan's envisaged justifications of inegalitarian schemes of domestic cooperation will be legitimately grounded, will remain within the limits of public reason, and will be accessible by both the subjects/citizens of the society in question (since it will invoke only *public* forms of reasoning), as well as the reasonable Society of Peoples which, presumably, must also accept the argument as valid.

I certainly agree with Buchanan's key insight that, in order to invoke properly *public* forms of reasoning in international relations (and hence to remain within the limits of public reason), a sophisticated account of the epistemological implications and methodological understandings which must pertain to any reliance on shared understandings in an account of practical reason appropriate to international relations is very definitely needed. This, I believe, is where Kratochwil is key, and I will consider the epistemological element of Buchanan's justificatory theory in detail below and compare such with Kratochwil's arguments concerning the normative nature of practical reasoning in the next section. I also think it likely that many justificatory arguments actually employed to support extreme inequalities harbour questionable empirical claims (Buchanan himself admits that his claim is a suggestion, not a justified argument[25]). However, one immediate question which arises from Buchanan's argument above is: Will the 'background culture' of international relations, which I certainly agree does exist, be enough to ground a justificatory defence of inequality which conforms with his robust egalitarian standards of international justice? As we shall see, Buchanan's robust form of institutional egalitarianism incorporates a conception of practical reasoning which is *not* invoked in a justification of his moral claims regarding the equal status of human beings. These moral claims are, explicitly, *assumptions*, justified through a combination of negative inference (Buchanan assumes that claims to normative inequality, rather than normative equality, are in need of justification) and the fact that Buchanan tends to address his arguments to a particular audience for whom his moral claims will, he anticipates, be antecedently justified. As suggested above, my claim is that without a fully fledged conception of public reason, as worked out by Rawls, Buchanan's account of normative justification will ultimately lack the force of the constructivist approach I espouse in the justification of normative claims in a manner appropriate to considerations of international justice. While Buchanan's *empirical* conception of practical reasoning contains many valuable insights (including the need for a sophisticated account of social epistemology as part of a conception of normative reasoning), and his claims concerning the fundamental importance of institutions in any justificatory theory of international relations are capable of taking seriously the significance of intersubjective structure (which I argue any true understanding of international relations must do), the lack of a constructivist justification for his *moral* claims will be controversial once Buchanan moves beyond a theoretical community which already accepts the ethical consequences of universal vulnerability.

Buchanan's 'egalitarianism' critique of Rawls is furthered and expanded on when he considers Rawls' claims regarding the sufficiency (or lack of) of Rawls' list of human rights in meeting the standard of 'fair terms of cooperation'. Again, Buchanan claims that implicit in the idea of fair terms of cooperation is the basic assumption that 'everyone's basic interests are to count for something and that everyone is to have moral obligations and duties'[26] – as revealed by the idea of a common good conception of justice. He therefore asks: 'How are inequalities (regarding gender, race, ethnicity, caste, or the distribution of political power) compatible with the terms of cooperation being fair?'[27] Rawls, he claims, has not appreciated the difficulty of justifying significant domestic inequalities in terms consistent with the idea of fair cooperation (and thus in terms which can be considered reasonable):

> Rawls seems to be insufficiently appreciative of how difficult it would be to justify the extreme inequalities of the Taliban regime or of the traditional Hindu caste system by appeal to the idea of fair cooperation. It is interesting to note that in general, it is efficiency, or the maximisation of the social good, that is typically appealed to in order to justify such inequalities when anything beyond purely religious 'reasons' are offered in support of them. I have already suggested that such appeals to efficiency or the optimal social good appear invariably to rest on false empirical claims (about what is needed

> for economic stability or for development or about the natural differences between those at the top and those at the bottom). Quite apart from this, however, the crucial point is that if we take Rawls's reasonableness criterion seriously, any attempt to justify inequalities by appeals to efficiency or the maximisation of the common good is ruled out as irrelevant if the inequalities in question cannot be shown to be compatible with the terms of cooperation being fair. Rawls is on very shaky ground when he assumes that the extreme forms of discrimination that are compatible with his account of a well-ordered hierarchical society can be reconciled with a commitment to fair terms of cooperation.[28]

Thus, Buchanan's critique of Rawls allows a glimpse into his commitment to a more or less fully liberal commitment to justice in international relations. His claim is that Rawls' commitment to even a basic set of human rights, and his conception of reasonableness in international relations, lead to the conclusion that, notwithstanding the indeterminate nature of what a 'consultation hierarchy' involves, a democratic society will more effectively secure its citizens' basic rights than a consultation hierarchy (this also indicates Buchanan's insistence on an 'institutional' conception of justice which takes seriously the central role of institutions in any account of the human rights and moral obligations conferred on citizens):

> Rawls assumes, without argument, that a society that includes what he calls a consultation hierarchy will reliably secure what he calls the human rights properly speaking, even in the absence of a multiparty political system, liberal-style freedom of expression and association, and a universal or even broad franchise that empowers citizens to vote at least on who will represent them in the making of the most basic laws. It is hard to evaluate this assumption, in part because Rawls says so little about what a consultative hierarchy includes. He does say that judges and other officials in a consultation hierarchy are bound to listen to voices of dissent. However, the idea that consultation is hierarchical seems to imply that persons are not allowed to address officials at the upper end of the hierarchy directly, and the qualifier 'consultative' presumably implies that dissenters have no institutionally recognised power to try to influence social policy, as they would have if they had the right to vote and to form political parties. If this is so, then it appears that the government of a society that includes only a consultative hierarchy is less likely, other

things being equal, to be held accountable by its citizens than one that is democratic. Therefore, it would also appear that, other things being equal, Rawlsian human rights will tend to be more secure in a democratic society than in a society that includes only a consultation hierarchy.[29]

Buchanan's institutional conception of justice – the Modest Objectivist View/The Natural Duty of Justice

Buchanan develops his Modest Objectivist View – his preferred framework by which to ground authoritative claims to human rights – in two essays in *Human Rights, Legitimacy, and the Use of Force*: one of which attempts to reconcile the 'minimalist egalitarianism of human rights' with 'the more robust egalitarianism of contemporary philosophical views of equality'[30]; the other of which addresses the 'parochialism objection' (the charge that 'what are called human rights are not really universal in the sense of being rights of all individuals but instead merely reflect (1) an arbitrarily restricted set of moral values; or (2) an arbitrary ranking of certain moral values'[31]). As we shall see, the *context* within which Buchanan's justificatory theory is set out becomes important.

The Modest Objectivist View sets out three assumptions on which claims regarding the authority of human rights norms rest:

1. Every person counts equally in some morally fundamental sense, and this basic equality of moral worth grounds an entitlement to conditions needed to secure the opportunity to live a decent or dignified life (the equal regard assumption).
2. Certain things can be done to human beings or certain deprivations they can suffer that generally undercut the opportunity for their living a decent life (the standard threat assumption).
3. Feasible and morally acceptable social institutions and practices can significantly reduce these standard threats (the institutional response assumption).[32]

Buchanan states the following about the Modest Objectivist View (the 'MOV'):

> Assumption 1 is one way of capturing the idea that the obligations in question are owed to individuals on their own account, and to that extent it is consonant with the idea that human rights are

> grounded in the inherent dignity of human beings. Assumptions 2 and 3 make it clear that this view of human rights has a substantial *empirical* component and that a list of human rights cannot be derived from a concept of human nature alone. More precisely, the MOV implies that sound justifications for assertions about the existence of human rights will rely significantly on factual premises, both about standard threats to basic human interests and about how these threats can be countered. According to the MOV, human rights are bundles of normative relations, primarily entitlements and duties. When these normative relations are realised – when human rights are respected – human beings enjoy powerful protections against the standard threats to their basic interests, the constituents of a decent human life.[33]

The equality assumption flows from Buchanan's commitment to a form of justificatory reasoning which is 'framed primarily in terms of the interests of human beings', as we saw in the context of his critique of Rawls' claims about the consequences of recognition of the burdens of judgment. In 'Equality and Human Rights', Buchanan further elucidates the normative underpinnings of the basic moral assumptions on which his justificatory theory rests which, as should already be clear from the preceding, is fundamentally egalitarian in its moral, and descriptive, essence:

> The Modest Objectivist View does not take human rights to be basic in the sense of being moral axioms. Instead, human rights norms are understood as requiring justification, and the justification appeals to basic human interests, to the idea that these basic interests ought to be protected, to assumptions about what threatens these interests, and to assumptions about what is needed to protect them.
>
> The conventional understanding of human rights is essentially egalitarian in two respects: human rights norms not only assume that there are some characteristics shared by all human beings (the Descriptive Equality Assumption), but also that a proper recognition of the moral significance of these characteristics requires that they be treated in certain ways and that this places significant restrictions on permissible inequalities among them (the Moral Equality Assumption). According to the Modest Objectivist View, the Moral Equality Assumption that grounds the conventional conception of human rights can be formulated as follows: each of us has an

> obligation to help ensure that every individual has the opportunity to have a minimally decent human life. If it is to ground the commitment to human rights and convey the moral priority that the conventional conception of human rights claims, the Moral Equality Assumption must be understood as a fundamental moral obligation that falls on all individuals, though fulfilling it ... typically requires appropriate institutions.[34]

As can be seen from this extended analysis, the Moral Equality Assumption is bound up with the Descriptive Equality Assumption – essentially, the assumption that all human beings are vulnerable in equivalent ways. Crucially, however, the Moral Equality Assumption is not *constructed from* the Descriptive Equality Assumption – that is, Buchanan does not start with the Descriptive Equality Assumption and proceed, through an appropriate conception of practical reason, to construct the normative qualities inherent in the Moral Equality Assumption. Rather, the Moral Equality Assumption appears just that – an *assumption* that *if* the Descriptive Equality Assumption is correct and human beings *are* all vulnerable in the same way, this fact alone necessarily creates morally significant obligations to help ensure that each individual is afforded the opportunity for a minimally decent human life. Essentially, Buchanan wants to argue that, *intuitively*, it follows from the fact of universal vulnerability that universal moral obligations are created.

The essence of Buchanan's *intuitive* claims regarding the moral underpinnings of authoritative rights/norms claims can additionally be gleaned from his earlier major work on international law. Interestingly, Buchanan also here argues, contrary to theorists such as Thomas Pogge, that the 'Natural Duty of Justice' (as a slight variation of the Modest Objectivist View which is referred to in this work) is *not* dependent on the fact of interaction across borders for its existence ('even if there were no global basic structure of cooperation or any form of interaction whatsoever among individuals across borders, we would still have a limited obligation to help create structures that provide all persons with access to just institutions'[35]).

In contrast to the Modest Objectivist View, which contains distinct normative and empirical elements, the Natural Duty of Justice is conceptualised as a moral obligation which itself *contains* empirical premises:

> The Natural Duty of Justice is the limited moral obligation to contribute to ensuring that all persons have access to just institutions,

> where this means primarily institutions that protect basic human rights. The Natural Duty of Justice assumes that securing justice for all persons requires institutions, but this is not an unreasonable assumption;

And:

> [T]he Natural Duty of Justice is not a rock-bottom, basic moral principle, though it is close to it. It rests on three premises, one factual, the other two moral. The factual premise is that ensuring that all persons are treated justly requires just institutions (including legal institutions). The first moral premise is that all persons are entitled to equal respect and concern – or, as Kant would say, that each is to be treated as an end. The second moral premise is that treating persons with equal concern and respect requires helping to ensure that they are treated justly, where this primarily means helping to make sure that their basic human rights are not violated (not merely refraining from violating them ourselves). Call the first moral premise the Moral Equality Principle (or the Equal Moral Consideration or Equal Regard Principle).[36]

Thus the formulations of the Modest Objectivist View and the Natural Duty of Justice are slightly different, but essentially they get at the same thing – that a respect for the Moral Equality Principle (that all persons' basic interests are to count for something) necessitates an *active* approach to ensuring that persons' basic rights are upheld:

> Taking the Moral Equality Principle seriously commits us to the Natural Duty of Justice, because a proper understanding of the Moral Equality Principle implies that to show proper regard for persons we must help ensure that their basic rights are protected. And this in turn requires us to embrace a cosmopolitan view of international law, rejecting both the idea that states are moral persons and the position that states are merely institutional resources for their own people.[37]

Thus, claims Buchanan, a commitment to the Moral Equality Principle will have far-reaching consequences and will require a progressive, cosmopolitan conception of international law, which includes a requirement of just institutions through which all individuals are afforded the opportunity to live a decent life. For Buchanan, the factual assertions (i.e. the acknowledgement that institutions have a far-reaching determinative effect on whether a person is afforded the opportunity to live a decent life, and the corresponding requirement that institutions containing the necessary tools to protect the basic rights of all are established and maintained) are as important as the moral assertion in any justificatory account of international justice.

In order to ensure that the institutions we support are endowed with the characteristics necessary to protect the basic rights of all – and thus to ensure that everyone is afforded the opportunity to live a decent life – Buchanan believes that a sophisticated social epistemology of human rights is needed. This, he claims, is required in order to avoid the traps of parochialism which, informed by the essentially empirical nature of political justification, is applied to conceptions of human rights in a purely *empirical* manner (e.g. a conception of human rights would be parochial if it: (1) 'were based on an unduly narrow understanding of the conditions that typically undercut a human being's opportunities for a decent life'; (2) 'were based on an unduly restricted view about which institutional arrangements can effectively counter a particular standard threat to basic human interests'; (3) 'if it incorporated a one-sided understanding of the effects on basic human interests of the enforcement of some of the rights it encompasses'[38]). For Buchanan, charges of parochialism in the *realisation* of rights in order to protect the basic interests of all are a real threat to the integrity of a just international order. In order to minimise the risks of empirical parochialism, he claims, institutions must adequately reflect what he calls a 'normative' conception of social epistemology (i.e. 'the comparative evaluation of alternative institutional arrangements according to their tendency to foster true or justified beliefs'[39]):

> [I]nstitutions that contribute to the articulation of human-rights norms ought to provide venues for deliberation in which the authority of good reasons is recognised, in which credible efforts are made to reduce the risk that strategic bargaining or raw power will displace rational deliberation, in which principled contestation of alternative views is encouraged, in which no points of view are excluded on the basis of prejudicial attitudes toward those who voice them, and in which conclusions about human rights are consonant with the foundational idea that these are moral rights that all human beings (now) have, independent of whether they are legally recognised by any legal system. Such arrangements could significantly reduce the risk that the underlying conception of a decent life would be subject to serious distortions of parochialism.[40]

Buchanan's social epistemology of human rights goes even further – he argues that international institutions are in a unique position to 'authoritatively specify' the 'interpretation of a particular human right when there is a plurality of reasonable interpretations'.[41] Thus, as is the case with the state in questions of domestic justice, a 'legitimate' institution can create a 'normative coordination point' by 'authoritatively specifying one arrangement from among the acceptable alternatives'.[42] This way, international institutions are capable of offering a principled, authoritative specification of an interpretation of what is to count as a human rights norm, and are able to do so on the basis of publicly available, reliable factual information. Buchanan's assertion seems to be that the basis of a publicly available account of human rights is a public form of justification which is both culturally inclusive and factually accurate, and that, once this has been established, institutions are in a position to articulate an authoritative interpretation of the norm in question:

> Properly designed institutions can reduce the risk of parochialism in the articulation of human rights norms and thereby contribute to establishing the legitimacy of an international legal order that is centrally committed to the protection of human rights, in at least the following ways:
>
> (1) They can access and utilise reliable factual information crucial for the justification and/or specification of human rights norms.
> (2) They can achieve a more inclusive representation of interests and viewpoints than is likely to be available at the domestic level and to that extent can mitigate the risk of culturally biased understandings of basic human interests, of what threatens them, and of what institutional arrangements are needed to counter the threats.
> (3) They can help us know what our obligations are regarding human rights by providing principled, authoritative specifications of human rights when there is a range of reasonable alternatives.[43]

There are several interesting aspects to this formulation which are worth noting at this stage:

1. In point (1), Buchanan is arguing that the justification of human rights norms crucially relies on 'reliable factual information' concerning those norms and institutional arrangements which will best protect the basic interests of all;

2. Again, at point (2), Buchanan's claims about the need to avoid 'culturally biased understandings' appears to relate to the need to avoid empirical claims which are conditioned by cultural bias, and hence are in danger of manipulation or, ultimately, untruth; and
3. Buchanan's use of 'reasonable' in point (3) is not defined, but appears to relate to any specification of human rights which takes the moral, and descriptive, equality assumptions seriously.

Buchanan further develops his account of social epistemology. He argues that, in order to ground a sufficient justification of *human rights norms* (which Buchanan views as a particularly vociferous form of norm-claim[44]), a 'provisional core conception of human rights' is needed, one that is able to flesh out an understanding of what is bound up with the specific idea of a human rights claim (institutions' 'epistemic adequacy depends in part on the particular character of the norms they are supposed to articulate'[45]) but, crucially, one that is capable of revision, adaption and (Buchanan will need to claim) abandonment as our confidence in the epistemic virtues of the institutions we support develops and shows our initial core conception to be in need of adaptation (thus avoiding 'vicious circularity' between the initial conception and the epistemic assessments we make about institutions). Buchanan's assertion is that the Modest Objectivist View is capable of grounding a core conception of human rights, from which the epistemic adequacy of international institutions can begin to be assessed, leading (potentially) to the revision of the core conception:

> To take the MOV as our provisional starting point is *not* to assume that it can provide by itself a fully adequate justification and specification of human-rights norms. Instead, the idea is to use the core conception to make a *Provisional* assessment of the plausibility of the lists of human rights that are contained in the major human-rights treaties. Once this is accomplished, we can then begin to make provisional assessments of the epistemic adequacy of existing institutions in their role of specifying and supplementing these rights without any vicious circularity – so long as we take seriously the possibility that the workings of these institutions may in turn require revisions in our initial conception of human-rights norms and even in the core conception itself.

Vicious circularity is avoided, then, if two conditions are satisfied:

(1) We have a provisional core conception of human rights that is both morally plausible and sufficiently contentful to guide the

formulation of a list of rights and an initial evaluation of the epistemic adequacy of the relevant institutions.

(2) We have reasons to be confident in the epistemic virtues of these institutions, reasons that are independent of the congruence between their specification of human rights norms and our initial core conception of human rights.[46]

For Buchanan, a commitment to the MOV as a provisional conception of human rights leads to a reasonable expectation that the 'institutions that articulate human-rights norms' should 'have provisions for accessing reliable factual information and correcting errors regarding the facts when they make them, given how crucial reliable factual information is to the justification and specification of human rights according to our core conception of human rights, the MOV'.[47] The relevant factual information will be information about what constitutes threats to basic human interests and, correspondingly, what combinations of human rights norms and institutional arrangements will be required to minimise such threats. The crucial point for Buchanan is that the epistemic adequacy of international institutions can be assessed *independently* from the provisional conception of human rights adopted:

> The crucial point is that whether the institutions have this epistemic virtue can be assessed independently *without* assuming that the particular conception of human rights norms we are now operating with is the correct one. What matters is whether the institutions have what it takes to produce or access reliable factual information *of the sort* that is likely to be relevant for specifying and justifying claims about human rights from the perspective of *something like* our core conception of human rights.[48]

Buchanan's arguments about the need to locate a sophisticated conception of social epistemology *within* a normative theory of justification allow an insight into the conception of practical reason employed therein. As can be drawn out from the analysis above, practical reason will necessarily feature in Buchanan's theory in at least two fundamental, and connected, respects:

1. *Public reason.* In assessing the best 'fit' between the identified threats to basic human interests, and the most appropriate institutional responses by which to effectively counteract such threats, a conception of public practical reason will be required in order to determine

the effectiveness with which specific patterns of human rights norms, as well as the institutional structures which protect and articulate them, adequately embody the most effective means by which basic interests can be protected. Without such a conception, we would not possess the tools required to assess the relationship between a particular institutional structure (and the particular pattern of human rights norms it embodies) and the specific threat to basic human interests which we are trying to minimise. Such reason must accord with the limits of public reason as worked out by Rawls: it must form part of a public basis of justification and must draw its content from publicly shared, inclusive, and non-parochial ideas;

2. *Practical/legal reason.* In assessing the epistemic adequacy of institutions to effectively utilise reliable factual information, engender an inclusive representation of interests, and ultimately provide principled, authoritative specifications of human rights, a conception of legal and practical reasoning will be required in order to accurately assess the ability of a particular social epistemology to gauge the epistemic effectiveness of a particular institutional structure to authoritatively select from a range of reasonable alternatives. Without such a conception, we would not be in a position to adequately assess the epistemic qualities of a particular institutional structure, because we would lack the tools required to make a connection between the epistemic characteristics of the institutional structure and an authoritative account of social epistemology. This, claims Buchanan, is fundamentally linked with processes of legalisation, and thus practical and legal reasoning are intimately intertwined as part of the justification of a particular institutional structure in international relations (he claims, 'we should not assume that legal processes are merely mechanisms for translating independently justified moral rights into legal ones; they can constitute modes of public practical reasoning that contribute to our understanding of moral rights and to their justification'[49]).

Buchanan's account of reasonableness in international relations is fundamentally linked to his claim that a standard of *legitimacy* is required in order to adequately assess the appropriateness of a particular institutional structure as part of the framework of international relations. In *Human Rights, Legitimacy, and the Use of Force,* Buchanan fleshes out the requirements of such a standard of legitimacy for institutions which, he claims, 'must provide a reasonable public basis for coordinated support for the institutions in question, on the basis of moral reasons that are widely accessible in spite of the persistence of significant moral disagreement – in particular, about the requirements of justice'.[50] Thus, claims Buchanan, '[g]lobal governance institutions... must not persist in committing serious injustices', which includes 'the violation of human rights'.[51] The violation of human rights will form part of what is meant by the term 'injustice' due to the existence of 'moral reasons that are widely accessible'.

We can see here that Buchanan is employing a conception of *public reason* as part of his wider conception of reasonableness. This conception is further shored up by Buchanan's frequent references to the idea of a public justification. However, the key feature of Buchanan's use of the idea of public reason in the context of a public form of international justification is that it is *necessarily linked to institutions which themselves articulate the idea of human rights*. Crucially, the idea of public reason in Buchanan's theory is not employed to justify the existence of human rights, nor to justify the moral assumptions which ground his assertion that everyone's basic interests count. Buchanan does not feel the need to offer a robust justification of these moral assumptions, and certainly does not do so by recourse to the idea of public reason. For him, they are an essential part of any legitimate conception of morality:

> In my judgment, the Moral Equality Principle itself is fundamental to any conception of morality worth seriously thinking about. Notice that it not only requires that in some basic sense we treat all persons equally (which is compatible with treating them all badly), but also that we treat them well, that we show a high regard for their basic interests, an equally high regard.
>
> Because I have no intention of systematically engaging those who are sceptical about morality altogether or about the fundamental moral equality of persons in this work, I will make no effort to argue for the Moral Equality Principle.[52]

For Buchanan, only those who already accept the basic moral contention that the basic interests of all should be treated with an equally high regard are worth engaging with. This claim antecedently given, he therefore justifies his more demanding moral claim – that each of us is obligated to ensure that all basic human interests are protected – by the assertion that it is logically incongruous to accept the first moral premise without accepting the second.

This theoretical reliance on an *assumption* that all must accept the basic moral premise that everyone's basic interests should be treated well (an extension of the assumption that everyone's basic interests are to count) continues into Buchanan's work in *Human Rights, Legitimacy, and the Use of Force,* and here it is informed by the *context* within which Buchanan's project is placed. As was noted earlier, the Modest Objectivist View is discussed in the context of an attempt to effectively combine the robust egalitarianism found in political philosophy with a conventional account of human rights, and then in an attempt to show how an institutional justification of human rights which begins with the Modest Objectivist View can overcome the parochialism objection (as formulated in the manner set out above). In each of these cases, the scope of Buchanan's project is limited; he is addressing a particular literature, or a particular charge, and therefore it is relatively easy to assume that the respective audiences he is addressing already accept the basic moral assumptions which guide his work.

However, once the scope of address is broadened, it may be more problematic to rely on an egalitarian assumption about the normative importance of all persons' basic interests (and the obligation to treat them with high regard) which, ultimately, arises from a fairly thick commitment to liberal values and moral sensibilities, rather than the public political culture of international relations. With respect to this claim, the conceptions of public practical reason employed in Buchanan's justificatory theory do not assist. The importance placed on the development of a sophisticated account of social epistemology in any justification of human rights norms is, I think, extremely insightful and Buchanan is right to claim it as an intrinsic part of a conception of practical reason appropriate to international relations. But the problem as I see it is that, in the manner employed by Buchanan (i.e. in the assessment of the effectiveness of institutional structures in adequately realising a normative objective which rests on an antecedently given moral assumption), a sophisticated account of practical and legal reasoning will *not* extend to considerations of the authority of the ethical underpinnings of the entire project.

Buchanan's conception of public reason is designed to assess the legitimacy of institutional structures, understood as their ability to effectively articulate authoritative specifications of human rights norms which most ably guarantee the protection of the basic interests of all. While again this is an extremely valuable use of the idea of public reason, the fundamental distinction between Buchanan's conception and the manner in which it is employed by Rawls is that, in Rawls' theory, it is designed to ground a substantive political conception of justice (albeit one worked out from within political liberalism) which itself specifies the ethical considerations which underpin assessments of the institutional structures which pertain in international relations. Moral commitments are constructed through the use of public reason (as part of a more general commitment to reasonableness); they are not antecedently given. Thus, in Rawls, public reason does not *rely* on predetermined, substantive moral assumptions; rather it relies on an account of reasonableness which specifies the formal requirements citizens/peoples must necessarily conform to in working out the substantive moral commitments which ground a political conception of justice. The subtlety lies in the fact that, for Rawls, a conception of reasonableness must necessarily contain the *motivational* considerations which citizens and/or peoples must connect with in order to be moved to act reasonably (i.e. a common good conception of justice; a willingness to offer fair terms of cooperation). This, however, is distinct from Buchanan's account of reasonableness in the following ways:

1. Buchanan does not claim that the Moral Equality Assumption arises from within a conception of reasonableness. It is a foundational assumption;
2. Rawls' motivational requirements specify the *types* of qualities which citizens/peoples will possess if they are motivated by a desire to act reasonably. This is wholly distinct from Buchanan's formulation which relies on substantive ethical assumptions which precede, rather than follow from, his account of reasonableness;
3. Correspondingly, while Rawls' account of public reason is designed to do the justificatory work in a *normative* sense, Buchanan's is designed to do the justificatory work in a *descriptive* sense. By drawing on ideas inherent in the public political culture of international relations, an account of public reason will, for Buchanan, serve to ensure that the *empirical* effectiveness of institutional structures in articulating inclusive and authoritative principles of human rights is adequately assessed.

6
Philosophical Constructivism and Critical Constructivism Combined: Kratochwil's Account of the Conditions of Practical Reasoning and the Rawlsian Conception of Public Reason

Buchanan's claim that an account of political justification needs to incorporate a sophisticated account of institutional and legal reasoning is certainly one I wish to take seriously. An account of the underpinnings of normative claims in international relations cannot but engage with the fact that normative projects must find a way to dispel boundaries between moral, practical, legal and institutional reasoning, all of which will play crucial roles in the construction and actualisation of normative structure. An account of international relations predicated on the concept of the reasonable must, therefore, find a way to incorporate these apparently divergent and distinct elements of the idea of reason into an enhanced or 'complete' account of political justification. At this point, Walker's claims about the presence of arbitrary, spatiotemporally conditioned distinctions between concepts, built on boundaries which, once scrutinised, can be seen to be predicated on illegitimate foundations, is key. The insistence on a delineation between various forms of reasoning into unique 'categories' (e.g. the category of practical reason; the category of institutional reason; the category of legal reason) can, I will argue, be undone. This is not to claim that normative forms of reasoning are completely analogous and contain no unique characteristics at all. On the contrary, what I want to argue is that the various forms of normative reasoning we have considered (and will consider further below) can be conceptualised in a continuous, and mutually supportive, manner rather than being thought of as distinct ideas speaking to distinct realms of normative focus. As we shall see, a project such as this will have profound and enhancing effects on the theories of social and philosophical constructivism I have considered above, and will ultimately serve to ground a theory of international politics capable of truly transcending the poststructuralist critique.

To reemphasise the importance of a consideration of Buchanan's critique of Rawls, and his own form of international political justification: Buchanan's most fundamental claim, for my purposes, is that an account of normative reasoning necessarily includes empirical and institutional elements, which themselves require a sophisticated account of practical and legal reasoning which:

1. Is capable of accommodation within a wider political constructivist framework, backed by a normative conception of reasonableness appropriate to the conditions of international relations;
2. Is capable of accommodation within (and, in a fundamental sense, capable of integration with) a conception of public reason by which international actors can draw on a rich and normatively significant array of ideas inherent in the 'public political culture of international relations' in order to provide the content of a 'shared basis of justification', as Rawls states,[1] as well as the content of debates among reasonable conceptions of justice (which, again as claimed by Rawls, is informed by 'the history and usages of international law and practice' which reasonable agents imbue with normative significance through a 'reflect[ion] on the advantages of the principles of equality among peoples'[2]). My argument will be that, in drawing on ideas inherent in the public political culture of international relations, actors will need to engage with the essentially *normative* nature of the structures and rules which anchor the intersubjective meanings of actions, principles, opinions and beliefs; and
3. Does not perpetuate the inside–outside dichotomy, or the other tenets of the critique of International Relations identified by Walker and Ashley.

My contention is that, in contrast with the foundational use of normative concepts as worked out by Buchanan, Rawls' conception of public reason *is* capable of accommodation within an account of international relations which takes seriously the need for an *appropriate* standard by which to ground normative claims for the regulation of world politics. Such a conception will need to be located within a more general standard of reasonableness which is capable of producing both appropriate and authoritative international normative principles via a sophisticated conception of normative reasoning. I want to argue that, given the inherent nature of international relations as it exists today (which I have identified through my consideration of Walker/Ashley, Wendt/Kratochwil, and Frost in earlier chapters), Rawls must engage with Buchanan's claim that political justification must necessarily contain empirical and institutional elements and that, in order to provide a sophisticated account of institutional reasoning and social epistemology (both of which are requisite to a true understanding of the nature of international relations), both Rawls and Buchanan can and must engage with the complex and sophisticated account of normative reasoning worked out by Kratochwil in *Rules, Norms and Decisions*.

Kratochwil's account of practical/legal reasoning

I have considered Kratochwil's holistic constructivism in detail in Chapter 2. To recall the essence of Kratochwil's theory – his fundamental claim is that

> human action in general is 'rule-governed', which means that – with the exception of pure reflexes or unthinking conditioned behaviour – it becomes understandable against the background of norms embodied in conventions and rules which give meaning to an action. Thus, not only must an actor refer to rules and norms when he/she wants to make a choice, but the observer, as well, must understand the normative structure underlying the action in order to interpret and appraise choices. Norms are therefore not only 'guidance devices', but also the means which allow people to pursue goals, share meanings, communicate with each other, criticise assertions, and justify actions.[3]

Given Kratochwil's assertion that 'rules and norms influence choices through the *reasoning process*', he claims that

> the processes of deliberation and interpretation deserve further attention. While various choice models have attempted to give a coherent account of certain aspects of choosing, such as specifying rational action as a maximising choice under certainty, risk, or even certain conditions of interdependence, these models are of limited help in understanding the reasoning procedures we use when we argue about our grievances. In that case the reasonableness, fairness, or

> appropriateness of our valuations and their attendant claims to priority are at issue. Here rational-choice models are of little help precisely because the criteria of traditional rationality presuppose the independent and fixed valuations of the actors. However, most of our arguments concerning policy or rights are not so much about the determination of the likely result, *given* a certain distribution of 'preferences', as they are debates over which preferences deserve priority over others, which ones ought to be changed, and which judgments deserve our assent. Here the overall persuasive 'weight' of claims rather than their logical necessity or aggregation is at issue.[4]

We can immediately see in these initial citations the fundamental connection between Kratochwil's conception of the role of norms in influencing action, his account of practical reasoning and, ultimately, the epistemological implications of a holistic norm-governed conception of action. Thus, I will proceed by considering Kratochwil's claims concerning the nature of norms and their effect on action and knowledge, and will then go on to consider Kratochwil's consideration of the nature of practical and legal reasoning (which, I believe, represent the deepest and most fundamental elements of *Rules, Norms and Decisions*). Finally, I will consider how Kratochwil's conception of normative reasoning can be accommodated within the framework of political constructivism and, ultimately, how a Kratochwilian conception of normative reasoning can provide mutual support for, and ultimately legitimate (in the context of international relations), a Rawlsian conception of public reason.

In laying the conceptual foundations for his unique form of constructivism, Kratochwil investigates 'three world-images and their corresponding concepts of knowledge'. These are:

1. The world of observational facts;
2. The world of 'intention and meaning'; and
3. The world of institutional facts.[5]

These distinct but at least partially translatable 'worlds' produce correspondingly distinct forms of knowledge and 'epistemological puzzles', which Kratochwil considers in turn.

The world of observational facts, dependent on 'an exhaustive description of these facts and on the establishment of certain regularities among them',[6] is of limited assistance within the social sciences, claims Kratochwil, precisely because 'usually we do not know what the data mean even if they come in quantified form'.[7] Thus, while data collecting and analysis may provide *some* assistance in the development of a true understanding of international relations, without some additional analytical tool (with a corresponding awareness of the epistemological implications of distinct types of 'facts'), we are not too well served.

The world of intention and meaning, claims Kratochwil, is 'no longer one of measurement but rather one in which the reconstruction of the parameters of action is at issue. Within such a horizon an actor's choice and his/her subjective intentions and motives can be understood'.[8] Thus, 'the appropriate model of knowledge is one in which the reconstruction of a subjective interpretation of a coherent (rational) course of action discloses the motive which "appears to the individual involved, or to the observer, to be a sufficient reason for his conduct" '.[9] This category of action, with its accompanying model of knowledge, includes a subcategory of 'social action', which is action 'requiring that an "individual's conduct is meaningfully oriented towards that of others" '.[10] Thus, claims Kratochwil, '[t]he differences to the world of observational facts becomes obvious. It not only contains mental terms, such as intention, wishing, and wanting, but the *interactions* among the social subjects are norm-governed'.[11] The fact that 'causal explanations within the action-perspective are fundamentally different from the causes of nature' leads to 'difficulties in explaining human action, if done purely in physicalist terms'.[12] Therefore:

> Meaningful action is created by placing an action within an intersubjectively understood context, even if such imputations are problematic or even 'wrong' in terms of their predictive capacity. To have 'explained' an action often means to have made intelligible the goals for which it was undertaken.[13]

The distinction between 'causal explanations' in the world of observation, and that of intention, is therefore that

> [i]n the case of natural phenomena (that is, in a physicalist framework), cause and effect have to be determined *independently* from each other through neutral measurements. But the same is *not* true in the case of motivational accounts, where 'causal' motives can only be imputed by the observer *after* a goal is assumed to be controlling.[14]

The world of 'institutional facts', claims Kratochwil, corresponds with a set of facts that 'are not well explained either by the theory of meaningful action or by theories relying on observational facts'.[15] Kratochwil's examples here include the act of marriage (i.e. stating 'I do'), or promising (i.e. stating 'I promise') since, in both instances, 'the language of intention does not seem to be appropriate to capture some of the essential features'.[16] Kratochwil claims:

> [R]ules are intrinsically involved in speech acts... [and]... their character is quite different from that of regulative rules, which serve as our usual model of rules. Regulative rules such as 'thou shall not kill' are constraining in that they order us to adopt a certain behaviour. Usually they can be expressed as imperatives, and it is this fact that gave rise to the Austinian mistake of conceptualising law as a 'command of the sovereign'. If imperative regulations are our paradigm of rules, constitutive rules which specify, i.e., what counts as a checkmate, a treaty, a vote, etc., strike us as somewhat curious. Therefore, there is an understandable tendency to amalgamate constitutive (or 'enabling' rules, as Hart has called some of them), with the paradigm of constraining or regulative rules. Nevertheless, there exist important differences between regulative and institutional rules, differences which have decisive epistemological implications.[17]

Thus, 'even descriptive terms such as "offside", "checkmate", "home run", etc., are not simply labels for a state of affairs but attain their meaning by pointing to further consequences within the game structure, such as choosing a move, making a point, having to pay a penalty'.[18] Ultimately, 'neither the model of instrumental rationality nor that of empathy, reconstructing the purposes of the actor, adequately explains a practice such as promising':

> The meaning of the act – or the illocutionary force of the utterance – 'is more than a matter of mere intention; it is at least sometimes a matter of convention and a correct analysis will have to capture both the intentional as well as the *conventional* aspects of such a speech act'.[19]

Thus 'knowledge of the game structure' becomes crucial in affording a context and a meaning to action, speech and knowledge. Kratochwil emphasises the importance of 'everyday language' in situating an action (or speech act) within a particular context and, thus, imbuing that action (or speech act) with meaning. Through everyday language, the 'structure of the discursive interaction and not the semantics or the manifest aspects of the sentences'[20] control the meaning of the speech act, which can include 'indirect' speech acts (i.e. where meaning is conveyed implicitly within the utterance, rather than in the semantics of the words used). Essentially, Kratochwil is arguing for a pragmatic approach to the investigation and location of meaning in speech actions, and it is through the anchor of everyday language (essentially, practical discourse) that this pragmatism reveals itself.

Once Kratochwil has established the basis for determining the meaning afforded to a particular speech action (through knowledge of the underlying normative structures by which the practice within which the speech act is made comes to be imbued with meaning), he asks: '[w]hy can rational actors give assent to statements made by someone else?'[21] The inducing of consent to statements concerning logical propositions, or practical judgements, can, claims Kratochwil, 'be attacked through a variety of strategies: through restrictions in meanings; through the acceptance of "evidence" for what is the case; or through the stabilisation of normatively secured expectations'.[22] The last of these strategies, the 'stabilisation of normatively secured expectations', applies to the 'pragmatic dimension of languages', which 'becomes most noticeable in deliberations about practical matters':

> Common understandings can be arrived at through the stabilisation and evocation of certain generally shared expectations among actors in a specific situation. The medium of understanding is then neither logical cogency nor semantic truth, but rather *claims to the validity of norms* on the basis of which actors can communicate, coordinate their actions, and adjust their preferences.[23]

Thus the 'problem of adducing consent' (which is critical, in the context of my book, in understanding why peoples would be motivated to take seriously the limits of public reason and not locate argument within the parameters of their own comprehensive doctrines[24]) specifically with regards to practical matters, gives rise to the conditions of practical reasoning as claims to the validity of those norms which underpin the social structures (and, ultimately, institutions) by which practical actions in international relations are imbued with meaning. Kratochwil argues that '[i]nstead of making "consistency" and "truth" the paradigmatic case for deciding validity-claims, as logic and positivism demand, we had better use the model of deciding such questions *discursively* as our "normal case" '.[25] Thus, he claims:

> [S]ince the basis of validity-claims remains problematic in cases of normative statements, as neither an external check nor internal

> logical criteria are available to settle 'practical' matters unequivocably, the issue of why and how certain 'opinions'... become authoritative has to be investigated. In particular, one has to inquire into the ways in which traditions, historical experiences, past cases, practices, ideologies, etc., provide support for 'reasons' that become socially dominant. Consensus, after all, does not simply emerge out of various debates but is dependent on the availability of cultural, historical, and philosophical experiences by which members of a society share meanings and find solutions to their problems.[26]

This passage goes to the heart of Kratochwil's conception of normativity and normative reasoning. It also provides an early indication of the conceptual similarities between practical reasoning in Kratochwil (and, to a reasonable extent, Frost), and public reason in Rawls. For Rawls, citizens draw on the ideas inherent in the 'public political culture' of a constitutional democracy (as, I would argue, do peoples in international relations in drawing on ideas inherent in the public political culture of the international realm[27]) and frame their proposals concerning principles of justice in such a way as to be reasonably acceptable to other reasonable peoples. Kratochwil, additionally, is here claiming that an inquiry into the intersubjective experiences by which consensus regarding authoritative expressions of opinion is reached will be crucial in order to understand claims to the validity of practically oriented norms (which themselves ground an understanding of the meaning of action and speech in practical contexts). This, I argue, leads to the conclusion that Kratochwil and Rawls conceptualise the *source* of the content of their respective approaches to practical (public) reason in a comparable way and, crucially, that the conceptions of normative reasoning developed by both can be amalgamated into a 'completed' theory of normative reasoning which will not only be able to combine the distinct strands of practical reason identified by Kratochwil, but will also be able to locate the conception within a wider conception of the reasonable, formatted to take into account the conditions of international relations (and therefore not susceptible to a charge of unvindicated liberalisation), which will ground the motivation for agents to engage in reasoning about the *moral* nature of the structures of IR.[28] I will develop this claim further below.

Norms and practical reason

Kratochwil's discussion of the normative nature of practical deliberations and 'institutional facts' feeds in to his consideration of the particular 'style' of practical reasoning (i.e. ' "deliberation", which deals with things which are judged to be in our control'[29]). As stated above, practical reasoning is, for Kratochwil, fundamentally bound up with legal reasoning.[30] He distinguishes between three 'contexts' of law, with three correspondingly different relationships between the context and the role of norms:

1. The 'first-party context ("first-party law") is characterised by the issuance of commands which may or may not have generalised character'.[31] Kratochwil claims: 'what is crucial for the first-party context is the *Imposed* character of the norm, i.e., that the interests, objections, or claims of the addressee(s) are at a minimum, as they are not admitted to an argumentative exchange on an equal basis'[32];
2. The 'second-party context is characterised by "strategic" behaviour among the parties, i.e., by the recognition of interdependence of decision-making, and – in many circumstances – the existence of "mixed motives", or even the perception of common interest'.[33] Kratochwil claims: 'Rules and norms *can, but need not, figure prominently in the actors' choices* since the bargaining between them might include coercive moves. Thus, the resort to norms can be – and frequently is – subsidiary to the process of "breaking the other's will" in order to arrive at a decision'[34]; and
3. 'Third-party law', which 'is the conventional conception of law, i.e., it covers the cases in which a third party applies *pre-existing rules* to a given controversy in order either to mediate or settle the submitted issues authoritatively'.[35]

Kratochwil is careful not to argue that not *all* applications of antecedently established norms can be classified as law:

> It is precisely the task for any serious analysis to make distinctions and develop a conceptual apparatus in which differences as well as commonalities of norms and their varying impact on decision-making can be assessed. Since actors normally *do* make distinctions between the prescriptive force of legal norms and imperatives of 'comity' or 'morality', the distinction between legal and non-legal norms is important for practical as well as theoretical reasons.[36]

Thus, Kratochwil's particular conception of the effect of norms on reasoning is identifiable. Legal norms and non-legal norms will have a particular effect on the style of reasoning employed by the actor-deliberator, with a corresponding effect on the decision reached and ultimately the action carried out. Additionally, first-party, second-party and third-party norms will influence the *style* of the reasoning process in particular ways and provide particular 'types of guidance'. Ultimately, 'rules and norms which are used for arriving at a decision do not function in this choice-process like logical terms or causes but rather as persuasive reasons'.[37]

Kratochwil frames his consideration of the particular characteristics of practical reason within a consideration of the differences between practical and 'theoretical' (or purely logical) reasoning. Thus, claims Kratochwil, in the case of practical reasoning the 'finding of the relevant "starting-points", rather than the stringency of the final logical deduction, is the important part'.[38] Correspondingly, in the case of practical reason the actor will rely on a variety of practical judgements which that actor will employ as part of an attempt at persuasive argument designed to foster 'rational' assent for the decision made:

> In arriving at a particular decision a judge, as well as, in most cases, an actor who follows (or decides to break), a rule, will seek assent to a variety of *practical judgments* which are logically independent of the relevant rule or norm... [a] good (i.e., persuasive) decision will be one in which... a rational assent can be gained through the giving of persuasive reasons why these rather than other practical judgments – which would have been possible – were held to be decisive and deserve support.[39]

It is at this point that Kratochwil introduces the concept of 'topoi', or 'commonplaces', stating their importance within the concept of practical reasoning:

> Commonplaces are not only helpful in the discovery of the *starting-points* for practical arguments... [t]opoi, as 'seats of arguments', are also decisive for attaining *assent to choices* based on a series of practical judgments.[40]

The conception of 'commonplaces' plays a hugely important role within Kratochwil's conception of practical reason. The interplay of specialised and practical ('commonplace') topoi provide the starting points for practical debates, as well as informing the *path* the debates will follow in order to arrive at an authoritative – and acceptable – decision:

> The topoi, or commonplaces, and the various 'catalogues' of topoi provide pointers for discursive strategies by which crucial facets of a practical problem can be examined and subjected to various challenges in the process of deliberation[41];

And:

> [W]hile 'practical arguments' within a discourse of grievances are potentially interminable, since each party can challenge the arguments of the opponent, more specialised techniques are necessary in order to lend persuasiveness to the finality of an authoritative decision. In law, these specialised techniques are based on certain topoi that are *specific to legal orders*. Their function is largely to justify *exclusions* and thus to limit the range of relevant facts and proofs.[42]

We see here the fundamental connection between practical and legal reasoning; legal reasoning is a form of practical reasoning which relies for its authority on specialised legal topoi. We also see that topoi serve to *exclude* various arguments, or bases for arguments, and, correspondingly, will also serve to justify the prioritisation and ordering of particular practical considerations as being of relevance to the practical or legal (or both) issue under consideration. Kratochwil claims that practical reason and his related conceptualisation of law are bound up with the *use* of practical and more specialised legal norms – as is the communication of the use of those norms as a fundamental component of the reasoning involved in reaching the ultimate decision – and that the invocation of particular practical or legal norms rely for their intersubjective validity on the determining presence of practical or legal topoi. It is important to note the distinctions Kratochwil draws between norms and topoi. Topoi are not, in themselves, norms. I will consider their genesis and character in detail below, but the important point to note here is that the development of historically and culturally conditioned topoi over time give meaning and structure to normative frameworks, which themselves serve to characterise the path of reasoning about practical issues.

Thus, Kratochwil has developed a wholly unique approach to the conceptualisation of law as a style of (essentially a form of practical) reasoning (and makes the concept of law and legal reasoning fundamentally relevant to my study). It also provides a sophisticated account of institutional reasoning and international law creation – and the fundamental role of norms in both – which can (1) speak directly to these elements of Buchanan's justificatory system as set out in the last chapter and (2) provide a means by which the traditional dichotomy between the domestic and international realms can be overcome:

> [T]he legal character of rules and norms can be established when we are able to show that these norms are *used* in a distinct fashion in making decisions and in communicating the basis for those choices to a wider audience. Note that such a characterisation of law is independent of formal institutions, levels of analysis, or the existence of logically closed systems.... [A]scertaining the *impact* different rules and norms have on any particular move in international relations or in the domestic arena can only be decided through an empirical investigation. Here the 'standard operating procedure' by which governments dispose of routine decisions are particularly relevant. Furthermore, the investigation of crises – in which these procedures break down and a redefinition of the game is sought – provides us with evidence on the role of norms under non-routine conditions. Such investigations could demonstrate the irrelevance of established norms when high political interests are at stake, although the picture, as it emerges from the concrete studies of crisis-bargaining, is quite different from the widely held belief of the irrelevance of norms in these situations. Even if we agree on the marginal, rather than central, importance of norms in moulding the *outcome* of international crises, such an assessment is quite different from the facile dichotomy between the 'domestic' and 'international arena where norms count or do not count respectively'.[43]

The nature of topoi, the path of legal argument and the characteristics of legal and normative reasoning

As should be clear from the above, Kratochwil conceptualises law as a particular 'style' of reasoning which, while being fundamentally connected with practical reasoning in the ways outlined above, remains subtly distinct from reasoning with moral (or indeed other non-legal) norms:

> [R]easoning with legal rules differs substantially from the type of reasoning appropriate for making policy decisions. The specificity of guidance of legal rules when contrasted with 'policy' can be seen when we consider changes in decision-making which deviate from established rules. Thus, we speak of a 'violation' of legal rules; policies, on the other hand, are not violated but changed, precisely because the discretion allowed makes implementation usually solely

> a matter of the unilateral calculus of the actor. Similarly, when a moral norm is transgressed, the justification for either condemning the conduct or excusing it will be substantially different from breaking a legal rule.... [M]oral arguments utilise mostly 'principles' rather than specific rules. This, however, means that much of the argument will turn on the questions of applicability of a principle, since principles do not specify their range of application. It is the specificity of legal rules, most obvious in the cases of setting definite deadlines for legally relevant actions, or for specifying the conditions of the validity of an action, that leads often to divergent assessments of the 'legality' versus the 'morality' of an action.[44]

Notwithstanding the significant differences Kratochwil identifies between legal and moral reasoning, the fact that they are both subsumed within the wider category of practical reason – and thus rely on the reason-providing characteristics of particular types of norms – necessarily means that 'a considerable overlap also exists between law and morals'.

Thus the *principled character of application*, and the reliance of both on the historical and cultural development of specialised and practical 'commonplaces' (which subsume both ethical and legal reasoning within the wider remit of practical reasoning), is a fundamental characteristic of both legal and normative reasoning. As we have seen, Kratochwil tends to conceptualise moral norms in a particular way – that is, as being principle-based, relatively indeterminate and imprecise when compared with legal norms. However, the key characteristic uniting legal and moral norms – their mutual application in a principled manner – is, I think, fundamentally bound up with the orientation of both within the bounds of Kratochwil's conception of practical reasoning (and, as we shall see below in Kratochwil's consideration of the profound constitutive role played by the institution of promising, are crucially linked concepts). Both moral and legal norms will provide contextual, path-dependent reasons for action which will depend for their communicative success on the underlying topoi (both specialist and 'commonplace') which will link the particular specialised (i.e. legal/philosophical discourse) and 'everyday' (i.e. practical discourse) in order to arrive at an authoritative decision. The analogous, interconnected and historically conditioned natures of moral, practical and legal reasoning (as well as the significant epistemological effect of conceptualising these realms of reasoning in a norm-oriented way) can, I think, be discerned from the following passage, in which Kratochwil addresses the 'rule of law' topos:

> [T]he concept is part and parcel of our heritage and o our way of tackling certain practical issues by making claims and counter-claims. Thus, in spite of a lack of stable reference, the term plays a decisive role in the realm of *praxis* where we try to work out our legal and political problems. Its meaning therefore consists in its *use* and in the connections it establishes to other concepts within a semantic field, and in the way in which certain actions and practices are thereby authorised or prohibited. Thus any analysis of this *problematique* must always be historical as well as analytical and must be alert to its 'ideological' dimension. Because it addresses practical issues, the rule of law is bound to deal with political projects, and these, in turn, always transcend the world as observed from an (allegedly) 'objective' point of view.[45]

For Kratochwil, practical argument proceeds by the use of a 'rhetorical proof' or 'enthymeme'. The enthymeme consists of two parts: 'the conclusion... and the "backing"', and must necessarily 'start with "things as they really are"' rather than from 'mere assumptions which are true by definition'.[46] The 'backing' is provided by way of the 'commonplaces', or 'topoi', of everyday language which I have discussed above. Crucially, commonplaces built in to rhetorical proof will express 'some shared interpretation of actions on the basis of certain practical experiences. Such a topos is therefore a *shared judgement* in a society that enables the respective actors to back their choices by means of accepted beliefs, rules of preference, or general classification schemes'.[47]

Thus, 'rhetorical syllogisms connect statements which are substantively based on only probable imputations expressed in the topos. In other words, *both the premises as well as the connection*... are only likely'.[48] The 'reasoning from the particular to the particular connected by a commonplace or topos'[49] is, for Kratochwil, the distinguishing nature of practical (as opposed to logical) reasoning. He claims:

> Topoi, or commonplaces,... not only establish 'starting-points' for arguments, but locate the issues of a debate in a substantive set of common understandings that provide for the crucial connections within the structure of the argument. Precisely because topoi reflect our commonsense understandings, these general topoi are 'persuasive' and can easily be resorted to when technical knowledge about

> an issue is lacking or has become problematic. It is through such a topical 'ordering' that everyday language can mediate between different areas of knowledge. Everyday language, therefore, also is able to bridge the gaps between various, more specialised 'discourses' which have emancipated themselves from the 'imprecision' of ordinary language through the creation of specialised systems of signs and meanings. However, commonplaces also play a part in more specialised discourses. They give structure and coherence to certain areas of practical reasoning.[50]

Thus the 'persuasive' nature of those topoi which reflect our 'commonsense understandings' will drive and inform the progress of practical (and legal) reasoning, and the role of topoi will be present both in everyday, and specialised, discourses. Kratochwil speaks of the importance of 'analogies' to the process of the application of norms to practical (and legal) issues:

> [N]orm-application is never a mere subsumption, but always entails an evaluation on the basis of analogies which are held to be relevant.[51]

Analogies, when invoked as an essential part of legal reasoning, are designed 'to establish similarities among different cases or objects in the face of (striking) dissimilarities. The similarity established thereby concerns a (partial) equality among the compared objects or phenomena in regard to a relevant aspect'.[52] Although Kratochwil does not explicitly extend their import to the wider category of practical reasoning, it is clear that analogies will function as part of the genesis of practical topoi, given that practical topoi function to contextualise and anchor common understandings (and, therefore, that analogies will feature heavily in the anchoring of common understandings). Thus practical reasoning, at least insofar as it is based on Kractochwil's conception of 'third-party law', will generally utilise the power of analogies in normatively securing common expectations. Analogies will therefore have a significant effect on the category of institutional reasoning which, again, is analogous with Kratochwil's conception of rule-based practical – or even legal – reasoning:

> [A]s soon as the process of reasoning with rules is institutionalised, i.e. a special class of 'rules-handlers' has developed, and the community has made retaliation increasingly dependent on antecedent

> authoritative determination as to what the 'relevant' issues are, requirements of formal justice attain new importance. This means, however, that analogies as a special technique of reasoning with rules become an indispensable tool for arriving at a decision. Historically we notice the shift from a 'second-party' law to a 'third-party' law with the emergence of explicit third parties'[53];

And (again, I would argue, relevant in the wider context of third-party institutional practical reasoning):

> Precisely because legal norms do not *refer* to objects existing irrespective of the understandings of the norm-addressees, a clear meaning of legal terms simply signifies that there is no doubt or disagreements among the members of an audience.[54]

Thus legal norms, being dependent for their validity on the intersubjective, culturally determined establishment of the underlying topoi (and the pathways by which the topoi are connected by way of practical argument), acquire clear meaning through the force of profound agreement among actors as to the meaning of the norm (with a corresponding clear use of the norm as part of legal reasoning). Again, I would make the point that, while Kratochwil's conception of law and legal reasoning has profound implications for the idea of institutional reasoning in international relations (for example, the problems associated with a conception of law as the command of a sovereign can now be overcome; the legitimacy of legal claims in the international context can be analysed through the lens of an inclusive and intersubjectively valid form of practical reasoning; the epistemological implications of institutional reasoning can be effectively assessed), not all institutional reasoning will be conceptualisable as legal reasoning.[55] However, given the fundamental links Kratochwil has drawn between legal and practical reasoning (both being bound together as forms of normative reasoning, or reasoning with norms), I would argue that the claims he makes regarding the role of topoi and analogies as fundamental constituents of legal reasoning are also directly applicable to non-legal, institutional reasoning (insofar as the latter is concerned with reasoning with rules), with the significant distinction that legal reasoning is concerned with the application of more precise and 'specific' formulations of the shared understandings which give rise to practical topoi.[56] Kratochwil's characterisation of a 'legal order' in *The Puzzles of Politics* provides clarification on this point:

> [A] legal order can be conceived of as a particular system of communicative action. It informs the participants about the nature of the game by determining the type of actors who can make claims; it sets the range of permissible goals the actors can pursue, specifies the steps necessary to insure the validity of their acts and assigns priority and weight to different claims. The legal order represents one of the primary means of organising social life because it makes more specific the shared general notions in practical matters which allow for interdependent decision-making. Finally, the legal order deals with the problems that arise due to scarcity and the non-identical preferences of a multiplicity of actors.[57]

Next, Kratochwil addresses the particular functions of topoi as 'means for appraisal'. He asks:

> Given that any action or event is susceptible to a variety of 'descriptions', how do we choose among the various characterisations, and how can we defend the appropriateness of our choices? Since the characterisation of an act stands in a close nexus to relevant norms governing a case, these issues are not merely of peripheral interest.[58]

The importance of successfully capturing an appropriate means by which to characterise action lies in the fact that 'the characterisation of actions whether in the legal or in the practical discourse is not a description at all, but rather an *appraisal*; it is an evaluation of "facts" in terms of some normative considerations'.[59] Kratochwil claims:

> We might take issue with a specific characterisation, bracket the implicit evaluation, or make it the explicit topic of our dispute; but what does not seem possible – unless we leave the practical discourse – is the reduction of the characterisation to a description in a language of pure observation. On the contrary, what acquires here the status of an 'objective' fact is not the thing described but rather the intersubjective *validity* of a characterisation upon which reasonable persons can agree.[60]

Kratochwil's claim is that the 'discursive application' of specialised topoi is crucial to the process by which appraisals of specific actions become possible. Again, Kratochwil's argument is conducted through the lens of legal reasoning – but I would argue that, given the passage above (in which the importance of appraisals to the *practical* discourse was acknowledged), and given the fundamental connections between the ways in which legal and practical reasoning operate (as set out in detail above), the functioning of the more specialised practical topoi (a range of which will be embedded within the public political culture of international relations), as part of practical reasoning, will be coterminous with the legal discourse:

> I shall argue that a specific appraisal becomes possible only through the discursive application of more specialised (legal) 'topoi' for which the laws of pleadings are a good example. Furthermore, the enumeration of legal topoi contained in procedural rules and settled practices provides not only instructions as to how a practitioner is to go about a case, but also assurances that in the process, a case is looked at from different angles. Finally, the 'authoritative' decision which establishes the holding by either subsuming the case under a certain norm or by stating the applicability of rule of *stare decisis* (together with the relevant facts and *obiter dicta*) depends for its persuasiveness largely upon a careful weaving, into one strand of thought, of legal and common-sense arguments. They 'back' the decision and its characterisation of the case. It is through this embeddedness of the specialised 'legal' language in the practical discourse that the importance of topoi as backings or groundings for decisions becomes visible.[61]

The existence of 'procedural rules' and 'settled practices' in the practical discourse of international relations means that, beyond the legal examples cited, topoi will function in the domain of international practical reasoning in the manner identified by Kratochwil above. Thus, 'a careful weaving, into one strand of thought', of specialised practical arguments and 'everyday', common-sense arguments will allow for the subsumption of a particular practical issue under a certain norm, or the stating of the applicability of a particular rule (the latter of which, as I have argued, will be particularly relevant to institutional reasoning in international relations). The importance of embedded specialised practical topoi, and their connection through practical argument based on the application of more 'common-sense' commonplaces (within which the idea of analogies plays a decisive role) has, I think, been established. As Kratochwil states,

> it is only on the basis of the presumption that such intersubjective characterisations *are* possible and that they can, at least in principle, be reasonably debated, that we can communicate about practical matters and attribute praise or blame[62];

And,

> interpretations and topical argumentation require attention to the reasonable expectations of others, to basic rather than transient interests, impartiality, and to stability of attitudes.[63]

As stated above, my contention is that Kratochwil's conceptions of legal and practical reasoning, and his account of the genesis of each, necessitates the existence of explicitly *moral* elements within his general account of normative reasoning. The presence of moral principles within the genesis of legal and reasoning can be discerned at various points in *Rules, Norms and Decisions* (most notably within Kratochwil's discussion of the 'discourse on grievances', which I will consider below). For example, when discussing the path of legal argument, Kratochwil states as follows:

> Through a series of 'turning-points', competing interests and interpretations can be taken into account, and can then be either rebutted or accepted. Thus, the judicial decisions are path-dependent, and it is this characteristic that distinguishes them from mere random choices, or from an unsystematic subjection of the subject-matter to competing evaluations. Nevertheless, such paths are not the result of a strict logical algorithm for decisions. Furthermore, the path, as established through the process of legal arguing, is additionally controlled by certain ethical principles that the participants have to heed – even the adversary attorneys are, after all, officers of the court. Both elements serve as a backdrop to understanding and as a 'frame' for the practice of legal arguing.[64]

Thus ethical principles play a role in establishing the pathway followed by legal reasoning. Such principles do not form part of the process of legal argument by accident; they are built in to the pathway-determining characteristics of the shared understandings, anchored around the existence of procedural topoi, which serve to delineate the course of argument in a manner which will instil acceptance and thus garner legitimacy (precisely *because* of the fact that the argument follows a pathway which is determined through the acknowledgement of normatively shared expectations).

For Kratochwil,

> the legitimacy of 'rational' legal order relies on a procedural notion, namely the process of norm creation. In this sense, law and politics

> are not only intrinsically linked through the concept of the 'state', where legislation is produced, but the state itself derives its legitimacy 'from' the people – or even understands itself as an expression of a particular people (nation state). Consequently, legitimisation deficits will appear in all instances of institutionalised inter-state cooperation that go beyond the classical alliance patterns or *ad hoc* limited purpose arrangements.[65]

This argument is, in my contention, fundamentally linked with the normative importance Rawls places on the principles which comprise his 'Law of Peoples'. For Rawls, the principles modelled in the 'second original position' [populated by peoples rather than persons] should comprise those principles drawn 'from the history and usages of international law and practice'. This is normatively significant, and backed by a constructivist normative justification. It is not simply an indication of conservative thinking. For Rawls, the requisite nature of the second original position (requisite due to the fundamentally *normative* character of international relations) requires that

> the parties are not given a menu of alternative principles and ideals from which to select, as they were in *Political Liberalism*... Rather, the representatives of liberal constitutional democracies reflect on the advantages of the principles of equality among peoples. The principles must also satisfy the criterion of reciprocity, since this criterion holds at both levels – both between citizens as citizens and between peoples as peoples. In the latter case it requires that, in proposing a principle to regulate the mutual relations between peoples, a people or their representatives must think not only that it is reasonable for them to propose it, but also that it is reasonable for other peoples to accept it.[66]

Thus the principles espoused by Rawls are drawn from the intersubjectively anchored, historically developed processes of norm creation (both in terms of international legal norms and the norms which underpin international social structures) will necessarily inform the content of the Law of Peoples.[67] This conception of the nature of morality and legality in international relations accords, in my contention, with the Kratochwilian account of practical, legal and moral reasoning (and the fundamental connection between each) as considered above. Moreover, the implicit connection between legal and moral reasoning, as mutual elements of the wider category of *practical* reasoning, and the normative development of both in the manner set out by Kratochwil, necessitate the existence of intersubjectively established moral constituents (or, in other words, intersubjective agreement on moral meanings and analogies) as part of the procedural topoi which ultimately come to shape the course of legal argument.

Additionally, through a consideration of an 'ordering and discursive treatment', through substantive principles, of claims in respect of particular grievances, the moral qualities inherent in Kratochwil's conceptualisation of normative reasoning come to the fore. One of his key claims in this section is that an intersubjective, rule-based approach to the question of how to order and regulate claims to rights, duties and particular grievances will avoid the problems faced by more formalistic theoretical models:

> [T]he process of arriving at a decision [concerning grievance-claims] has to be guided by certain criteria, and in addition, assent to practical judgments must be gained in a noncapricious fashion. It is here that rules which constitute such a discourse and make non-idiosyncratic assent possible attain their great importance.[68]

In this context, Kratochwil sets out the intersubjective effects reasoning will have on the 'moral' discourse (again, he conceives of moral reasoning as being less determinate than, but still akin to, legal reasoning):

> Reason is . . . concerned with the pre-conditions (or 'transcendental' conditions, we might say) of a 'moral' discourse, in which the effects of our actions on others can be assessed. Although not necessarily providing compelling solutions, it imparts at least a certain order and persuasiveness to the process of arguing and to its outcomes.[69]

As is clear from this passage, an action is, according to Kratochwil, imbued with moral qualities due to the 'attitude people take towards the action, rather than the act or its physical properties'.[70] Citing Pufendorf, Kratochwil claims that '[r]easoning about moral matters . . . is characterised by its claim to universal validity among all human beings . . . , by the recognition that actions arise out of the free determinations of the actors, and by the realisation that their moral character cannot be derived from the perception of their physical characteristics'.[71] Thus, as in the case of legal and (more generally) practical reasoning, moral reasoning is defined by its norm-oriented, intersubjective qualities. Kratochwil explicitly draws attention to the analogous nature of moral and legal reasoning, referring to

> a substantial similarity between legal and moral reasoning insofar as both involve judgments on practical matters, and both have to be arrived at through a process of *principled argumentation*. Second, since both moral and legal reasoning are designed to lead to principled choices, the element of 'heteronomy' that is involved in the decisions is different from the imposition of a superior will. The heteronomy refers to general principles which are constitutive of the individual 'self' as well as of the existence of society.[72]

The institution of *promising*, according to Kratochwil, gives us a crucial insight into the *intersubjective* nature of moral reasoning (and thus establishes its link with practical and legal reasoning). Promising, which, as we have seen, provides evidence of the fundamental link between moral and legal reasoning (being an example of a matter internal to both) is dependent on the *illocutionary* force of the utterance which establishes the promissory obligation.[73] It is also, claims Kratochwil, such a vociferous form of moral obligation precisely because it speaks to the very *constitution* of the moral nature of the promisor:

> [I]t is exactly the 'uptake' of the obligation, i.e., its *il*locutionary force rather than the *per*locutionary effect, which is crucial.... Unless we do not want to have anything to do with the other person, we cannot simply ignore or belittle the illocutionary effect of the promise. Doing so would mean that we do not take the person seriously, that we deny him/her the status of a moral agent by discounting his/her utterances, or that he/she is like a child or an imbecile who does not know what he/she is doing[74];

And:

> [I]t is our common conception of the freedom and responsibility of moral agents that *precedes*, and has to be logically prior to, any attainment or utility of goals that agents choose to undertake, singly or in conjunction. It is our notion that there is a 'self' which remains the same, despite a variety of changes in desires, moods, intentions, and circumstances, that is at stake as much as is the possible harm we do to others by misleading them or inducing their reliance on us. To that extent promising is constitutive of 'agency' and of our

> ability to bind or commit ourselves by an act of will. Conversely, it is through the giving of reasons indicating the lack of free will or the impairment of an actor's agency, or through the intervention of an unforeseeable event, that we allow promisors to modify or abrogate their obligations. Precisely because the uptake of an obligation is so fundamental to our basic moral conceptions, promising is most probably paradigmatic for a wide variety of rule-bound actions, including the institution of asserting something (telling the truth).[75]

Kratochwil's conception of moral reasoning, its status as being intimately linked with his conceptions of practical and legal reasoning, and the crucial importance of institutional structures to the moral constitution of agents (expressed by Kratochwil through an analysis of the institution of promising) will have profound implications on Rawls' conceptualisation of the Society of Peoples, the idea of public reason, and the publicly justified construction of principles of international law in *The Law of Peoples*. In particular, Kratochwil's conception of normative reasoning – and the profound effects normative structures and reasoning have on the moral constitution of agents – will determine the nature and scope of the Society of Peoples, which (as we saw above and will reconsider below) will include those peoples who, through a willingness to engage with other peoples on terms publicly available to each, become participants in the construction of normative social structures (contextualised by the existence of practical, moral and legal topoi and commonplaces, linked together through the use of analogies and intersubjectively valid forms of practical reasoning), and will thus be capable of being constituted as fully moral agents. For Rawls, the Society of reasonable Peoples is a society of moral agents who, through engagement with other reasonable peoples through the adoption of reasoning about matters of basic justice in international relations *predicated on publicly available terms*, not only constitute themselves as moral agents but also justify the construction of principles of international justice and law which are, in important respects, *legitimate*. This is achieved and contextualised through recourse to publicly available ideas – as Rawls notes:

> Public reasoning aims for public justification. We appeal to political conceptions of justice, and to ascertainable evidence and facts open to public view, in order to reach conclusions about what we think are the most reasonable political institutions and policies. Public justification is not simply valid reasoning, but argument addressed to

> others: it proceeds correctly from premises we accept and think others could reasonably accept to conclusions we think they could also reasonably accept.[76]

The essential feature to note about the Society of Peoples is that it is a *normative community*. This is, in essence, why Rawls chooses peoples as the normatively significant representatives of agents in international relations, who will ultimately deliberate about and decide on those principles which will come to comprise the Law of Peoples. As Rawls notes, '[l]iberal peoples have three basic features: a reasonably just constitutional democratic government that serves their fundamental interests; citizens united by what Mill called "common sympathies"; and finally, a moral nature'.[77] The idea of 'common sympathies' is key: Rawls claims that 'the Law of Peoples starts with the need for common sympathies, no matter what their source may be'.[78] Equally as important, however, is the idea that liberal peoples (and we can assume that Rawls would extend this characteristic to decent peoples as well, hence their inclusion in the Society of Peoples) have a moral character:

> Like citizens in a domestic society, liberal peoples are both reasonable and rational, and their rational conduct, as organised and expressed in their elections and votes, and the laws and policies of their government, is similarly constrained by their sense of what is reasonable. As reasonable citizens in domestic society offer to cooperate on fair terms with other citizens, so (reasonable) liberal (or decent) peoples offer fair terms of cooperation to other peoples. A people will honour these terms when assured that other peoples will do so as well. This leads us to the principles of political justice in the first case and the Law of Peoples in the other.[79]

Kratochwil is also concerned with the establishment of a normative community. As we have seen, for Kratochwil, a normative community is one in which meaning and, ultimately, authoritative decisions, are established on the basis of intersubjectively constructed norms and rules, functioning in a particular way to influence the style of reasoning by which the normative community in question is able to arbitrate problems and solve political puzzles. For Kratochwil, again as we have seen, the idea of a *normative* community is fundamentally linked to the idea of a *legal* community via the styles of practical reasoning involved in each and the effect on such reasoning played by the presence of norms and rules. Given the claim that the concept legal reasoning is fundamentally bound up with the concept of practical reasoning (both bound up with the idea of a normative community and its ability to construct meaning through interaction with normative structure), the idea of a legal community will be fundamentally linked with the idea of a normative community (as with Rawls).

The similarities between the underlying projects of Rawls and Kratochwil should be obvious here. Both are concerned with the analysis and development of ideas about what it means for members of a normative community to address reasonable, publicly available argument to other members of such a community, by recourse to the intersubjective elements of shared society which provide meaning and context to any discussion of public political concepts. My argument is that Rawls' conceptualisation of a reasonable Society of Peoples (that is, a society of peoples united by a common commitment to frame argument concerning public political considerations within the limits of public reason[80]) can only be possible if he takes seriously the subtle considerations regarding practical, moral and legal reasoning developed by Kratochwil. Crucially, by linking moral and legal reasoning through their mutual constitution via the existence of intersubjectively anchored shared understandings, and by contextualising practical reason through the specialised topoi and commonplaces which *all* members of the Society of Peoples can access,[81] questions concerning the *legitimacy* of the argument made by Rawls are effectively dealt with. The idea of a reasonable Society of Peoples, and an international public reason, are enhanced by situating a theory of normative social structure, which itself relies on an account of the intersubjective creation of meaning among agents engaging with one another via the medium of practical reasoning (in all its forms), *within* a Rawlsian account of normative reasoning. The effects will be profound: Buchanan's insistence on an institutional, social-epistemological and legal presence within a public form of political justification will be answered by an extremely sophisticated account of the relationship between each; the idea of a Society of reasonable (and decent) Peoples will be vindicated through recourse to the fact that such a Society includes those peoples willing to engage with one another on publicly available terms (and thus will participate in the constructive processes whereby intersubjective meaning – and normative social structure – are created); and an account of public reason which takes seriously the context and constitution of *practical* reason – essential, I would argue, in any account of normative reasoning – will be properly 'formatted' to take into account the conditions of international relations (as opposed to domestic liberal institutions).

Moreover, Kratochwil's theory will have a significant effect on the idea of international law (the medium by which the content of the Law of Peoples is populated) in Rawls' political constructivism at the international level (and will, in my contention, ground a theory of international relations more *appropriate* to the unique conditions which pertain in world politics than the theory worked out by Buchanan[82]). International law is fundamentally bound up with the existence of normative social structures in international relations, as well as the conceptions of moral, practical and institutional reasoning developed by Kratochwil. As we have seen, these social structures are constituted by (and obtain their legitimacy from) the existence of norms which are themselves constituted through intersubjective understandings, contextualised through the existence of publicly available topoi and analogies. Legal reasoning is a form of practical reasoning and is therefore intimately bound up with the processes of construction through which norms, rules and structure are imbued with meaning. Thus, the Society of Peoples – and the international law it produces and agrees on (the Law of Peoples) – is inherently bound up with the idea of norms, commonplaces, common understandings and social structure. Further, the *moral* constitution of the agents of normative focus in international relations (which is crucial to Rawls' political constructivism) depends on the institutional structures within which actors act, and thus an account of how these structures are imbued with meaning (and their effect on practical and legal argument) will become crucial. The relationship between the *moral* and *legal* conceptualisations of the Law of Peoples will thus be properly drawn out and explained by Kratochwil's theory.

Ultimately, I would argue, the 'combined' account of normative reasoning developed here and below should be embedded within a Rawlsian account of political constructivism, grounded in an underlying conception of reasonableness. Such an account of justification in international political theory would thereby proceed from a consideration of those attributes of agents (i.e. citizens in the domestic case; peoples (constituted by citizens) in the international), and their engagement with practical reasoning, which allow for a *capacity* to engage with other agents in such a way as to establish the existence of a normative community. The crucial question 'Why should agents engage with other agents in a reasonable, publicly accessible way?' should then be answerable. A conception of reasonableness which is *appropriate* and *properly formatted* to account for the conditions of international relations will, I argue, be capable of grounding a theory of international politics which can transcend the poststructuralist critique in a legitimate manner. This conception will be fleshed out further in the next chapter. For now, I consider the combination of a Rawlsian conception of public reason and a Kratochwilian conception of practical reason.

Practical reason and public reason combined

I have now considered in detail Kratochwil's conception of practical reason which, as we have seen, is fundamentally linked with his conceptions of legal and moral reasoning. I have also considered how the ideas of public/practical, moral, legal and institutional reasoning developed by Kratochwil and Rawls, contextualised through the idea of a normative community (the Society of Peoples in Rawls/the community of rational agents through which shared expectations are constructed in Kratochwil), can have profound and mutually supportive effects on one another. I now turn to a consideration of the conceptual similarities in the theories of normative reasoning developed by Rawls and Kratochwil, and how a combined version of public/practical reason might be embedded within the framework of a Rawlsian version of political constructivism.

I now turn to a comparison of Kratochwil's conception of practical reasoning, and Rawls's conception of public reason.

Recall the 'publicity conditions' which Rawls set down as fundamental requirements for a well-ordered society underpinned by a truly *public* form of political justification (these are cited above, but I reproduce them here for ease of reference):

> The first...is achieved when society is effectively regulated by public principles of justice: citizens accept and know that others likewise accept those principles, and this knowledge in turn is publicly recognized. Further, the institutions of the basic structure of society are just (as defined by those principles) and everyone with reason recognises this. They do so on the basis of commonly shared beliefs confirmed by methods of inquiry and ways of reasoning generally accepted as appropriate for questions of political justice.
>
> The second level of publicity concerns the general beliefs in the light of which first principles of justice themselves can be accepted, that is, the general beliefs about human nature and the way political and social institutions generally work, and indeed all such beliefs relevant to political justice. Citizens in a well-ordered society roughly agree on these beliefs because they can be supported (as at the first

> level) by publicly shared methods of inquiry and forms of reasoning.... I assume these methods to be familiar from common sense and to include the procedures and conclusions of science and social thought, when these are well established and not controversial....
>
> The third and last level of publicity has to do with the full justification of the public conception of justice as it would be presented in its own terms. This justification includes everything that we would say – you and I – when we set up justice as fairness and reflect why we proceed in one way rather than another.[83]

Recall also Rawls' arguments concerning the *source* of the content of a properly *public* form of reasoning which, *because* it is public reason, takes seriously the 'values of political justice'[84]:

> [I]n discussing constitutional essentials and matters of basic justice we are not to appeal to comprehensive religious and philosophical doctrines – to what we as individuals or members of associations see as the whole truth – nor to elaborate economic theories of general equilibrium, say, if these are in dispute. As far as possible, the knowledge and ways of reasoning that ground our affirming the principles of justice and their application to constitutional essentials and basic justice are to rest on the plain truths now widely accepted, or available, to citizens generally. Otherwise, the political conception would not provide a public basis of justification.[85]

Now consider the following passage considering Kratochwil's constructivism, written by James W. Davis:

> [H]ow do individuals affix values to events and institutions and are the processes and outcomes necessarily historically unique? Without access to mental states and processes and realising that observable behaviour can be the product of a variety of antecedent factors, the proper focus of such investigation is discourse, namely the reasons that are given and accepted by social actors as a sufficient justification for compliance or noncompliance... The giving of reasons involves discursively linking some particular features of the case at hand with a general rule, and thus constitutes a mode of reasoning *from the particular to the general*. And although we cannot predict the path an argument will take, and even if ultimate judgments regarding the meaning of a rule or norm in a particular context are in this sense 'path dependent', it does not follow that the process and result of

arguing is arbitrary... Hence, analysing and evaluating the path and outcome of arguments over the applicability of norms in a particular historical case can lead to general knowledge, albeit of a different sort than is the focus of adherents to statistical or deductive reasoning.[86]

My argument in this section is as follows:

1. My central claim is that the conceptions of normative reasoning worked out by Rawls and Kratochwil are (a) capable of mutual accommodation (and display a range of analogous characteristics), and (b) both contain fundamental characteristics which serve to *strengthen* and *complete* the opposing conception of normative reason. Essentially, the idea of public reason provides for the scope within which reasoning will proceed from those predicates – and will remain within those limits – which reasonable agents will reasonably believe other reasonable agents will reasonably accept (again, all uses of 'reasonable' are here necessary). Such an idea can accommodate a Kratochwilian account of practical reason which locates the 'reasonableness' requirements of public reason within normative structures determined by the communicative power of rules and norms – themselves contextualised by the existence of underlying topoi or commonplaces which serve to shape common understandings and shared meanings (which, as we have seen, underlies both Rawls' account of public reason, and Kratochwil's account of practical reason). In so doing, the content of public reason will be imbued with practical – and normative – meaning and crucial considerations concerning the practical and institutional realisation of a realistic utopia can be fleshed out;
2. I also claim that both theorists locate the source of the *content* of deliberations through the use of public/practical reasoning in the same way – that is, both conceive of agents drawing the content of ideas which will inform deliberations through the use of practical reason from the *public political culture* inherent within the 'basic structure' of political society. Such will involve agents drawing on 'commonplace' ideas (topoi) which inform the path of commonsense argument (as Rawls notes, 'presently accepted general beliefs and forms of reasoning found in common sense'[87] or 'ascertainable evidence and facts open to public view'[88]), as well as the more specialised discourses of science, legal reasoning, technical knowledge etc which have, through the intersubjective, historicised constitutive processes captured by Kratochwil, and the availability of

publicly accepted evidential underpinnings, become accepted among agents and actors in world politics (for example, again as noted by Rawls, 'the methods and conclusions of science when these are not controversial'[89]);

3. As was noted above regarding Kratochwil's conception of practical reasoning, the ideas which inform argument will necessary contain *moral* considerations as these become part of the fabric of international relations through intersubjective experience. Rawls' theory, however, here provides a solid framework for the construction of a set of normative principles suitable for the regulation of international relations. Crucially, the underlying moral principles which will ultimately inform the path of practical reasoning will depend on the establishment of a principle of *legitimacy* among the actors and agents of world politics, backed by a more general but fundamental conception of *reasonableness* in international relations;
4. Both Rawls and Kratochwil locate the justification of normative principles within a criterion of legitimacy; Rawls through the 'liberal principle of legitimacy' which determines the circumstances which give rise to the legitimate use of coercive political power[90]; Kratochwil through a consideration of the means by which practical argument can 'induce consent' through the invocation of claims to the validity of norms which are themselves constituted by the 'stablisation and evocation of certain generally shared expectations among actors in a specific situation'[91];
5. My argument is that, by invoking Kratochwil's detailed considerations of the means by which reasoning with norms fosters acceptance and legitimacy among agents *within* the context of a Rawlsian political constructivist framework, the key problems faced in any attempt to divorce the idea of public reason from political *liberalism* will be overcome. Through *Kratochwil's* normative theory, we can arrive at a concept of legitimacy in international relations which does *not* depend on the acceptance of liberal predicates for its theoretical force; this is crucial in the context of international relations in which, as Rawls attempts to show via the concept of a decent non-liberal people, it is not only liberal societies who would take seriously the idea of public reason, and hence accept the principles of the Law of Peoples;
6. Through Kratochwil's theory, we can also flesh out a conception of political justification which, crucially, can take seriously Buchanan's arguments concerning the need for an *institutional* element (and a correspondingly sophisticated understanding of the social-epistemological implications of a *normative* account of

international relations) in any attempt to justify principles in world politics;

7. Locating a conception of practical reason within a Rawlsian framework will ultimately provide the context for a justification of the need for agents to respect the limits of public reason when debating 'matters of basic justice' (which, as we have seen, underpins the Rawlsian constructivist project since it addresses the crucial question: *why* should agents respect the limits of public reason?); and
8. A unified theory of public/practical reason will be capable of location within a wider conception of reasonableness (again made possible by the normative framework offered by Rawlsian political constructivism) which can ground moral claims in international relations in a manner not susceptible to the poststructuralist critique. I will consider the work of McKinnon and Roberts (the latter of which, I argue, develops a reading of the Rawlsian account of reasonableness which is capable of grounding moral claims in a manner *appropriate* to international relations) in the next chapter.

Practical reason and Rawlsian constructivism

As noted by O'Neill, the idea of public reason is arguably one of the deepest and most fundamental ideas inherent within Rawlsian constructivism. It is worth reminding ourselves of the essence of the idea and its place within an account of political society:

> A political society, and indeed every reasonable and rational agent, whether it be an individual, or a family or an association, or even a confederation of political societies, has a way of formulating its plans, of putting its ends in an order of priority and of making its decisions accordingly. The way a political society does this is its reason; its ability to do these things is also its reason, though in a different sense: it is an intellectual and moral power, rooted in the capacities of its human members.[92]

As was considered above, the idea of public reason arises out of a conception of the reasonable which, in contrast to the conception of the *rational* employed by Rawls, is by its nature a *moral*, and *public*, conception:

> [T]he reasonable is public in a way the rational is not. This means that it is by the reasonable that we enter as equals the public world of others and stand ready to propose, or to accept, as the case may be,

> fair terms of cooperation with them. These terms, set out as principles, specify the reasons we are to share and publicly recognise before one another as grounding our social relations. Insofar as we are reasonable, we are ready to work out the framework for the public social world, a framework it is reasonable to expect everyone to endorse and act on, provided others can be relied on to do the same.[93]

One of the significant aims of *The Law of Peoples* is the task of extending the political constructivism worked out by Rawls in *Political Liberalism* to the realm of the international, or, as Rawls describes it, the 'Society of reasonable (liberal and decent) Peoples'. Given that, as we saw in *Political Liberalism,* the idea of a political conception of justice[94] is intended to apply to the 'basic structure' of society,[95] Rawls is concerned to work out the proper scope of the 'basic structure' of the Society of Peoples in *The Law of Peoples* (without which, as Rawls notes, the idea of a political conception of justice could not arise). The idea of the basic structure in international relations will be, as Rawls notes, fundamentally distinct from, though analogous to, the idea of the basic structure within a constitutional democracy. Thus, for Rawls, the idea of the basic structure of international society is bound up with the respect for the self-determination and cultural heritage of other reasonable peoples, *even where those peoples do not respect fully liberal principles and ideals* (described by Rawls as 'decent' reasonable peoples):

> Certainly the social world of liberal and decent peoples is not one that, by liberal principles, is fully just. Some may feel that permitting this injustice and not insisting on liberal principles for all societies requires strong reasons. I believe that there are such reasons. Most important is maintaining mutual respect among peoples. Lapsing into contempt on the one side, and bitterness and resentment on the other, can only cause damage. These relations are not a matter of the internal (liberal or decent) basic structure of each people viewed separately. Rather, maintaining mutual respect among peoples in the Society of Peoples constitutes an essential part of the basic structure and political climate of that society. The Law of Peoples considers this wider background basic structure and the merits of its political climate in encouraging reforms in a liberal direction as overriding the lack of liberal justice in decent societies.[96]

This idea of a 'basic structure' of the Society of Peoples – and the companion idea of a standard of 'decency', which liberal peoples are committed, by their own standards of reasonableness, to tolerate – can best be conceptualised as Rawls' extension of the idea of public reason to the international. Given that decent non-liberal peoples will embody the fundamental requirements of a 'member in good standing in a reasonable Society of Peoples',[97] they will be capable of framing argument concerning matters of 'basic justice' within the limits of public reason and will, crucially, be able to justify their own internal arrangements/external relations through reasoned argument which *itself* remains within the limits of public reason. Interestingly, although decent societies will fulfil the two conditions for acceptance as a member of good standing within the reasonable Society of Peoples, Rawls claims that the idea of decency is *not* subsumed within his general conception of reasonableness:

> I think of decency as a normative idea of the same kind as reasonableness, though weaker (that is, it covers less than reasonableness does). We give it meaning by how we use it. Thus a decent people must honour the laws of peace; its system of law must be such as to respect human rights and to impose duties and obligations on all persons in its territory. Its system of law must follow a common good idea of justice that takes into account what it sees as the fundamental interests of everyone in society. And, finally, there must be a sincere and not unreasonable belief on the part of judges and other officials that the law is indeed guided by a common good idea of justice.[98]

Thus the 'decent common good idea of hierarchical peoples is a minimal idea. Its being realised by a society renders its institutions worthy of toleration'.[99] This, I would argue, is characterised by Rawls' project in *The Law of Peoples*, which is designed to work out how a theory of political constructivism to apply to the relations between peoples can be worked out from *within* political liberalism. My argument is that, when properly formatted so as to be appropriate to a conception of political constructivism in international relations (and hence divorced from political liberalism), the concept of decency *is* located within a conception of reasonableness and (crucially) *is* capable of adopting the idea of public reason. My understanding of this element of Rawls' international theory is, therefore, as follows:

1. The *practical effect*, rather than the essential nature, of a society's institutions are what is important in determining whether

that society contains the necessary elements for qualification as a 'member in good standing of a reasonable Society of Peoples';

2. Thus, the key question will be: Can a society's internal arrangements, and external relations, be justified by recourse to argument which remains within the limits of public reason?;
3. Additionally, in agreeing to frame argument concerning matters of 'basic justice' within the limits of public reason, a society will qualify as a member in good standing of a reasonable Society of Peoples;
4. Rawls' claim is that decent non-liberal societies will affirm the principles alluded to in 2 and 3. Argument for the decent society's derivation from stringent liberal requirements of justice will, Rawls claims, be framable in such a way that it can be conceived of as argument which reasonable peoples will reasonably expect others to reasonably accept. Additionally, a decent society will be one which is sufficiently motivated by its common good conception of justice to seek to enter into reasonable argument concerning matters of 'basic justice' to govern its relations with other peoples. Hence, such a decent society will be reasonable in a sense sufficient for qualification as a 'member in good standing of a reasonable Society of Peoples'.

Following this line of reasoning, it becomes clear that the vital qualifying factor for inclusion within a reasonable Society of Peoples is the normative and institutional capacity for a society to be *motivated* to engage in argument framed in the language of public reason. The motivational force is here provided by the presence of a common good conception of justice which delineates the decent from the non-decent. Coupled with this, we can add a sufficient respect for the burdens of judgement for a decent society to be sufficiently motivated to refrain from couching argument concerning matters of basic justice in the language of its own comprehensive doctrine. Finally, it is important to note the *moral-institutional* requirements of a decent society. Its system of law must be such as to impose *bona fide* moral duties and obligations on all persons within the people's territory (and must be fundamentally linked with the decent society's common good conception of justice via the connections between legal and moral reasoning as elucidated by Kratochwil). Since the members of the people are viewed as decent and rational, as well as responsible and able to play a part in social life, they recognise these duties and obligations as fitting with their common good idea of justice and do not see their duties and obligations as mere commands imposed by force. Judicial officers must reasonably believe that the law must be guided by the common good conception of justice.

Such a conception, while (as we have seen) not necessarily comprising a 'fully reasonable' idea of justice from the point of view of political liberalism (due to the potential absence of specifically liberal values inherent within a fully liberal conception of reasonableness, such as the stipulation that citizens be conceived of as 'free and equal' which, as Buchanan noted, is not necessarily appropriate in the context of international relations), will contain the grounding for a sufficient motivation to engage in reasoned argument concerning matters of basic justice, and thus the *effect* of the society's common good conception of justice will be a willingness to respect the limits of public reason. This claim regarding the moral status of law (i.e. as arising from the common good conception of justice) will, correspondingly, require an *institutional* commitment on the part of decent peoples, since the machinations of law within the society in question will need to take seriously the role of the common good conception of justice in the historical determination of the principles of such law. As Buchanan noted, institutional claims of this kind will require a sophisticated social epistemology if it is to adequately translate moral principles and ideals into institutional reasoning. Moreover, in taking seriously Buchanan's general claims regarding the necessity of an institutional component in any account of political justification, and given the fact that we are here concerned with the *practical* effect of the characteristics of a decent society (as set out above), I would contend that the requirements of decency as set out by Rawls will *all* require a consideration of the institutional means by which the moral considerations he specifies in *The Law of Peoples* can be effectively realised. Rawls will, therefore, need a sophisticated account of the nature of institutional reasoning (and one which is capable of uniting conceptions of moral, legal and institutional reasoning into a uniform conception of practical reason) as well as the social-epistemological effects of adopting a *normative* account of such reason. Kratochwil, as we have seen, has provided just such a theory.

As already stated, Rawls is concerned to work out the conditions for achieving a 'realistic utopia' among the reasonable Society of Peoples as it exists today. As we also saw, he claims that such an idea is 'importantly institutional'. To recall:

> In the domestic case it connects with the way citizens conduct themselves under the institutions and practices within which they have grown up; in the international case with the way a people's character has historically developed. We depend on the facts of social conduct as historical knowledge and reflection establish them.[100]

The 'facts of social conduct', locatable through 'historical knowledge and reflection', will inform the content of the Law of Peoples. A range of important questions follow:

1. How will these 'facts' be drawn on and employed by peoples engaged in public reason?
2. How does 'historical knowledge and reflection' uncover socially constructed 'facts'?
3. What are the epistemological implications of the historical construction of institutional 'facts'?
4. How can reasonable peoples invoke such socially constructed 'facts' as the starting points for a public justification of political principles?
5. How will the path of argument framed by the limits of public reason proceed in a legitimate manner?
6. How will the principles ultimately agreed on be realised, in a practical sense, in international relations?

Three claims follow. Firstly, I contend that these questions are crucial to the proper realisation of a *realistic* utopia. Secondly, my claim is that Rawls' theory does not contain the necessary tools with which to provide answers to them. Thirdly, I would claim that, in addressing these questions, Kratochwil's theory has developed a sophisticated array of theoretical tools with which to fill the gaps in Rawls' conception of normative reason and, alongside the fact that Rawls provides an account of reasonableness which provides the motivational requirements for a desire to locate a 'utopia', a combined conception of public/practical reason, underpinned by a conception of reasonableness appropriate to international relations, will form a 'completed' theory of normative reasoning.

Let us work through such a 'combined' conception:

1. Reasonable societies in international relations contain the requisite moral components (including a common good conception of justice), actualised through appropriate institutional structures, to be sufficiently motivated to seek to engage in reasoned argument with other reasonable societies (each with its own comprehensive conceptions of justice), and will seek to do so within the limits of public reason;
2. In order to remain within the boundaries of public reason, argument will need to be grounded in publicly available starting points; proceed by the use of publicly accepted modes of reasoning; and

ultimately reach determinate decisions (in the form of proposed principles of justice) which are publicly acceptable (i.e. which the proposer reasonably believes will be reasonably acceptable to other reasonable peoples);

3. In order to ensure the proposal of *publicly* acceptable principles, reasonable peoples will draw from the facts of 'social conduct' (i.e. the public political culture or 'basic structure' of international relations);
4. In order to locate publicly available starting points, and to ensure that argument proceeds in a logically coherent and publicly acceptable manner, a conception of practical reason, itself intimately bound up with the facts of social conduct, is necessary. Such a conception will need to be connected with a parallel conception of *moral* reasoning (since the motivating force behind the engagement in reasonable argument is located within a range of *moral* characteristics inherent in any reasonable (including decent) society). Additionally, given that a realistic utopia can only be effectively realised through appropriate institutional structures, capable of providing authoritative determinations in cases of normative uncertainty, a practical conception of institutional reasoning is also necessary (with a correspondingly sophisticated account of the epistemological status of 'social facts' and the requirement for a sophisticated social-epistemology as part of institutional reasoning);
5. Kratochwil's theory provides an account of practical reason which combines all these required elements and which, through the use of intersubjectively constructed norms, conditions a conception of practical reasoning intimately connected with the 'facts of social conduct', as specified by Rawls as informing the content of public reason;
6. The pathway-oriented construction of practical (and legal) reasoning in Kratochwil's theory is conditioned through reliance on the existence of specialised topoi, linked through the communicative power of everyday language which effectively 'fills the gaps' in specialist discourse and links argument in a logically coherent manner. The use of analogies, as was noted in the context of Kratochwil's consideration of the path of legal argument, will play a crucial role in the evocation of intersubjective experience and common understandings and will ultimately ground a norm-based conception of reason which will foster acceptance and legitimacy among reasonable and decent peoples;

7. Such a conception of practical reason remains within the limits of public reason. As Kratochwil claims, the communicative power of everyday language (which conditions the legitimacy of normative validity-claims) relies on the illocutionary force of the utterance which itself serves to constitute the agent as a moral being. In parallel, the act of proposing those principles which the proposer reasonably believes would be reasonably accepted by reasonable peoples constitutes the proposer as a member in good standing in the Society of Peoples. Thus, crucially, the limits of public reason and the effect of norms on practical reasoning function in a comparable manner. Moreover, recourse to specialised (i.e. non-public) discourse is perfectly compatible with the requirements of public reason so long as it is done in a manner which accords with its limits (i.e. so long as it is done in a manner which is capable of public justification[101]);
8. Both conceptions of normative reasoning draw on the existence of the 'facts of social conduct', or 'commonplaces' – that is, the existence of historically developed, socially constructed background knowledge which is generally accepted and relatively uncontroversial – in locating the starting points for argument and in informing the content of public reason. They are therefore mutually compatible;
9. Through the location of Kratochwilian practical reason within the framework of Rawlsian political constructivism (itself underpinned by the idea of public reason), the moral underpinnings of a motivation to engage in reasoned argument concerning matters of basic justice – itself grounded in a moral conception of reasonableness in international relations – has now been realised. This creates the conditions necessary for the realisation of a realistic utopia and, thus, the structure of normative reasoning is imbued with *philosophical* meaning;
10. However, by combining Rawls' account of public reason, and his philosophical constructivism, with Kratochwil's account of practical reason, the crucial questions set out above regarding such essential issues as the *way* in which the 'facts of social conduct' will inform the content of public reason (i.e. through recourse to analogies, specialised topoi and 'commonplaces'), the path the reasoning will follow, the fundamental link between moral, practical, institutional and legal reasoning and the effect of reasoning through recourse to norms will be answered;

11. We therefore have a conception of practical reasoning, located within a philosophical constructivist framework, which can adequately explain the means by which a realistic utopia, through the use of public reason, can be realised.

One key problem faced by Rawls' international project is the danger of reliance on a *liberal* conception of legitimacy in working out the content of public reason. As we saw earlier, a conception of legitimacy is required in order to work out those principles which will be reasonably acceptable to reasonable peoples. Rawls' arguments in *Political Liberalism* relied to a large extent on the 'liberal principle of legitimacy'. However, by incorporating Kratochwil's account of practical reason as part of Rawls' constructivism, this problem falls away. Kratochwil's theory incorporates a conception of legitimacy which, I would argue, is entirely appropriate for international relations in that it is fundamentally bound up with the anchoring of common understandings around intersubjectively conditioned (and, hence, intersubjectively *legitimate*) norms and rules. The effect of locating the underpinnings of a conception of legitimacy within the normative effects of shared understandings on practical reasoning is to wholly divorce the idea of legitimacy from a fully liberal conception of reasonableness. As we saw in my analysis of Kratochwil's consideration of the nature of 'institutional facts', a norm-oriented approach to international relations will provide an account of how norms, and therefore reasoning, are imbued with intersubjective meaning and are ultimately capable of grounding argument which will be perceived as legitimate by other reasonable actors.

7
The Concept of the Reasonable in International Political Justification: A Rejoinder to the Poststructuralist Critique

In the last three chapters I have attempted, through detailed expositions and parallel readings of the work of Rawls, Buchanan and Kratochwil, to conceptualise the structure of a 'complete' account of normative reason. Such an account, I argued, has the potential to augment synthesised conceptions of practical, moral and legal reasoning, anchored around an account of normatively secured common understandings (as developed in detail by Kratochwil), within the framework of a Rawlsian form of political constructivism. By so doing, I claimed, Kratochwil's arguments concerning the presence and effects of norms (and the contextualising effects of the historically conditioned 'commonplaces' of practical discourse) in influencing the orientation, pathways and legitimacy of practical reasoning[1] allow for the development of an account of how normative reasoning functions within the context of intersubjective normative structure, and which is crucially capable of accommodation within the framework of a Rawlsian political constructivism. The latter is vital because of the need to provide a justificatory context by which the idea of public reason (which I have claimed forms the core of Rawls' constructivist project), as a normatively significant and justifying concept, is vindicated. Without such a framework (and, crucially, the underlying concept of the reasonable which I will consider in this section), crucial questions concerning the *ways* in which the limits of public reason provide the means for a strong, *legitimate* form of justification that can validly be invoked in justifying principles of *international* justice will remain unanswered. Notwithstanding the fact that Kratochwil's conception of practical reason provides a sophisticated account of the processes by which normative reasoning anchored around intersubjective understandings can proceed in a legitimate and meaningful manner (thus providing an understanding of the contextualising processes by which reasoning with norms begins and proceeds to an authoritative determination), without locating such an account within a more general conception of the reasonable (as we have seen in Rawls), the task of providing the *most robust* tools by which a normative account of political justification *capable of answering the poststructuralist critique* (the crucial purpose of my study), and which can ground the construction of *legitimate* and *publicly acceptable* principles of international justice, will be incomplete. The crucial purpose of Rawls' constructivist framework, I have claimed, is the development of an account of public reason that grounds his political conception of justice. My task in this chapter is to explore whether Rawls' wider conception of the reasonable, which grounds his ideas of public reason and a political conception of justice, contains the theoretical strength and legitimacy necessary to form a valid response to the challenge of poststructuralism.

The presence of intersubjective norms anchored around the historically developed and contextualising effects of the 'facts of social conduct' is crucial to an understanding of *how* practical reasoning operates within the context of intersubjective normative structure. In order to properly understand *how* agents will engage with one another by recourse to common understandings and meanings drawn from shared experiences as participants in the (legal, institutional) structures of contemporary international relations, Kratochwil's conception of the conditions of practical reasoning becomes crucial. I have argued in the last chapter that the subject matter of the *content* of Kratochwil's account of normative reasoning (i.e. his account of the orientating and contextualising effects of topoi, commonplaces and analogies on practical reasoning) function in a remarkably similar way to the ideas inherent in the background culture of political society which inform the subject matter of Rawls' account of the *content* of public reason. Owing to these crucial and fundamental analogies between the two conceptions, I argued that they could be effectively combined into a 'completed' account of normative reasoning. Both theories, I claim, contain crucial elements by which to augment its counterpart: Kratochwil through a sophisticated account of *how* practical reasoning functions within the context of normative (including legal and institutional) structure; Rawls through the justificatory power of the framework of his political constructivism and the crucial idea of public reason contained within it. The *limits* of public reason assume paramount importance in the context of normative justification – they determine the boundaries of reasoning which can be afforded a legitimate justification by effectively determining the limits of reasonableness in international relations.

What is still needed is an analysis of the basis on which Rawls believes that agents will be motivated to respect the limits of public reason; his conception of the reasonable. Kratochwil's account of practical reason is effective in describing the nature of reasoning with rules and norms, and the effects those rules and norms will have on the meanings employed by the reasoner. It also offers a crucial account of the fundamental connection between the various categories of practical reason considered in the last chapter (thereby responding to Buchanan's arguments about the need for an institutional component *within* an account of normative justification). However, it is through a robust yet legitimate account of the basic conditions of reasonableness that a truly objective and authoritative account of *why* agents will be motivated to engage with others by recourse to the use of public reason becomes possible. The framework of Rawlsian constructivism, and its grounding idea of the reasonable, allows just that.

I have used the term 'appropriate to international relations' in many instances in this book, particularly in the context of an account of political principles of justice which are identified through the use of normative reason and which are subject to a standard of legitimacy. By 'appropriate to international relations', I mean that the principles in question are subject to an appropriate standard of *legitimacy* – in other words, a standard of legitimacy applicable to, and likely to adduce consent and foster legitimacy among, the reasonable peoples of the world. Kratochwil's theory, as I have claimed, conceptualises an account of normative reasoning which, I believe, is consistent with just such a standard – essentially one that yields reasoning which accounts for the complex ways in which practical reasoning interacts with the intersubjectively anchored common understandings which typify reasoning with norms, but which can also provide a vindication for the Rawlsian insistence on addressing others from within the limits of public reason.

As we saw in Chapter 4, Rawls claims that the Law of Peoples arises out of a liberal conception of justice (essentially the extension of a liberal conception of justice to the international) but that it represents a corpus of principles that would be reasonably acceptable – and hence justifiable – to decent non-liberal peoples. The latter characteristic – the fact that liberal peoples can reasonably expect that *all* reasonable peoples would accept the principles of the Law of Peoples is, for Rawls, the key to a corpus of principles which are *objectively* justified:

> In developing the Law of Peoples I said that liberal societies ask how they are to conduct themselves toward other societies from the point of view of their *own* political conceptions. We must always start from where we now are, assuming that we have taken all reasonable precautions to review the grounds of our political conception and to guard against bias and error. To the objection that to proceed thus is ethnocentric or merely western, the reply is: no, not necessarily. Whether it is so turns on the *content* of the Law of Peoples that liberal societies embrace. The objectivity of that law surely depends not on its time, place, or culture of origin, but whether it satisfies the criterion of reciprocity and belongs to the public reason of the Society of liberal and decent Peoples.
>
> Looking at the Law of Peoples, we see that it does satisfy the criterion of reciprocity. It asks of other societies only what they can reasonably grant without submitting to a position of inferiority or domination. Here it is crucial that the Law of Peoples does not require decent societies to abandon or modify their religious institutions and adopt liberal ones. We have supposed that decent societies would affirm the same Law of Peoples that would hold among just liberal societies. This enabled that law to be universal in its reach. It is so because it asks of other societies only what they can reasonably endorse once they are prepared to stand in a relation of fair equality with all other societies. They cannot argue that being in a relation of equality with other peoples is a western idea! In what other relation can a people and its regime reasonably expect to stand?[2]

This passage offers a crucial insight into Rawls' conception of the idea of reasonableness as applied to international relations. Firstly, Rawls claims that the grounds of our political conceptions of justice must be constantly reviewed to 'guard against bias and error'. Second, Rawls claims that the key to a political justification orientated around the idea of public reason is the principle of reciprocity – in other words, in formulating a conception of justice to apply to its foreign policy a liberal peoples (and ultimately the Society of liberal Peoples) should ask reasonable non-liberal peoples to adopt only those principles which they genuinely believe could reasonably be adopted, while at the same ensuring a relationship of equality between liberal and non-liberal but decent peoples.

Given that Rawls' stated project (as reflected in the opening sentence of the citation immediately above) in *The Law of Peoples* is to work out those principles of international justice by which liberal peoples should engage with non-liberal, decent peoples,[3] the 'objectivity' of the Law of Peoples highlighted above must presumably refer to the following:

1. 'Objectivity' in the sense that, in order to be accepted by decent non-liberal societies, the principles which constitute the Law of Peoples must overcome the charge of ethnocentrism or cultural bias. This is clearly the sense referred to above and flows from the fact that it would be unreasonable to expect decent non-liberal peoples, in equal standing with liberal peoples in the Society of Peoples, to reasonably accept as reasonable a corpus of principles which they deem to be peculiarly liberal-centric in nature. Rawls believes that, because the principles he outlines satisfy the principle of reciprocity and are justifiable from within the limits of public reason, this charge is overcome; and
2. 'Objectivity' in the sense required by the political justification *internal* to a liberal political conception of justice. As we saw in the extended analysis of the concept of the reasonable and the idea of public reason in *Political Liberalism* above, a liberal political conception of justice requires commitment to principles of toleration and equality, and a respect for the burdens of judgement and the limits of public reason. Rawls' claim regarding objectivity in *The Law of Peoples* is therefore that a liberal people's own political conception of justice dictates that it be committed to proposing principles which it reasonably believes to be reasonably acceptable to all reasonable peoples. In this sense, the means by which principles of international justice proposed by liberal peoples are constructed will need to be 'objective', and such principles will need to be justifiable from within the limits of public reason.

I want to claim that an account of normative justification which can overcome the challenge of poststructuralism can best be grounded on a Rawlsian conception of the reasonable properly formatted to take account of the conditions of international relations. Additionally, it is crucial to show that Rawls' conception of reasonableness can support an account of normative reason which augments the distinct yet vitally comparable conceptions of normative and public reason developed by Kratochwil and Rawls. As should be clear from my extended exposition of Kratochwil's theory, the account of normative reasoning he develops is designed as an *objective* account of the conditions of practical reasoning within normative structure (replete with intersubjective norms and rules). The fact that Kratochwil's account of practical reason is based on the existence of intersubjectively conditioned, shared understandings, oriented around the existence of norms and contextualising topoi, does not detract from this fact; rather, it offers an explanation of the development over time of normative structure – and the institutions which actualise such – in international relations. An account of international relations which did not accept that shared understandings and, in turn, normative structure, arise over time and are bound up with historical experiences in the relations between peoples and states would not, in my contention, embody a true understanding of the nature of international practice. Rawls himself acknowledges the need for an account of how the content of political principles of justice (such as the principles of the Law of Peoples) arises out of the 'facts of social conduct' and is drawn from ideas inherent in the background culture of political society. Kratochwil provides such an account and provides an understanding of how reasoning within the context of intersubjectively established meanings gives rise to the development of legal and institutional structure. My argument is that, in order to be considered a truly objective and authoritative account of the nature of international relations (thereby transcending the poststructuralist critique), the conception of normative reasoning I espouse must be grounded in an objective account of the nature of the reasonable which can be shown to be appropriate to international relations.

Rawls' conception of the reasonable can ground an account of normative reasoning capable of bearing the following characteristics:

1. *Objectivity*. Rawls considers his project in *The Law of Peoples* to arise out of his constructivism in *Political Liberalism*. The crucial purpose of the former, however, is the construction of a political conception of justice that is reasonably acceptable to all reasonable peoples. In this sense, Rawls' project in *The Law of Peoples* can properly be thought of as objective. I wish to show, via Roberts' formulation of a Rawlsian conception of the characteristics of reasonableness, that the minimal constraints of practicality can ground an *objective* (in the first sense highlighted above) account of public/practical reason;
2. *Authority*. Rawls' political constructivism must be grounded on a conception of reasonableness which renders practical reason *authoritative*. An authoritative means by which to ground justificatory debate in international relations will foster legitimate principles of political justice and will take seriously Kratochwil's 'problems of adducing consent', which I argued *must* be taken seriously in any account of normative reasoning. Again, through the minimal constraints on reasoning identified by Roberts, an account of the *authority* of normative reasoning can be given which can also accommodate

Kratochwil's account of the nature of reasoning within normative structures;

3. *Appropriateness/legitimacy*. Given the fact that I consider Rawls' conception of the reasonable to be capable of grounding an account of normative reason which is both *objective* and *authoritative*, and which takes account of the nature of reasoning within the context of normative structure, I consider that the standard of reasonableness identified by Rawls is both appropriate to international relations and itself capable of grounding legitimate principles of political justice for the international. Thus the poststructuralist charge of illegitimate foundationalism will have been overcome.

In this chapter I will subject the heart of Rawls' constructivism to critical scrutiny through a reconsideration of the essential characteristics involved in his conception of the reasonable, and through an examination of McKinnon's critique of Rawls' reliance on the conception of the burdens of judgement (respect for which forms a crucial part of his conception of the reasonable), which she believes provides for an account of the reasonable which places too high a demand threshold (and hence too high a demand for uniformity) on agents. I will consider whether McKinnon's critique of Rawls' conception of reasonableness is sound, and whether her alternative 'many flowers' view (which attributes agents' acceptance of the fact of reasonable pluralism to their acceptance of the importance of self-respect for themselves and others) is necessary in order to ground a conception of reasonableness appropriate to international relations. Ultimately, I will consider Roberts' minimalistic account of a Rawlsian conception of reasonableness, and his arguments concerning the objectivity and authority of practical reason. I will argue that, via Roberts, we can ground an undemanding (and hence legitimate) account of the nature of the reasonable in international relations which does not rely on McKinnon's 'many flowers' conception. In my contention, an argument which relies on notions of 'primary-goods' (such as McKinnon's account of the importance of self-respect) and thick conceptions of the attributes and evaluative tendencies of agents (which McKinnon's account necessitates) are *less* likely to be acceptable – and hence less likely to adduce consent and foster legitimacy among reasonable peoples – than an argument which grounds reasonableness in the minimal constraints of practicality. Therefore, and after showing how Roberts' conception of Rawlsian reasonableness can be considered objective and authoritative, and hence legitimate, I claim that Roberts' formulation contains all that is necessary to overcome the challenge of poststructuralism.

Rawls' conception of the reasonable re-examined

To recall the essence of Rawls' conception of the reasonable in *Political Liberalism*:

> The reasonable is an element of the idea of society as a system of fair cooperation and that its fair terms be reasonable for all to accept is part of its idea of reciprocity... Reasonable persons, we say, are not moved by the general good as such but desire for its own sake a social world in which they, as free and equal, can cooperate with others on terms all can accept. They insist that reciprocity should hold within that world so that each benefits along with others[4];

And:

> [I]t is by the reasonable that we enter as equals the public world of others and stand ready to propose, or to accept, as the case may be, fair terms of cooperation with them. These terms, set out as principles, specify the reasons we are to share and publicly recognise before one another as grounding our social relations. Insofar as we are reasonable, we are ready to work out the framework for the public social world, a framework it is reasonable to expect everyone to endorse and act on, provided others can be relied on to do the same[5];

And:

> The second basic aspect [of the reasonable]...is the willingness to recognise the burdens of judgment and to accept their consequences for the use of public reason in directing the legitimate exercise of political power in a constitutional regime.[6]

These elements of the reasonable flow from Rawls' more fundamental conception of the person – or, as McKinnon states, his conception of the 'ideal person' – by which principles of justice will be worked out through the application of practical reason. McKinnon summarises the characteristics of Rawls' conception of the person as follows:

1. Persons have the capacity for a conception of the good.
2. Persons are reasonable:

    (a) they have the capacity for a sense of justice;
    (b) they accept the consequences of the burdens of judgement; and

(c) they subscribe to a (full or partial) reasonable comprehensive doctrine.

3. Persons are rational.
4. Persons conceive of themselves as equal *qua* citizens.
5. Persons conceive of themselves as free *qua* citizens.
6. Persons value the conditions of their self-respect *qua* citizens.
7. Persons have a reasonable moral psychology.
8. Social co-operation is guided by publicly recognised rules which each person regards as appropriate and proper.
9. The terms of social co-operation are such that each person can reasonably accept them, as long as all others do.
10. Persons engaged in social co-operation have an idea of their own rational advantage.[7]

The concept of the reasonable is a fundamental constituent of these 'ideas of practical reason'[8] and essentially regulates the public aspect of a person's willingness to enter into reasoning about justice with others. McKinnon describes elements (a) and (c) thus[9]:

> (a) *Persons possess the capacity for a sense of justice.* This is 'the capacity to understand, to apply, and to act from the public conception of justice which characterises the fair terms of social cooperation ... a sense of justice also expresses a willingness, if not the desire, to act in relation to others on terms they can publicly endorse'. When people have the capacity for a sense of justice they want to find publicly acceptable and mutually advantageous solutions to problems of social co-operation: they are not stubborn, manipulative, dishonest or perverse. The capacity for a sense of justice is one of the two 'moral powers' that characterise persons in ideal theory. The other is the capacity for a conception of the good.[10]
>
> ...
>
> (c) *Persons subscribe to a (full or partial) reasonable comprehensive doctrine* which informs each of their conceptions of the good: 'We ... connect with ... a conception [of the good] a view of our relation to the world – religions, philosophical and moral – by reference to which the value and significance of our ends and attachments are understood'.[11]

Thus, reasonable persons will be motivated[12] to engage with others in order to find publicly acceptable means by which they can co-exist, and their own conception of the good will be regulated by a reasonable comprehensive doctrine which will essentially ensure that such conceptions of the good are realised in a reasonable manner (i.e. one which is consistent with the wider public conception of justice acceptable to all).

Given the analogies drawn by Rawls between the idea of a reasonable citizen and the idea of a reasonable people (which we saw in Chapter 4), the conception of the reasonable in *The Law of Peoples* functions in the same way as in *Political Liberalism*. To recall, Rawls claims that

> [l]iberal peoples have three basic features: a reasonably just constitutional democratic government that serves their fundamental interests; citizens united by what Mill called 'common sympathies'; and finally, a moral nature. The first is institutional, the second is cultural, and the third requires a firm attachment to a political (moral) conception of right and justice.[13]

The third aspect of this formulation is the most interesting for present purposes. Rawls claims:

> Like citizens in domestic society, liberal peoples are both reasonable and rational, and their rational conduct, as organised and expressed in their elections and votes, and the laws and policies of their government, is similarly constrained by their sense of what is reasonable. As reasonable citizens in domestic society offer to cooperate on fair terms with other citizens, so (reasonable) liberal (or decent) peoples offer fair terms of cooperation to other peoples. A people will honour these terms when assured that other peoples will do so as well. This leads us to the principles of political justice in the first case and the Law of Peoples in the other.[14]

Thus, as in the domestic case, the willingness to propose fair terms of cooperation (so long as reciprocity is assured) forms the heart of Rawls' conception of the reasonable. This willingness, alongside a reasonable people's respect for the burdens of judgement (which I discuss further below), will provide the crucial basis for explaining *why* a reasonable people will respect and adhere to the limits of public reason when engaging with other societies in matters of basic justice. Essentially, as we have seen, a willingness to propose fair terms of cooperation means to propose only those principles which the proposer can reasonably expect the proposee to reasonably accept (or, put another way, not to unreasonably reject[15]). The elements of the reasonable identified above provide the necessary normative backdrop for such a willingness. Only if agents are imbued with a capacity for a sense of justice; a respect for the burdens of judgement; and a subscription to a reasonable comprehensive doctrine (the latter of which serves to contextualise an agent's conception of the good) will a respect for the limits of public reason be explained in normative terms. As I have already argued, such a conception – and the respect for the limits of public reason to which it gives rise – can itself support the conception of normative reasoning (contextualised through the presence of norms and normative structure – and ultimately, I claim, principles of justice – in international relations) as developed by Kratochwil.

A respect for the burdens of judgement is a fundamental element of the concept of the reasonable and is also crucially linked to the companion conception of toleration.[16] I considered Rawls' characterisation of this element of the reasonable in the last chapter, but in order to recap, McKinnon provides an instructive summary of the burdens of judgement which plays on the summary offered by Rawls in *Political Liberalism* (as cited in Chapter 4):

The burdens of judgement are that:

a. 'The evidence – empirical and scientific – bearing on the case is conflicting and complex, and thus hard to assess and evaluate'.
b. Agreement on the considerations relevant to a particular judgement does not guarantee agreement with respect to how these considerations should be weighted in judgement.
c. The concepts appearing in judgement 'are vague and subject to hard cases', making interpretation unavoidable.
d. 'To some extent…the way we assess evidence and weigh moral and political values is shaped by our total experience, our whole course of life up till now: and our total experiences must always differ'.
e. Normative considerations in cases of judgement are hard to assess, both on their own, and in relation to one another when they are in competition.
f. '[A]ny system of institutions has, as it were, a limited social space'. In the same way that a person cannot guarantee the realisation of

> everything she values in her own life, given the practical restrictions that a limited life span places on the number of ends and plans that a person can pursue, so political institutions cannot be guaranteed to protect all our 'cherished values'. We find choices between these values hard to make precisely because they are deeply cherished, and disagreement among reasonable people on which value is to be prioritised is inevitable.[17]

McKinnon states that '[t]he burdens of judgment explain why rational people committed to finding publicly acceptable principles of justice, and with the best will in the world, cannot be expected to come to unanimous, or even near unanimous, agreement on important matters involving the use of judgment'.[18] Essentially, acceptance of the burdens of judgement entails a respect for reasonable pluralism. As Rawls states:

> As reasonable and rational we have to make different kinds of judgments. As rational we have to balance our various ends and estimate their appropriate place in our way of life; and doing this confronts us with grave difficulties in making correct judgments of rationality. On the other hand, as reasonable we must assess the strength of peoples' claims, not only against our claims, but against one another, or on our common practices and institutions, all this giving rise to difficulties in our making sound reasonable judgments. In addition, there is the reasonable as it applies to our beliefs and schemes of thought, or the reasonable as appraising our use of our theoretical (and not our moral and practical) powers, and here too we meet the corresponding kind of difficulties. We need to keep in mind these three kinds of judgments with their characteristic burdens.[19]

As should be clear from the above, the fact of *reasonable* pluralism is not to be regretted, in Rawls' contention. It is *not* a product of flawed practical reasoning, or confusion, or irrationality, or an epistemic failure to understand the truth concerning matters of basic justice. Rather, Rawls' claim is that acceptance of the burdens of judgement 'means that not all forms of pluralism can be explained in terms of the irrationality, stubbornness or stupidity of those who hold diverse views: some forms of pluralism are reasonable, and therefore not to be regretted as a side-effect of epistemic failure'.[20] McKinnon's claim is that, in Rawls' constructivism, the ideas of toleration and public reason flow directly from acceptance of (or respect for) the burdens of judgement:

1. *Toleration* because

> [i]f a reasonable person realises that she and all other reasonable people are under the burdens of judgment then, when other reasonable people disagree with her, she does not conclude that these people are stupid, wilful, obstructive or misinformed, even though she thinks that these people have false beliefs with respect to the issue over which they disagree, given that for her to believe something is for her to believe it to be true.[21]

I fundamentally disagree with McKinnon's formulation of the principle of toleration at this point. Firstly, in my contention, political constructivism is not intended to speak to the kind of moral beliefs which an agent might believe to be 'true', and which would lead that agent to consider that others have false beliefs (even if those beliefs are to be tolerated). Political constructivism is silent on these substantive moral issues and makes no judgement about them whatsoever. In terms of the issues which political constructivism *does* speak to – matters of basic justice – these are not issues which can sensibly be thought of as giving rise to true or false beliefs. They are the product of the realisation, via practical reason, of a means by which reasonable peoples can live justly and peacefully together in a shared space and communicate with each other on reasonable terms. Nothing about Rawls' constructivism, therefore, speaks to the truth or falsity of beliefs arising within reasonable or even unreasonable comprehensive doctrines;

2. *Public reason* because

> [a]ccepting the fact of reasonable pluralism means accepting that the free exercise of reason creates a plurality of comprehensive views about justice, and other matters, and thus that reasonable people cannot be expected to reach agreement on comprehensive matters. In that case, any reasonable person engaged in justificatory debate must offer others justificatory reasons which she sincerely and genuinely takes to be reasons that others could accept as justificatory reasons through the free use of their reason, given their willingness to propose and abide by fair principles of justice.[22]

The idea that reasonable persons (and peoples) will accept and respect the consequences of the burdens of judgement forms the backdrop for McKinnon's critique of Rawls' conception of the reasonable (and, as we shall see, the springboard for McKinnon's discussion of her own, alternative, conception). Her argument proceeds thus:

> Rawls' characterisation of persons as accepting the consequences of the burdens of judgment... is ambiguous between three interpretations. On two of these readings, justificatory reasons appear worryingly demanding,[23] but on the alternative less demanding reading, it is left unclear why ideal persons could not reject reasons to practice toleration and endorse public reason. However, unless there are grounds for claiming that persons facing problems of justice *qua* reasoners could not reject toleration and public reason, the critical potential of Rawlsian justificatory reasons is lost. If we advocate the least demanding reading... then we must provide alternative grounds for thinking persons *qua* justice-seeking practical reasoners could not reject reasons to practise toleration and endorse public reason.[24]

McKinnon's 'three interpretations' of Rawls' characterisation of reasonable peoples as accepting the consequences of the burdens of judgement (in essence, interpretations of agents' beliefs as to the reasons why, given that practical reason is subject to the burdens of judgement, reasonable pluralism is permanent) are as follows:

1. 'The first interpretation is that pluralism is permanent because reason underdetermines belief, especially belief about values. Call this the "underdetermination view". The view is that reason has limits, and once those limits are reached, the paths to beliefs are diverse and no longer track the demands of reason. Thus, once the limits of reason have been reached, pluralism is reasonable, because all belief sets within pluralism are consistent with reason, even though none of them is demanded by reason. With respect to (at least) beliefs about value, reason runs out without uniquely specifying any one set of beliefs. Beyond reason, belief sets vary according to the demands of faith, habit, upbringing and other paths to belief which do not track reason'.[25]

McKinnon's claim is that support for the underdetermination view can be found in a passage in Rawls' 'Justice as Fairness: Political not

Metaphysical'[26] which, she contends, lends support to the following argument:

> Rawls explains the permanent fact of pluralism by reference to the incommensurability of peoples' conceptions of the good, even in the best of conditions. This means that conceptions of the good cannot be ranked according to a master value, or ranked by comparison with one another. This can be seen as a version of the underdetermination view because once reason reaches its limits it can specify no value according to which different conceptions of the good can be ranked, and neither can it guide comparisons of conceptions of the good in the absence of a master-value. There are many accounts of incommensurability in the literature, and not all of them cast incommensurability in terms of the underdetermination of beliefs about value by reason. But this is how incommensurability must be cast if it provides the key to understanding why the operation of reason makes pluralism a permanent fact, and it is this that we are trying to understand by looking at Rawls.[27]

McKinnon's own claims regarding the underdetermination interpretation are as follows:

> There are two problems with the underdetermination view. First, I have argued elsewhere that imputing to ideal people a belief in the incommensurability of conceptions of the good has no consequences for whether stage 1 reasons [i.e. justificatory reasons for the adoption of a conception of political justification] to practise toleration are motivationally adequate for these ideal people. Incommensurability is a view about the *nature* of pluralism, whereas the motivation to practise toleration must respond to beliefs about the *character* of pluralism. With respect to the character of pluralism, theses of incommensurability remain silent: the truth or falsity of theses of incommensurability is simply irrelevant to the question of whether principles of toleration are justified.
>
> More germane to my topic here, however, is a problem with the demandingness of the underdetermination view. On this account, we must assume that stage 2 people [i.e. the hypothetical agents of justice in Rawlsian political constructivism] believe that reason runs out before any one set of beliefs about value is specified as uniquely reasonable. This belief entails a belief that reasonable pluralism is

permanent. So, for ideal people to be motivated by stage 1 reasons to practise toleration (ignoring the criticism above) and to endorse public reason requires that they all believe:

(a) that different belief sets ought not to be subject to criticism through the use of reason, because their incommensurability means that they cannot be ranked against one another through the use of reason; and that
(b) as a consequence, reasonable pluralism is a permanent fact.

The worry about the underdetermination view is the demandingness of (a). Theses of incommensurability are highly controversial. To acquire that all people accept the truth of these theses – that all people become uniform in their beliefs about the limitations of reason – is very demanding. But according to the underdetermination view, stage 2 people not only agree that reason has limits. According to this view, they also agree about what these limits are; that is, they agree about the point at which reason runs out with respect to beliefs about value. Again, this is deeply controversial, even among philosophers who accept theses of incommensurability in principle.[28]

2. The second interpretation is what McKinnon terms the 'burdens of judgment' reading, authority for which she claims arises in the opening lectures of *Political Liberalism*[29]:

On the burdens reading, stage 2 people accept that pluralism is permanent *because* they believe that the exercise of judgement is subject to certain burdens which make disagreement inevitable in ideal conditions: they all accept the same explanation of why they cannot expect to convince one another of their views through the exercise of reason, even in the best of conditions. In that case, people who recognise these burdens of judgment accept that reasonable pluralism is ineradicable.... The burdens view is less demanding than the underdetermination view because the beliefs it requires that people come to acquire in order for it to be possible for them to be motivated by justificatory reasons are less controversial than the theses of incommensurability. For example, that 'the evidence – empirical and scientific – bearing on [any] case is conflicting and complex, and thus hard to assess and evaluate', and that, 'to some extent... the way we assess evidence and weigh moral and political values is shaped by

> our total experience, our whole life course up till now: and our total experience must always differ'. These are statements that many people with different beliefs could come to share without relinquishing these beliefs. Nevertheless, once we pick apart the burdens view it becomes clear that the demands it makes are not insubstantial.[30]

McKinnon's arguments concerning the demandingness of the 'burdens' view are as follows:

> On the burdens view each person must accept the same explanation of the permanence of pluralism, and accept that this explanation applies not just to others, but also to herself. Given that acceptance of an explanation involves the acquisition of beliefs, the burdens view – like the underdetermination view – demands some uniformity of belief with respect to the sources of pluralism. The thought behind the burdens view is that it is only if people accept pluralism as permanent in virtue of the fact that everyone stands under the burdens of judgment that people will restrain themselves with respect to the use of power to suppress the view of others – i.e. practise toleration – and present their political reasons to others in terms they take to be acceptable to them (i.e. be committed to public reason).[31]

3. Given the demandingness of the 'underdetermination' and 'burdens' view, as outlined by McKinnon above, the third interpretation – and the one she herself ultimately adopts – is what she calls the 'many flowers' view. This interpretation is designed to explain agents' acceptance of the permanence of pluralism *without* demanding the sort of uniformity of belief which McKinnon claims is symptomatic of the two previously considered interpretations:

> Is there a less demanding account of the permanence of pluralism which nevertheless explains why reasons for practising toleration and engaging in public reason could be motivating for stage 2 people? The final account I shall consider eschews appeal to theses of incommensurability or the burdens of judgment. Instead, this account allows that people will differ with respect to their explanations of why pluralism is a permanent fact, just as they differ in the paths they take to their most cherished and important beliefs. On this view, persons are as divided with respect to the explanation of the fact of pluralism as they are with respect to moral, religious and philosophical questions, and how they arrive at their answers to them.[32]

Thus, the 'many flowers' view allows for divergence on the causes of permanent pluralism. McKinnon's worry, in this instance, is not that the interpretation is *too* demanding (i.e. because it demands too great a level of uniformity among agents); rather, the worry is that it may not be demanding enough:

> On the many flowers view, the expectation is not that persons agree upon one explanation of the permanence of pluralism. Different people will explain the permanence of deep diversity in terms of scepticism, epistemic failure, human laziness, mass ignorance, etc. This creates a worry about the many flowers view: unless a person conceives of pluralism as (at least potentially) reasonable through acceptance of the burdens of judgment, her commitment to the permanence of pluralism will not be genuine. The fear is that unless we assume that persons accept the permanence of pluralism *as a consequence of* the proper exercise of reason itself, then we cannot assume that, should the balance of power between them and those with whom they disagree change, they will not attempt to use this power to correct, or just suppress, those who disagree with them. Without uniformity of belief here, uniformity of motivation with respect to toleration and public reason are not secured.[33]

McKinnon's proposed solution to this concern with the 'many flowers' view is to insist on a minimal but crucial demand which agents must accept if their acceptance of the permanence of pluralism is to be considered reasonable:

> The many flowers view must, I think, make at least this demand of people: that they acknowledge that whenever conditions of freedom have obtained in the past, beliefs about moral, religious and philosophical questions have diverged. The many flowers view means that people who accept this fact about human history will differ with respect to what makes it a fact. However, to be sure that they do not retain a secret glimmering vision of a world united behind their own beliefs, we must ask them to take the record of history seriously. This is a demand, but it is not one that discriminates between different philosophical accounts of pluralism (as the underdetermination view does), and neither does it require uniformity with respect to the way in which people conceive of the operation of their own understanding (as the burdens view does).[34]

McKinnon's claim is, thus, that so long as agents are required to take 'the record of history' regarding the necessary divergence of reasonable comprehensive doctrines in 'conditions of freedom', they will be motivationally committed to practising toleration and public reason – and hence will be reasonable. This minimal demand (i.e. the *recognition* that reasonable pluralism is permanent) is, in my contention, a crucial element in any conception of the reasonable and one which is particularly apposite and necessary to a conception of the reasonable designed to ground a conception of practical reason appropriate for international principles of justice. Crucial to the character of the conception of the reasonable, however, is the question of whether recognition of the permanence of reasonable pluralism is enough to ground a genuine commitment to public reason on the part of agents, or whether a further constructivist element is required in order to adequately ground such a motivational commitment. Given McKinnon's stated commitment to the 'many flowers' interpretation, her claim is that, since agents will be divided as to *why* they believe that pluralism is a permanent fact, a deeper account of why such diverse agents will be committed to toleration and public reason will be required. If such is not present, claims McKinnon, agents who recognise the 'record of history' – and are thus aware that agents will always differ with respect to comprehensive beliefs in conditions of freedom – 'may nevertheless believe that these means [i.e. reason, coercion or revelation] can be used to convince a large part of humanity, and they may believe that that part is the membership of their constituency of justification'.[35] This reflects the less demanding nature of the 'many flowers' view as opposed to the 'underdetermination' and 'burdens' views, claims McKinnon, and leads her to argue that the shortfall in the account of motivational adequacy engendered by the 'many flowers' view can be overcome by an account of why reasonable agents, with diverse reasons for accepting the permanence of pluralism, are all committed to toleration and public reason which is grounded on a conception of the 'personal bases of self-respect':

> I shall argue that, regardless of the differences in their paths to self-respect, stage 2 people should be thought of as motivationally uniform with respect to their self-respect. Diverse beliefs acquired through diverse means – reason, faith, habit, upbringing etc – can all supply the personal bases of self-respect. Given this uniformity of motivation, I shall argue that the social contexts in which self-respect is developed – the dynamics of close associational life and citizenship – explain why people deeply divided in their beliefs and

> paths to them could be motivated to practise toleration and endorse public reason.

If McKinnon is correct in her argument that the 'many flowers' view, combined with a conception of the personal bases of self-respect, gives rise to a conception of practical reason which is less demanding (in the sense of a requirement of uniformity of belief) on agents than Rawls' conception of the reasonable, then it may be the case that McKinnon's conception is, in fact, *more* appropriate for use in the context of an international political constructivism than Rawls'. Much rests on McKinnon's interpretation of Rawls' account of reasonableness and the burdens of judgement. As I will explore in the next section, McKinnon's formulation of political constructivism as being bound up with the personal and social bases of self-respect introduces a substantive argument concerning the intrinsic value of self-respect to agents, and necessitates a relatively thick and fully fledged account of the attributes of agents. While this is fruitful from the perspective of a liberal conception of justice, *if* it can be shown that McKinnon's arguments concerning the inherent demandingness of Rawls' conception of reasonableness are unsustainable (i.e. if Rawls' conception of reasonableness can be shown to be minimally demanding yet robust and objective), there is no need to introduce 'primary-goods'-style arguments (which Rawls explicitly seeks to exclude in his accounts of political constructivism in *Political Liberalism* and *The Law of Peoples*), and a complex account of the attributes and evaluative preferences of agents, into an account of political constructivism and practical reason. I claim that Roberts offers an interpretation of Rawls' conception of reasonableness which is undemanding enough to ground a robust account of practical reason and which can accommodate Kratochwil's account of the conditions of reasoning within the context of normative structure. I ultimately prefer Roberts' interpretation of Rawls' conception to the account of reasonableness provided by McKinnon.

McKinnon and the personal bases of self-respect

The account of self-respect developed by McKinnon in *Liberalism and the Defence of Political Constructivism* contains two basic elements: congruence and nonsubservience. In terms of congruence:

> A person's self-respect requires congruence between her self-conception and her self-expression; it depends upon her meeting standards with

> which she in some way identifies. Self-respect requires that a person act in ways at least consistent with and preferably supportive of her self-conception. In failing to act in these ways a person fails to be as she had thought she was or hoped she could be.[36]

'Standards of excellence' which inform a person's self-conception, claims McKinnon, will be relative to that person's self-conception. Success, and therefore congruence, will be achieved where a person realises the standards informed by her self-conception. Such realisation can be characterised in two distinct ways; either through an agent 'meeting social criteria for the activities she values' (the Nozickean formulation); or success according to what McKinnon terms 'individual criteria of excellence':

> Individual criteria of excellence relate to a person's conception of her 'ideal self'. This is not a person's conception of what she would be like were the world a perfect place and she had all the talents, abilities and social successes she could wish for, but rather a conception of what she can achieve – of what is possible for her – given her own particular and actual talents and abilities.[37]

The 'individual criteria of excellence' is essentially the realisation that the basis of an agent's self-respect may, but does not always and need not necessarily cohere with social standards of excellence. Both elements can be present – McKinnon claims that 'success can have both a social and a more private aspect; it is the latter kind of success that ultimately matters for self-respect'[38] and 'it is the fact that a person identifies herself with these standards that makes them relevant to her self-respect, not the fact that others with whom she associates judge success or failure according to these standards'.[39] Thus, the personal bases of self-respect may or may not cohere with the social bases – and indeed is likely to be at least partially linked with the same – but it is the personal bases which matter for congruence and ultimately for self-respect.

However, claims McKinnon, congruence on its own is insufficient to ground an account of self-respect; an agent's own conception of her status is equally as important. For McKinnon, the importance of an agent's self-conception of her own status is highlighted in the distinction between those who act (McKinnon considers those who starve themselves or those who self-harm) because of a low conception of their own status and those who take the same action for alternative (perhaps political) reasons, and the effect on the relative self-respect of each caused by that agent's reasons for acting. In the case of the agent motivated to act by a low conception of her own status, McKinnon claims that we would normally think of that agent's self-respect as being correspondingly low. Further, McKinnon claims that a low conception of one's own status is likely to lead to the belief that others have a higher status than oneself, which leads to subservience, formulated in the following manner:

> A person conceives of herself as having less status than others when she would judge as illegitimate any expectation of hers that others offer her justifying reasons why she should perform actions which she is expected by them to perform.[40]

Thus, the legitimacy of an *expectation* of the provision of justifying reasons for demands for a particular action, and the presence or absence of such within an agent's self-conception, forms the key to a nonsubservient self-conception.

McKinnon claims that such a self-conception, which contains a positive expression of the nonsubservience requirement, is crucial to the realisation of the personal bases of self-respect:

> We can put the claim positively: a person conceives of herself as having similar status to others when she would judge as legitimate any expectation of hers that others should offer her justifying reasons why she should perform actions which she is expected by them to perform, were she to have such an expectation. This characterisation of non-subservience is supposed to capture the idea that a person with a sense of her own status has a sense of herself as worthy of being given reasons.[41]

Ultimately, McKinnon's argument is that 'those who accept the permanence of pluralism in virtue of accepting the diverse ways in which self-respect can be developed and maintained could not reject reasons to practice toleration and to endorse public reason'.[42] The argument is framed within a consideration of the effect on practical reasoning which ensues if the conception of reasonableness which grounds practical reason is imbued with a respect for the diverse means by which self-respect is realised. From the perspective of my argument in this book, I believe that it is crucial to consider McKinnon's position for the following reasons:

1. If McKinnon is correct in her claim that her formulation of the concept of the reasonable – and the conception of practical reason which follows from such – is less demanding (in the sense that it requires less uniformity of belief) than Rawls' conception, it may be that McKinnon's conception of the reasonable is in fact *more* appropriate for political justification in the international context;
2. However, by considering the complex requirements concerning the conceptions of congruence and non-subservience, their respective effects on the evaluative component of practical reason, and the necessary skills and attributes of agents which flow from McKinnon's conception of reasonableness, I intend to argue that it introduces a vast array of substantive considerations into its account of practical reason which may render it *more* demanding, and hence less likely to adduce legitimacy, than Rawls' conception. I argue that Roberts' reading of the Rawlsian conception of reasonableness presents all the tools required for a robust understanding of international relations, which can transcend the poststructuralist challenge, *without* the inclusion of the requirement that agents accept the fact of reasonable pluralism on the basis that their judgement is burdened (which is the substance of McKinnon's critique of Rawls).

To begin, McKinnon considers Rawls' theory in *A Theory of Justice* concerning the congruence element of self-respect (which, she claims, is the 'most developed account in the literature' and which introduces the ideas about the interplay between personal self-respect and its social contexts which, McKinnon claims, are crucial in grounding her conception of practical reasoning). She claims:

> With respect to congruence, Rawls claims that self-respect depends upon '(1) Having a rational plan of life, and in particular one that satisfies the Aristotelian principle; and (2) finding our own person and deeds appreciated and confirmed by others who are likewise esteemed and their association enjoyed'.[43]

Hence, the 'three aspects of Rawls' characterisation of the success related to self-respect' that need clarification are as follows:

1. The sense of 'rationality': ' "Full deliberative rationality" refers to the choice of life plans in hypothetical conditions wherein all the facts relevant to that life plan are available to the chooser and the chooser takes the most effective means to the ends she adopts in the light of this knowledge'[44];
2. The Aristotelian principle: 'other things being equal, human beings enjoy the exercise of their realised capacities (their innate or trained abilities), and this enjoyment increases the more the capacity is realised, or the greater its complexity'[45];
3. 'For Rawls, self-respect involves a person being confident in her abilities to carry out her life plans, and involves a sense that these plans are worth carrying out. People normally engage in these activities in communities of shared interests, where they judge themselves more or less successful at these activities according to standards relativised to the abilities of members of these communities. A person's self-respect is supported by membership of such communities when she succeeds in activities around which the group is organised, and which, given her membership of the group, inform her self-conception'.[46]

With these clarifications in mind, McKinnon states as follows:

> Rawls' account of the congruence aspect of self-respect and its social contexts is psychologically plausible. So long as we remember that congruence must be achieved against the background of a non-subservient self-conception... the details of Rawls' account can be used to fill the motivational gap in the many flowers interpretation.[47]

McKinnon's conception of practical reason

McKinnon summarises her arguments concerning the effects of her self-respect based conception of reasonableness in grounding and contextualising a conception of practical reason[48] as follows:

(1) self-respect is an idea of practical reason as it addresses problems of justice;
(2) that the social contexts in which self-respect is developed mean that self-respecting people could not reject reasons to practice toleration and endorse public reason; and
(3) that these features of self-respect mean that those who seek an explanation of why ideal people accept the permanence of pluralism that is less demanding than the incommensurability or burdens view

> should make the self-respect of ideal people a prominent feature of stage 2 of the Constructivist procedure of justification.[49]

Thus, claims McKinnon:

1. Self-respect contextualises practical reasoning about matters of justice[50];
2. '[S]elf-respecting people could not reject reasons to practice toleration and endorse public reason in virtue of the social dynamics of self-respect'[51];
3. 'If the many flowers view which emphasises self-respect is less demanding than the burdens or incommensurability views, then it is to be preferred on the grounds that it allows for more diversity in the constituency of justification than the alternative views'.[52]

In order to assess the impact on practical reasoning which the presence of her conception of self-respect within the concept of the reasonable, McKinnon considers the effects of both key elements of self-respect – nonsubservience and congruence – on the resulting conception of practical reasoning:

1. *Nonsubservience and practical reasoning.* The effects of subservience on practical reason are clear: 'The subservient person would judge any expectation of hers that others give her justifying reasons to be illegitimate'.[53] Hence, subservience directly affects an agent's ability to assess justifying reasons because that agent would not even judge the expectation that such reasons should be provided as legitimate, and hence will not be in a position to engage in the process of justification at all:

> The problem with the subservient person is that she will not judge to be legitimate her expectations that those to whom she is subservient provide her with reasons for the demands they make of her (if, indeed, she has any such expectations). As these demands will relate to proposed solutions to problems of justice, the subservient person is not in a position to exchange political justifications with those to whom she is subservient.[54]

Hence, McKinnon's argument is that nonsubservience is a necessary condition in order for agents to engage in practical reasoning about questions of justice.

2. *Congruence and practical reasoning.* McKinnon's arguments concerning the effects of congruence on the conditions of practical reasoning are more complex. She begins with the following observation regarding the nature of practical reason:

> When a practical reasoner deliberates over the reasons supporting the various ends and means between which she must choose, she assesses ends and means by assessing the reasons which support the adoption of these ends and means. Ends and means supported by reasons which convince the person that these ends and means are appropriate for her are, all else being equal, the ends and means that she will adopt.[55]

Given this insight into the nature of practical reasoning, McKinnon considers the 'qualitative aspects' of the assessment of the reasons underlying the adoption of specific ends and means which agents undertake when engaging in practical reasoning:

1. Quantitative assessment:

> A person can be thought of as assessing reasons by comparing them in terms of a single value or good. On this account, one reason will be endorsed as better than another if the course of action it supports creates more of this value, or a greater amount of this good.[56]

Thus, '[q]uantitative calculation is a matter of comparing options along the same dimension of value. But the value in terms of which options are compared need not be particularly dear to the calculating person, in which case the options she evaluates may have little significance for her'[57];

2. Weak evaluation:

> In some cases of practical evaluation a person does not compare reasons along a single dimension of value, but rather chooses between reasons supporting courses of action which are contingently incompatible, and which express values that the person does not reduce to a master value. In these cases, a person acknowledges the values expressed by the competing reasons as values, but does not attempt to compare them in terms of a further value, as she would if she were assessing them quantitatively. Instead, she focuses on the value

> that would be realised by each course of action in its own terms, and chooses between the options understood as outcomes[58];

3. Strong evaluation:

> When a person evaluates strongly she assesses what action for the reasons under consideration would mean for her conception of herself as a certain sort of person, and for her hopes about the sort of person she might become. Given any person's self-respect supporting self-conception, motivations to act for certain reasons will be ruled out.[59]

McKinnon states of strong evaluation that '[u]nlike weak evaluation, reasons ruled out by strong evaluation are not excluded just in virtue of how they conflict with other reasons which are also valued. Rather, certain reasons are ruled out because action for them would destroy a person's self-respect'.[60] The concept of strong evaluation is intended to capture 'the sense in which we attribute significance to some choices and not others'.[61]

The idea of strong evaluation is essential in understanding the requirement of congruence as an essential condition of practical reasoning, claims McKinnon. This is the case because reasoning about questions which speak to a person's conception of her own self-respect require strongly evaluative assessment, which itself relies on a robust (i.e. congruent) self-conception in order to be practically possible. McKinnon states as follows:

> It is according to a person's robust self-conception that reasons are contrastively assessed in strong evaluation. When evaluating in this way, a person asks herself whether acting for any of the reasons under evaluation contrasts with the self-conception generated by congruence, and at the heart of her self-respect... Given the diversity of self-conceptions fit to ground self-respect, reasons which are strongly evaluated in a positive light for a person with one sort of self-conception may not receive a positive evaluation by a person with another sort of self-conception.[62]

A person's self-conception – and her corresponding 'vocabulary of worth'[63] – will 'disintegrate' where a total failure of congruence occurs. Moreover, an agent with a *weak* self-conception, underpinned by *damaged* or *limited* congruence, will be in a relatively weaker position with respect to strong evaluation (and, hence, to practical reasoning) than an agent with a *robust* self-conception, underpinned by strong congruence.[64]

McKinnon's central argument is that practical reasoning about questions of basic justice[65] is strongly evaluative, and that therefore 'congruence provides a context for such reasoning [i.e. by being a fundamental constituent of the concept of the reasonable], in which case self-respect as a whole is an idea of practical reason as it faces problems of justice'.[66] Further, McKinnon argues that

> a person's commitment to her self-respect and its social conditions, combined with an acknowledgement that all other people share these commitments, can be shown to yield commitment to principles of toleration and procedures of public reason, in the sense that reasons for practising toleration and endorsing public reason[67] could not be rejected by self-respecting people.[68]

The argument proceeds as follows:

> If deep diversity is permanent, all persons accept this, and all persons are assumed to be self-respecters, then no person can expect[69] others to strongly evaluate justificatory reasons with a vocabulary of worth identical to her own. Accepting the fact of deep diversity means accepting that self-respect can be achieved according to a plurality of individual criteria of excellence, and thus that each self-respecter will strongly evaluate justificatory reasons in a different way. In that case, any self-respecting person engaged in justificatory debate under these conditions must offer others justificatory reasons which she sincerely and genuinely takes to be reasons that others could accept as justificatory reasons through strong evaluation in a vocabulary of worth informed by their self-respect. In other words, self-respecters who bring their strong evaluations to public justification are committed to the use of public reason when engaging with other self-respecters in justificatory debates about problems of justice. This does not mean that justificatory reasons must always be presented in public reason in the first instance. As Rawls' 'proviso' allows, these reasons can initially be presented as thick, comprehensive reasons indexed to, and expressed in terms of, a particular conception of the good. But so long as these reasons are eventually presented in public reason they are appropriate as justificatory reasons.[70]

Thus, for McKinnon, *because* a requirement of reasonableness is that self-respecting agents accept that others achieve self-respect through a plurality (perhaps a reasonable plurality?) of diverse individual criteria of excellence, promulgated through vocabularies of worth unique to that agent, then reasonable agents will be committed to engaging in justificatory debate concerning matters of basic justice through public reason. McKinnon therefore adapts Rawls' account of the *ideal* of public reason to take account of her alternative formulation of the concept of the reasonable:

(1) Public officials – judges, legislators, candidates for public office, etc. – present their political justifications to citizens in terms of reasons which they sincerely and genuinely take to be reasons which the public, and other officials, could endorse through their strongly evaluative practical reasoning.
(2) Ordinary citizens 'view themselves as ideal legislators' in order to judge whether public officials satisfy (1), and do what they can to criticise and remove from office public officials who fail to satisfy (1).
(3) Ordinary citizens are willing and able to offer to one another only those justificatory reasons which they sincerely and genuinely take to be reasons that each could accept as justificatory reasons through strong evaluation, given that they accept that their self-respect related differences are permanent, which means that they will permanently differ with respect to the vocabulary of worth they bring to strong evaluation.[71]

The *fact* that agents acknowledge that other agents value their self-respect, realised through permanently diverse expressions of value, will, for McKinnon, trigger a commitment to public reason. She is concerned, however, to defend her argument from the possible objection that a commitment to public reason is at odds with agents' personal commitments to their own self-respect, either through a motivational conflict between both commitments, or else through the requirement of particular skills and qualities which self-respecters cannot be expected to possess. In considering and attempting to redress these potential objections, McKinnon states as follows regarding the qualities and skills required for a commitment to public reason on the part of agents:

Justificatory debate in public reason requires that a person have the following qualities and exercise the following skills.

- The ability to discern when another person's beliefs, values, wants and commitments differ from her own.
- The ability to tell how others differ from her by listening to their self-descriptions, and the terms of their vocabulary of worth, so as to be able to judge whether her strongly evaluative justificatory reasons are presentable in public reason to these other people.
- The capacity for empathy, enabling the person to imagine what it would be like for another self-respecting person to be presented with the strongly evaluative reasons which she proposes as justificatory reasons.
- An acceptance of the possibility that she might be mistaken about the extent to which her strongly evaluative reasons are in fact presentable in public reason. Without this, there is no possibility that any person can be brought to change her mind about solutions to problems of justice through justificatory discourse, whether or not it is framed in terms of public reason.
- Sincerity in the presentation of justificatory reasons in public reason: the reasons a person claims to sincerely and genuinely believe to be presentable in public reason must really be believed by her to have this character. Without sincerity, the whole procedure of public justification can become a sham disguising the machinations of those competing for power behind the scenes of fake justificatory procedures.[72]

McKinnon claims that the exercise of these skills in the context of justificatory debate concerning matters of basic justice within the limits of public reason can be thought of as a 'duty of civility' between agents. Her claim is that 'every self-respecting person has an interest in protecting procedures of justification governed by the ideal of public reason, even if not every person has a reason to engage actively in public reason herself'.[73] This argument clearly culminates in a weaker commitment to public reason on the part of agents of justice than in the constructivism of Rawls – however, McKinnon believes that it is necessary to weaken the commitment to public reason in order to explain its motivational adequacy without resorting to 'controversial' arguments concerning the reliance of self-respect on political society as a whole. In any case, she claims, if her argument is accepted, 'reasons for endorsing public reason governed procedures of justification is [*sic*] vindicated'.[74] This, combined with her claim that the 'many flowers' view is less demanding than the 'burdens' view (as expounded by Rawls), leads McKinnon to conclude that a conception of the reasonable which relies on the 'many flowers' commitment to accepting the permanence of pluralism, rather than an acceptance of the burdens of judgement, is to be preferred:

> The many flowers view is less demanding than the burdens view because of the difference between what the operation of judgment aims at and what the motivational commitment to self-respect aims at. The burdens view requires that people accept the possibility that they could never convince any other person of any of their beliefs, even in ideal conditions.... Most of us, when we believe that a belief of ours is true, believe that we could convince others to share that belief, if only conditions were ideal: we treat the truth of any belief of ours as evidence that the correct exercise of reason by others would bring them to see the truth of this belief. To require that people relinquish this conception of what it means for them to have true beliefs is demanding.[75]

McKinnon's conception of the reasonable – less demanding than Rawls'?

Through the detailed exposition of the constructivist theory of McKinnon above, I have considered a conception of the reasonable (and its grounding role within a constructivist form of political justification) which, on its author's explicitly stated aim, is designed to offer an account of political justification which is capable of explaining a commitment to public reason on the part of agents engaged in debates about justice, but which is purportedly less demanding (in the technical sense highlighted by McKinnon) than Rawls' account of the reasonable. The reason I have considered McKinnon's conception of the reasonable in such depth is simple: given the unique conditions which exist in the realm of the international – and, specifically, the presence of a wide-ranging and diverse mixture of reasonable (liberal and decent) comprehensive doctrines – a form of constructivist justificatory theory which is minimally demanding is likely to be appropriate in grounding a *legitimate* form of international political constructivism. A theory which begins with and takes seriously Rawls' arguments concerning the nature and structure of the concept of the reasonable, but which is crucially adapted so as to present a less demanding concept from which to construct an appropriate conception of practical reason will be crucial, for the purposes of my book, in grounding a theory of international relations which is capable of overcoming the poststructuralist critique. If McKinnon is correct in her claim that her account of reasonableness is less demanding than Rawls', McKinnon's account should be preferred as the basis of a response to poststructuralism. If, however, her claim is unsustainable, Rawls' conception of reasonableness will be defended.

McKinnon, as in the case of Rawls in *Political Liberalism*, presents her theory as a form of *liberal* political constructivism, applicable to the basic structure of the *domestic* society of a constitutional democracy. Correspondingly, the conception of the reasonable developed in detail by McKinnon is designed in her work to ground just such a liberal, domestic form of constructivism, and ultimately to justify liberal, domestic principles of justice. For my purposes, therefore, the following three questions become paramount:

(1) Is it the case that McKinnon's conception of the reasonable can be legitimately deployed in the context of a theory designed to construct principles of international justice (through an appropriate conception of practical reasoning)? The answer is: yes (McKinnon's 'Law of Peoples' project));
(2) Given that the answer to (1) is 'yes', the second crucial question becomes: Is it the case that McKinnon's conception of the reasonable can *only* ground an international constructivism which is appropriate when conceptualised as an extension of liberalism to the international? Or is it the case that McKinnon's conception of the reasonable can ground an international constructivism which is capable of an *objective* (in form 1 of the forms of objectivity identified near the start of this chapter[76]) form of justification? Here, the answer is: McKinnon develops her conception of self-respect in order to make it adaptable, and hence objective. However, the introduction of a substantive argument concerning the intrinsic value of a primary good (in this case, self-respect), and complex considerations of the skills and evaluative preferences which agents will need to possess, is theoretically risky insofar as political constructivism (as envisaged by the later Rawls) explicitly attempts to avoid recourse to arguments concerning comprehensive questions of value; and
(3) Is McKinnon's account of reasonableness really less demanding than Rawls'?

Recall the following claim made by Rawls in *The Law of Peoples*:

> [L]iberal peoples have a certain moral character. Like citizens in domestic society, liberal peoples are both reasonable and rational,

> and their rational conduct, as organised and expressed in their elections and votes, and the laws and policies of their government, is similarly constrained by their sense of what is reasonable. As reasonable citizens in domestic society offer to cooperate on fair terms with other citizens, so (reasonable) liberal (or decent) peoples offer fair terms of cooperation to other peoples. A people will honour these terms when assured that other peoples will do so as well. This leads us to the principles of political justice in the first case and the Law of Peoples in the other.[77]

The crucial idea linking *The Law of Peoples* with Rawls' constructivism in *Political Liberalism* is the idea that peoples can be both reasonable and rational *in an equivalent and directly comparable sense* to citizens in domestic society. Therefore, *The Law of Peoples* is not about working out a new conception of the reasonable by which to construct principles of justice for international relations; it is about working out how the conception of the reasonable developed in *Political Liberalism* can be legitimately deployed in a constructivist theory appropriate for international relations. The claim is not that peoples share identical characteristics with citizens of a constitutional democracy; rather, the claim is that both are conceived of as capable of embodying the fundamental characteristics of rationality and reasonableness worked out in *Political Liberalism*. The most fundamental point to notice about Rawls' argument in *The Law of Peoples* is that the conception of the reasonable incorporated therein is essentially the same as that developed in *Political Liberalism*. In both cases, citizen and people, the agent is conceived of as possessing the constituent requirements of reasonableness:

1. *It has the capacity for a sense of justice.*[78] As we saw in *Political Liberalism*, the capacity for a sense of justice, as distinct from the capacity for a conception of the good (the 'distinctive moral power' of rationality, which Rawlsian agents are also conceptualised as possessing), provides the normative force behind the willingness of agents to 'stand ready to propose, or to accept... fair terms of cooperation' which 'specify the reasons we are to share and publicly recognise before one another as grounding our social relations'.[79] The capacity for a sense of justice imbues the concept of the reasonable with its *public* nature (which, as we saw, again distinguishes it from rationalism). Agents are motivated to engage in public justificatory debate because they have a capacity for a sense of justice. In the case of peoples, then, as in the case of citizens, the idea of public reason arises out of the idea that reasonable agents possess a capacity for

a sense of justice. The Law of Peoples is the expression of this capacity, and this motivation to engage with others on publicly available terms when reasoning about matters of basic justice. To recall:

> I distinguish between the public reason of liberal peoples and the public reason of the Society of Peoples. The first is the public reason of equal citizens of domestic society debating the constitutional essentials and matters of basic justice concerning their own government; the second is the public reason of free and equal liberal peoples debating their mutual relations as peoples. The Law of Peoples with its political concepts and principles, ideals and criteria, is the content of this latter public reason. Although these two public reasons do not have the same content, the role of public reason among free and equal peoples is analogous to its role in a constitutional democratic regime among free and equal citizens.
>
> Political liberalism proposes that, in a constitutional democratic regime, comprehensive doctrines of truth or of right are to be replaced in public reason by an idea of the politically reasonable addressed to citizens as citizens. Here note the parallel: public reason is invoked by members of the Society of Peoples, and its principles are addressed to peoples as peoples. They are not expressed in terms of comprehensive doctrines of truth or right, which may hold sway in this or that society, but in terms that can be shared by different peoples.[80]

2. *It respects the fact of permanent pluralism.* In the case of peoples, a respect for the burdens of judgment (or the fact of permanent pluralism) arises within a 'reasonable idea of toleration' which, Rawls claims, is crucial to a reasonable political conception of justice appropriate for use in reasoning about matters of international justice. To recall, Rawls claims that the 'main points' of the idea of toleration are as follows:

> (1) Reasonable persons do not all affirm the same comprehensive doctrine. This is said to be a consequence of the 'burdens of judgment'. (2) Many reasonable doctrines are affirmed, not all of which can be true or right as judged from within any one comprehensive doctrine. (3) It is not unreasonable to affirm any one of the reasonable comprehensive doctrines. (4) Others who affirm reasonable doctrines different from ours are reasonable also. (5) In affirming our belief in a doctrine we recognise as reasonable, we are not being unreasonable.

(6) Reasonable persons think it unreasonable to use political power, should they possess it, to repress other doctrines that are reasonable yet different from their own.[81]

The manner in which Rawls' conception of reasonableness comes to be expressed in the case of peoples is captured early on in *The Law of Peoples*: liberal and decent peoples are characterised by their nature as reasonable. The character of a liberal or decent people, expressed through the three elements identified by Rawls ('a reasonably just constitutional democratic government[82] that serves their fundamental interests; citizens united by what Mill calls 'common sympathies'; and finally, a moral nature'[83]), is fundamentally bound up with the concept of the reasonable. Crucially, therefore, the most fundamental idea behind Rawls' theory in *The Law of Peoples* is comparable to the most fundamental idea in *Political Liberalism* – the concept of the reasonable and the idea of public reason which flows from such.

If we accept that peoples can be rational and reasonable in a comparable sense to citizens in domestic society, it follows that the idea of public reason will be applicable and appropriate to international relations. The concept of the reasonable vindicates the claim that agents – citizens or peoples – will be motivated to respect the limits of public reason when engaging in justificatory debate concerning matters of basic justice. The idea of public reason, as I argued in the last chapter, contains enough analogous elements and objectives when compared with Kratochwil's conception of practical reason to form a combined conception of normative reasoning which seeks to give a fuller account of the nature of the reasoning invoked by agents engaged in justificatory debate *within the context of normative structure* than Rawls' account of public reason alone can give. Crucially, Kratochwil's theory possesses the tools necessary in order to ground an *objective* account of the way justificatory reasoning concerning matters of basic justice can link with crucial considerations of practicality in realising the principles formulated by reasonable agents engaged in public reasoning. As I have previously argued, institutional and legal reasoning *must* feature in any realistic account of international political constructivism; they must be intimately bound up with, and capable of expression within, a conception of practical reason properly formatted so as to be appropriate to international relations. Given the undeniable role played by institutions and law in realising and giving expression to principles of international justice, a conception of normative reason which can bridge the divide between Rawlsian constructivism (based on the idea of public reason), on the one hand, and conceptions of institutional and legal reasoning, on the other, will be invaluable. Moreover, it will lend weight to the argument that Rawls' constructivism is capable of being genuinely *realistic*, as well as utopian. The danger is that an international theory premised on the idea of peoples which is both rational and reasonable may be subject to the charge that it does not reflect, and is therefore not appropriate to, the conditions of international relations. If one can argue, as I have attempted to do in the last chapter, that Rawls' constructivism can be effectively combined with Kratochwil's conception of practical reasoning, and reasoning with norms more generally, we have a genuine link between the idea of public reason, the construction of normative structure in international relations, and the expression of such structure through practical, legal and institutional reasoning anchored around the existence of intersubjectively anchored norms. This, as Buchanan identified (correctly in my contention) is fundamental to any account of international political justification.

The concept of the reasonable is a 'primitive' concept[84] or, as Rawls describes it, alongside rationalism it constitutes one of 'two distinct and independent basic ideas'.[85] It cannot be afforded an explanation by recourse to any external concept, only by reference to its constituent ideas which are themselves imbued with meaning *because* they form the basis of the concept of the reasonable. The idea of public reason flows from the concept of the reasonable. When justifying agents' commitment to engage in justificatory debate from within the limits of public reason, the concept of the reasonable can be invoked; agents are committed to public reason because they are reasonable. The driving force behind the justificatory power of the concept of the reasonable are the concepts' constituent parts; the idea that reasonable agents have the capacity for a sense of justice and respect the fact of permanent pluralism. Because these elements form the characteristics of a reasonable agent, they are imbued with normatively significant meaning, culminating in normative force. Therefore, the conception of public reason developed from within the concept of the reasonable will itself have normative force, and reasonable agents will be bound to accept it.

Because of the normatively 'basic' nature of the concept of the reasonable, it is not a concept which requires acceptance of substantive judgements of value originating from within the thick public political culture of any particular society to coherently and generally apply to *all* agents. Nor is it derived from the language of any particular comprehensive doctrine. Rather, the concept of the reasonable, and a reasonable agent, is capable of originating from within *any* particular comprehensive doctrine. *if* an agent has the capacity for a sense of justice, and *if* an agent respects the fact of permanent pluralism when considering matters of basic justice, that agent will be reasonable, and therefore capable of engaging in public justificatory debate. It is conceptually impossible, in my contention, to argue that a particular people could not have the capacity for a sense of justice. All peoples, and all comprehensive doctrines, whether liberal, decent or unreasonable, have the capacity for a sense of justice. As I have argued above, it is the second element, the respect for the fact of permanent pluralism, which I believe really reveals the normatively significant nature of the concept of the reasonable. A people may or may not engender this element of the reasonable when entering into relations with other peoples; those that do not, who either do not accept that normatively significant pluralism exists or else do not accept that such pluralism is reasonable and hence refuse to respect it, will be unreasonable peoples. But the crucial point is that all peoples are *capable* of respecting the fact of permanent pluralism when dealing with other peoples. Because of this fact, the idea of the reasonable *can* apply to peoples, and *is* therefore appropriate in grounding a theory of international relations.

Rawls conceives of his form of constructivism as being reasonably acceptable to all reasonable peoples, and thus of grounding a legitimate Law of Peoples. It should be clear from the detailed consideration I have afforded Rawls' conception of reasonableness that, in order to ground an inclusive and legitimate theory of political justification, Rawls has taken care to develop the conception of the reasonable in *Political Liberalism* from minimal and uncontroversial predicates. The capacity for a sense of justice, and a respect for the fact of permanent pluralism, are open concepts which do not require that agents accept any active form of judgements about value, or reasoning tied to any particular comprehensive doctrine (and thus do not require that agents subscribe to any particular comprehensive doctrine). However, as we saw above, McKinnon argues that the fact that the most significant element of Rawls' conception of reasonableness – a respect for the fact of permanent pluralism – is oriented around accepting the burdens of judgement creates a form of political constructivism which is demanding on agents insofar as the concept requires a strong uniformity of belief among agents as to why pluralism is permanent. By conceiving of agents as caring about their own self-respect, claims McKinnon, an explanation of why agents would accept the fact of permanent pluralism can be given without reliance on acceptance of the burdens of judgement. This formulation, claims McKinnon, is less demanding than

Rawls' formulation because it does not require a high degree of uniformity of belief among agents as to why pluralism is permanent. Thus, so long as a form of political justification based on a conception of the reasonable which is oriented around the idea of self-respect would be demonstrably appropriate for the construction of principles applicable to international relations, and so long as we accept McKinnon's argument that her conceptualisation of reasonableness is less demanding than that of Rawls, McKinnon's conception ought to be preferred for my purposes. I wish to consider the latter proposition below.

The fundamental distinction between McKinnon's conception of the reasonable and that developed by Rawls in *Political Liberalism* is as follows: McKinnon's conception ascribes to agents a particular judgement of value – namely, that all agents value and care about their own self-respect – and places it at the heart of a conception of practical reason. Agents must universally value self-respect as a 'primary good',[86] understood through the presence of congruence and non-subservience, and must possess the requisite skills and attributes and evaluate reasoning in the ways ascribed to them by McKinnon, in order for her argument as to why agents would be motivated to respect the limits of public reason to function. In applying McKinnon's theory of justification to the construction of international principles of justice, the argument must be that all reasonable peoples respect the fact that all other reasonable peoples care about their self-respect and may realise such in a variety of distinct and diverse (but reasonable) ways. This justifies McKinnon's claim that reasonable peoples will be willing to engage in public justificatory debate with reasonable others.

Is a recognition of self-respect as a primary good necessary to an account of reasonableness which is minimally demanding and hence capable of grounding a legitimate understanding of international relations by which to transcend poststructuralism? Can Rawls' account be defended and be shown to be undemanding yet robust, minimal yet legitimate, and capable of accommodating Kratochwil's account of the nature of reasoning within normative contexts? In the next section I will consider the Rawlsian account of reasonableness and practical reason developed by Roberts. Ultimately, I will argue that, through an analysis of Roberts' work, McKinnon's claim that Rawls' conception of reasonableness is too demanding can be dispelled. I also claim that Rawls' account of political constructivism (on Roberts' reading) is less demanding than McKinnon's, in that it does not rely on a substantive argument concerning the inherent value of self-respect and can ground an objective and authoritative account of practical reason *without* requiring uniformity of belief among agents.

Roberts' conception of reasonableness

Roberts' stated aim in his book *Political Constructivism*[87] is to develop a theory of political justification anchored around a Rawlsian conception of practical reason which 'is necessarily reflective' and which offers 'reasons to others'.[88] This minimal approach to the conditions of reasonableness and reasoning practically characterises Roberts' conception of constructivism and political justification – the aim is to develop a 'constructivist account... plausibly and independently arrived at through a series of quite natural steps',[89] oriented around a minimalist conception of practical reason. The conception of reasonableness at the core of Roberts' account of political constructivism flows from claims about the necessity of a sophisticated account of practical reasoning. Given that '[p]eople are always doing something or other, and in doing so, they are always doing that something with or around, perhaps as a response to, other people',[90] claims Roberts, 'justificatory questions are an unavoidable but everyday part of all our lives'.[91] Thus:

> An account of practical reasoning is necessary, as it both constitutes and explains how we think about questions [of justification for action], how we should think about these questions and perhaps what sort of reasons are proper and legitimate for action.[92]

Therefore, *given* the fact that agents act and act in such a way that their action will involve (in some capacity), and have an effect on, other agents, and *given* the fact that we are used to the idea, and even the practice, of providing reasons in support of our actions in our everyday experience, an account of the nature and conditions of justificatory reasons will need to take into account what Roberts calls the 'constraints of practicality'[93] (the specifics of which I discuss below). Crucially, therefore, for the purposes of Roberts' interpretation of Rawlsian constructivism, an agent is reasonable when he/she is willing to engage in justificatory debate with other agents by recourse to reasoning which is *Practical* (i.e. disciplined by the constraints of practicality).

Roberts distinguishes between our common understandings of reasoning which is idealistic by nature, and reasoning which is practical. 'If idealistic reasoning is in some way disconnected from the "real world" ', he claims, 'practical reasoning must at least be concerned with, adapted to, make reference to or relate to "the world" '.[94] This requirement – that practical reason be in some way connected to, or disciplined by, the world – is borne out in the stipulation that 'practical reasons, in order to be practical rather than idealistic, should identify reasons that are adapted to the situation in which they are to count as reasons'.[95] The claim does not require, claims Roberts, a 'privileged description of the world out there... [which] ... presents itself to all people with adequate powers of perception'.[96] Rather, the claim is that 'our reasoning, if it is to be practical, must avoid inconsistency with available information about the world, however that is presented to us'.[97] This requirement is expressed in practical reasoning by the following stipulation:

> Practical reasoning must 'fit', be guided by, or at least be appropriate to, the environment(s) within which it is to function as reasoning, as it is concerned to offer reasons for action or for the adoption of principles for action. Since actions at least possibly impinge on others, our reasoning must be responsive to the relative normative and political environments. We must therefore be prepared to offer reasons that are at least possible reasons given the range of expectations we can legitimately have of the environments in which these reasons are to count.[98]

Thus, practical reasoning must offer reasons which are 'at least possible' within the environment in which they operate in order to properly remain within the constraints of practicality. Given the further fact that 'the normative environment for practical reasoning consists of a plurality of competing and probably incompatible conceptions of the good life'[99] (the 'fact of reasonable pluralism', as we have seen in my analysis of Rawls'/McKinnon's consideration of the burdens of judgement/'many flowers' view above and in Chapter 4), Roberts further claims that 'if our reasoning is to be practical, to be disciplined by "the world", it must take account of this plural normative environment'.[100] Practical reason must acknowledge the plurality of political environments and must adapt itself accordingly – meaning that the reasons offered in support of particular actions must be at least possible across a plurality of normatively significant environments where such action has the potential to cut across political and normative boundaries and affect a plurality of others. Thus:

> Recognising that in order for our reasoning to be practical it must be responsive to the normative and political environments in which

> the reasons that it offers are to count as reasons is an important first step in ensuring that our reasons are disciplined by the world. This recognition involves the acknowledgement that we must *start from where we are* and that responding to our plural normative and political environments is one part of starting from where we are in our practical deliberations.[101]

'Reasoning in such a way that our reasons are disciplined by the world', claims Roberts, 'means that we must avoid making further assumptions that are not accurate of that world. Assumptions that are inconsistent with available information about the world are no basis for practical reasoning'.[102] Thus, assumptions which bear no relation to the real world (i.e. conceptions of society or the person which bear no relation to the actual characteristics of real world societies or people) are necessarily excluded from the scope of practical reason. This apparently simple observation has, claims Roberts, 'significant consequence[s]' for practical reasoning in a world characterised by the existence of a plurality of normative environments:

> If reasons are to 'fit' environments when environments are plural, then reasons may have to be adapted to suit the variety of environments we necessarily encounter. In order for our reasoning to be practical, we may have to offer different reasons in different environments. What might be a reasonable expectation of one normative or political environment may not be so of another.[103]

This observation requires that '[s]ome assumptions about the "facts" or relationships that constitute each environment must be regarded as "fixed" loosely in any justification appropriate to that environment',[104] but that the assumptions we make in addressing reasons to certain others may not be relevant under different circumstances (i.e. where reasoning is addressed to other categories of recipient). Agents offering reasons to others must therefore be sensitive to the assumptions underpinning their reasoning, and specifically must take care not to 'exclude' the intended recipients of their reasons on the basis that they have assumed certain underlying features of those others, or the particular environment they share with those others, which are not applicable or appropriate in the particular circumstances.

Given the stipulation that reasoning be disciplined by the world, Roberts claims that the assumptions on which reasons are based may either be shown to be mistaken (i.e. the fact that an assumption is untrue may be borne out during the process of offering reasons to others), or else may *become* mistaken as the conditions of the relevant normative environment change.[105] It is paramount, therefore, that the assumptions on which reasoning is based are themselves subjected to constant analysis and, where necessary, to revision and adaptation in light of the available information about the particular conditions of the normative environment in question:

> [E]nvironments are not static. It is clear that the relationships and groupings that constitute normative and political environments are not themselves fixed but shifting; they change and evolve over time, and our account of the conditions on practical reasoning must acknowledge this basic point[106];

And:

> Recognition of the necessity of revising basic assumptions is the recognition that our reasons and justifications may also change. This highlights the provisional or perhaps temporary nature of any properly practical reasons. Their dependency on environment ensures their provisional standing, as all environments and relationships change over time. No environment can be assumed to be fixed for all time, and therefore even our most strongly held reasons must be regarded as only provisionally held (even if it is difficult to imagine what criticism or novel encounter could cast doubt on them).[107]

Thus, to summarise the 'constraints of practicality', Roberts states:

> [W]e have found that reasoning practically involves recognising two simple injunctions. First, it involves ensuring that we *offer reasons that are disciplined by the world* to the extent that these reasons are at least possible reasons. Our reasons, if practical, should respond appropriately to the normative and political environments in which they are to function. Responding appropriately to the environments in which we find ourselves is a matter of starting where we are and, therefore, of making assumptions that are appropriate to our environments. We must also recognise that such environments are plural and that different assumptions might be appropriate in different environments, and so different justifications may have to be offered to different audiences. Second, reasoning practically involves recognising that the environments in which our reasons function are continually changing. Reasoning practically in a changing world is a matter of a willingness to revisit and revise basic assumptions, reasons

and principles to ensure that they remain appropriate as that world changes. Responding to these changes, coupled with a sensitivity to the possibility that our basic assumptions may be less appropriate than we thought, leads us to an understanding of reasoning practically as involving a central and basic commitment to a process of ongoing *critical reflection.*[108]

Theoretical, practical and motivational limits on reasoning

Once the minimal and uncontroversial formal requirements of reasoning which can properly be said to conform with the constraints of practicality are established, Roberts then goes on to consider whether the claim that 'reasons are linked to contexts' necessitates a 'relative or subjective conclusion from an account of practical reasoning'.[109] Such a conclusion, he claims, 'will rely on an account of the limits of practical reasoning' – that is, the claim that all reasoning is 'constrained within less-than-universal limits'.[110] The arguments concerning necessary limits to practical reasoning generally cite theoretical, practical and motivational limitations, claims Roberts. In each case, Roberts' counterargument is that the claimed limitations on reasoning do not, by necessity, apply, and that an account of the possibility of an *objective*[111] scope for practical reasoning is therefore possible:

1. *Theoretical limits.* Citing the work of 'communitarians and multiculturalists', Roberts claims: 'The basic argument is that there are certain assumptions that necessarily underpin our reasoning and that these assumptions are different for different people at different times and places. These assumptions function as "givens" for all our reasons and justifications, and they are "culturally bestowed or socially imposed" '.[112] Therefore, '[i]f our reasoning necessarily has certain basic assumptions given by context and our self-understanding is closely tied to a particular culture, then other cultures become unintelligible to us. We have no resources that enable us to make sense of what those in strange and unfamiliar contexts are doing or saying'.[113] The claim Roberts is here addressing is essentially that '[w]e cannot, either temporarily or permanently, escape from or even step outside of our particular context. Nor, as they are given, not chosen, are the features of that context and the way they shape and constrain us available for rational assessment'.[114] On this argument, practical reasoning rests on assumptions which are intelligible only within the constraints of particular cultural understandings, and therefore only within the bounds of a particular culture (or

perhaps a particular comprehensive doctrine). Not only can reasoning not be transmuted between the bespoke languages and understandings of particular cultures, but (and even more fundamentally) agents cannot critically assess the assumptions their culturally conditioned reasoning relies on via the medium of reflective reason. Alternatively, the argument can be recast as the claim that 'our reflective engagement with reasons is always culturally constrained'[115] (rather than wholly determined by context), and that, therefore, 'basic assumptions of our reasoning remain, in principle, beyond critical examination, and therefore unrevisable'.[116]

Thus, argues Roberts, cultural understandings will ultimately be informed and determined by engagement by agents in critical and reflective processes of practical reasoning:

> If someone has reason to reject certain cultural values as ones that they feel no reason to endorse, then this also gives them reason to reject or modify the social understandings tied up with those values. Obviously, an individual reflection on, and rejection of, a set of social or cultural understandings will not radically alter those understandings (although the reflection of many individuals might), but it does give a foothold to the idea that these understandings are under constant examination and may be subject to reasoned pressures to adapt or change. The relationship between cultural and individual reasons does not obviously involve a process of one-way determination of the individual by the cultural but may instead be a reciprocal relationship of mutual influence.[117]

This claim, coupled with the argument that 'reflective engagement with novel ideas and challenges to our current ways of thinking that originate from outside our cultural horizons'[118] bears no *conceptual* difference to reflective engagement with such ideas and challenges which originate *within* the applicable agent's particular cultural context, leads Roberts to conclude that the argument that practical reasoning cannot be divorced from the cultural constraints tied up with the particular context within which the reasoner is situated is unsustainable. In reality, he claims, cultural understandings overlap to a remarkable degree:

> What are claimed by some people to be radically different conceptual schemes are far better thought of as necessarily overlapping to an

> enormous degree. That 1 per cent of the time understanding or translating is difficult does not establish the claimed theoretical limits on our reasons and justifications.[119]

2. *Practical limits.* In the case of arguments concerning conceptual limitations on practical reasoning which do not attribute such limitations to either theoretical or motivational issues, Roberts considers these to be arguments concerning necessary practical limitations on agents' practical reasoning (i.e. the argument that, practically speaking, our reasoning is confined to a limited and exclusive, rather than wide and inclusive, remit). Arguments of this sort are simply and roundly rejected by Roberts:

> To the extent that this is not a claim about theoretical or motivational limits, it should not occupy much of our attention. There may indeed be very good reason for focusing the bulk of our reasoning locally. This is where our family and friends are, and we may feel that we owe them a special sort of concern and attention and that particular and very important obligations arise for us in this context. Also, we may feel that we have a range of particular and special obligations of limited extent that we incur as members of clubs and associations, as contractors with other individuals and groups, as citizens of particular states or as compatriots in the same community. Our attention really is overwhelmingly focused locally. However, there is no reason to think that the everyday limits that we quite naturally impose upon our reasoning are ever necessary limits, and it is this question of necessity that concerns us here.[120]

Given that '[t]oday, all others stand in some form of relationship with us, and we therefore make some sort of practical assumptions about them whenever we act', Roberts claims that 'there are no necessary practical limits to our reasoning'.[121]

3. *Motivational limits.* Arguments claiming necessary motivational limits of reasoning are potentially the most significant of the three categories considered by Roberts, and are dealt with at the most length in *Political Constructivism.*[122] They also represents the most significant form of objection to the scope and authority of practical reason from the perspective of my book since, as we saw in the arguments leveled against Rawls by O'Neill in Chapter 4 (and as I have been exploring in this chapter), the claim that Rawls' conception of public reason cannot

properly ground a theory of political justification without an additional and authoritative account of agents' *motivation* to frame justificatory debate concerning matters of basic justice within the limits ascribed to the concept by Rawls is a cogent one and must be addressed. It is therefore important, for my purposes, to consider in detail the propensity for claims to motivational limitations on practical and normative reasoning to carry weight. I have argued that an answer to the question: '*Why* would agents' respect the limits of public reason in engaging in justificatory debates concerning matters of basic justice with others?' is provided by the concept of a reasonable agent. I have also argued that, *contrary to* the charges leveled at Rawls' conception of public reason by O'Neill, the *fact* of agreement on the normative desirability of particular principles among agents is *extrinsic* to the idea of public reason and represents the *consequence* of agents framing their justificatory arguments in this way (rather than an *intrinsic* element of the conception). Both of these points speak to issues of motivation.[123] Thus, *because* I claim that the motivational work is done by the concept of the reasonable, and *because* of the sophisticated yet minimal and generally uncontroversial conceptions of the reasonable which, particularly Roberts, but also Rawls and McKinnon have been concerned to develop, my argument is that many of the motivational concerns leveled against political constructivism should be relatively easy to dispel. However, the claim to motivational limits which Roberts explicitly addresses speaks directly to the question: '*Why* would agents be motivated by reasons for action (i.e. in the sense which means that they actually *take* the particular action *on the basis of* such reasons) *unless* they possessed an existing interest or desire which would be furthered by acceptance of such reasons?' This is a related question to those set out above, but warrants a closer examination of the relationship between practical reason and desire and, ultimately, of the relationship between questions of justification and those of motivation. I will consider these issues through an analysis of Roberts' response to the claim that reasons for action will not motivate an agent to act unless that agent already has a pre-existing desire which would be furthered by acceptance of the particular reason in question.

In summarising claims to necessary motivational limits on reasons, Roberts states:

> Perhaps there is another form of limit to our reasons that is based on an understanding of the place of motivation in arguments for principles of justice. Perhaps it is necessary, in order to understand justice,

> to consider a person's motives for action, in particular, their possible motivation for acting justly. Is a commitment to justice premised on a coincidence between the dictates of justice and our pre-existing interests?[124];

And:

> The basic claim concerning the limits on reasons is a claim about what counts as a good reason. A good reason must be motivating and can only be so if appeal to it presupposes a pre-existing interest or desire that I have, such that acceptance of that reason as a reason for me would further that interest or desire. If I do not have the desire that is presupposed, then that reason cannot be mine. Reasons are limited by the extent to which people have the presupposed desire.[125]

The basic claim is therefore that 'principles of justice can only be justified... if they are motivationally sufficient, and they can only exhibit this characteristic if they coincide with a pre-existing desire'.[126]

Roberts' responses to this claim are threefold:

> First, I will suggest that this is a sort of non-question, as issues of justification and motivation come apart. Second, even if constructivism concedes (although I do not think it has to) that the motivational claim is important for justification, it can still go on to show that it is a non-question in a second way (as far as constructivist justification is concerned); constructivist justification finds its starting points in the moral and political practices that we are already tied into. Third, I am impressed with Scanlon's argument that the specific claims about the necessary role of interest or desire in motivation and justification that are assumed in the argument about motivational limits to reason are problematic. Together, these arguments will show that there do not appear to be any obvious motivational limits to reasons.[127]

Thus, the following arguments are provided by Roberts to dispel the claim to motivational limits on reasons:

a. We *should* be motivated by good reasons *even if* we currently are not[128];
b. There is nothing normatively significant in what we are currently psychologically motivated to regard as a good reason[129];

c. 'The starting points of constructivist justification are the moral and political practices in which we already find ourselves (and we are always already involved in some)'. Whether or not we challenge such practices, practical reasoning adopts a critically reflective attitude to such practices and the reasoning conditioned by such[130];
d. 'We have a stake in the principles that are justified by constructivist reflective reason because we are already intimately linked with moral and political practices that presuppose them'.[131]

The ultimate claim concerning motivational limits on reasons which Roberts considers is that desires or interests play a foundational or constitutive role in questions of both motivation and justification. In responding to this claim, Roberts considers:

> If reason (instead of or as well as desire) can be motivational, then the practical normative force of accepting and acting on good reasons that our prior commitment to moral practices may entail is not parasitic on pre-existing conviction or desire.[132]

In establishing that reason itself can be the source of motivation among agents, Roberts draws on the detailed consideration of the nature of reasons undertaken by Scanlon in *What We Owe to Each Other.*[133] Roberts' consideration of Scanlon's arguments concerning the nature of reasons are extremely instructive on this point and I want to visit Scanlon's text itself in order to flesh out his position on this point in greater detail. Additionally, Scanlon's arguments concerning the nature of motivation feeds in to my claim that, in order to truly understand the complex, intersubjective nature of international relations, a theory of political constructivism must engage with Kratochwil's sophisticated account of the nature of practical, legal and moral reasoning – thus providing a crucial link between Kratochwil's account of practical reason and Roberts' interpretation of the Rawlsian conception of reasonableness. This is because the normative social structures conceptualised by Kratochwil, and the style of reasoning associated with Kratochwil's account of the conditions of practical reasoning, operate on the basis of the normative authority of reasoning in Kratochwil's sense alone and do not carry an account of the role of interest or desire within a conception of motivation. My argument has been that, by situating Kratochwil's account of normative reasoning within the framework of Rawlsian political constructivism, with an appropriate account of the concept of the reasonable underpinning the justification of a combined account of public/practical reasoning, an account of the motivation of agents to engage in public justificatory argument concerning matters of basic justice will be supplied. Therefore, an argument which convincingly shows why a conception of pre-given interests or desires are not necessary to an account of motivation will lend weight to the claim that the combined account of the structure of normative reasoning which I advocate is wholly constructivist (and therefore legitimately transcends the poststructuralist critique). It does *not* rely on what Roberts terms 'contractarian' claims to the necessity of an antecedently established set of interests or desires. Such reliance would, in my opinion, be the type of foundationalist recourse which Walker and Ashley would vehemently attack as resting on an illegitimate account of the authority of an ontologically established set of interests, and should therefore not feature as part of the constructivist theory of international relations I am concerned to establish. Scanlon's arguments in this regard are therefore vitally important for consideration as part of my book. I also believe that Scanlon's consideration of the motivational qualities of reasons is more fundamental than Kratochwil's analysis of practical reason. Kratochwil's theory is concerned with identifying and explaining *how* a particular *style* of reasoning *within the context of normative structure* functions. Scanlon is concerned to identify the structural features inherent in the very idea of a reason generally. The two theories are therefore compatible.

Scanlon takes the idea of reasons, including practical reasons or reasons underpinning action, as 'primitive' and 'unproblematic'. He claims:

> I will argue that desires, insofar as they are distinguished from the recognition of reasons, have a much less fundamental role in practical thinking than is commonly supposed. Indeed, I have become convinced that insofar as 'having a desire' is understood as a state that is distinct from 'seeing something as a reason', it plays almost no role in the justification and explanation of action.[134]

This is a profound claim,[135] but one that effectively feeds in to my combined account of public/practical reason, and the concept of reasonableness, herein. It relies on Scanlon's particular conceptualisation of the nature of a reason – or rather, a reason in what he terms the 'standard normative sense':

> What I am concerned with... are reasons in the 'standard normative sense'. So when I say that something is or is not a reason I will not

> be concerned with whether it is or could be someone's operative reason but with whether it is a *good* reason – a consideration that really counts in favour of the thing in question.[136]

The idea of a reason in the 'standard normative sense' – that is, in the case of practical reasoning, a reason which genuinely counts in favour of a particular action – rests on Scanlon's belief that '[t]here is a difference between asking what reason there is for believing that P and asking what a given person's reason for believing it was'.[137] The latter is what Scanlon refers to as an agent's 'operative reason'. The distinction, essentially, rests on a distinction between objective and subjective reasons. Practical reasons in the 'standard normative sense' are reasons which *objectively* count in favour of a particular action; an agent's operative reasons are reasons which *subjectively* count in favour of it.

The category of phenomena which Scanlon believes that 'reasons in the standard normative sense' are applicable to are what Scanlon describes as 'judgment sensitive attitudes'[138]:

> What is the range of things for which reasons in the standard normative sense can be asked for or offered? States or occurrences that are independent of any conscious agent are clearly excluded. Most, perhaps even all, of the things that are included are attitudes of rational agents such as beliefs, intentions, hopes, fears, and attitudes such as admiration, respect, contempt, and indignation.[139]

Judgement-sensitive attitudes are therefore distinguished from *non* judgement-sensitive attitudes or more base or simplistic attitudes or feelings experienced by an agent (the example given is hunger). Judgement-sensitive attitudes involve more sophisticated processes of evaluation among agents. Scanlon claims:

> *Having* a judgment-sensitive attitude involves a complicated set of dispositions to think and react in specified ways. For example, a person who believes that P will tend to have feelings of conviction about P when the question arises, will normally be prepared to affirm P and to use it as a premise in further reasoning, will tend to think of P as a piece of counterevidence when claims incompatible with it are advanced, and so on. Similarly, a person who intends to do A will not only feel favourably disposed, on balance, to that course of action, but will also tend to be on the lookout for ways of carrying out this intention (finding means, looking for ways of fitting in with other

> plans, and so on), and will think of this intention as a prima facie objection when incompatible courses of action are proposed.[140]

Thus:

> An attitude is judgment-sensitive if it is part of being the attitude it is that this complex of dispositions should be sensitive to a particular kind of judgment. But having such an attitude involves not only being disposed to judge in certain ways but also being disposed to various patterns of unreflective thought, such as being disposed to *think* of the proposition believed or the course of action intended at the relevant moments.[141]

The idea of normative reasons as 'judgment-sensitive attitudes' assists in explaining, claims Scanlon, how agents can properly be said to be 'responsible' for, and hence potentially required to justify, their own attitudes and beliefs as well as, ultimately but more familiarly, their own action:

> Because 'being responsible' is mainly a matter of the appropriateness of demanding reasons, it is enough that the attitude in question be a judgment-sensitive one – that is, one that either directly reflects the agent's judgment or is supposed to be governed by it. For this reason, one can be responsible not only for one's actions but also for intentions, beliefs, and other attitudes. That is, one can properly be asked to defend these attitudes according to the canons relevant to them, and one can be appraised in the light of these canons for the attitudes one holds.[142]

Therefore, for Scanlon, the fact that an agent has an attitude or belief, or undertakes a particular action, is something *active* which, were the agent called on to provide a justification for so having, would need to be explained by reasons which, on an appraisal of such, could objectively be described as *good* reasons for having the particular attitude or belief, or undertaking the particular action, in question.

Given the active and complex nature of Scanlon's conceptualisation of normative reasons as judgement-sensitive attitudes, his fundamental argument concerning the nature of reasons and motivation is that, given the assumption that agents are rational creatures, an agent who judges the reasons in support of a particular attitude or belief, or in support of a particular action, will usually hold such attitude/belief, or normally forms the intention to do the particular action, and that the judgement itself is normally a sufficient account of the motivation of the agent to hold the attitude or belief, or form the intention to act:

> A rational person who judges there to be sufficient grounds for believing that P normally has that belief, and this judgment is normally sufficient explanation for so believing. There is no need to appeal to some further source of motivation such as 'wanting to believe'. Similarly, a rational person who judges there to be compelling reason to do A normally forms the intention to do A, and this judgment is sufficient explanation of that intention and of the agent's acting on it (since this action is part of what such an intention involves). There is no need to invoke an additional form of motivation beyond the judgment and the reasons it recognises, some further force to, as it were, get the limbs in motion.[143]

This conclusion flows, according to Scanlon, from his account of rationality (and, in particular, the claim that '[j]udgment-sensitive attitudes... are responsive to the agent's judgments about the adequacy of reasons'[144]). This is not to state, claims Scanlon, that there is no conceptual distinction between recognising something as a reason and being motivated to act on it; rather, the argument is that 'when a person not only recognises something as a reason but also is moved to act', the latter is not 'due to the presence of some further motivating element in addition to that recognition – something appropriately called a desire'.[145] Thus, '[j]ust as in the case of belief, there is no need to appeal to a further source of motivation to explain how a rational creature can be led to act'.[146]

Interestingly, and in contrast to Rawls, Scanlon's conception of reasonableness is afforded a less fundamental, but nevertheless still crucial place in his account of agents' motivation (and his account of *moral* motivation in particular) than his conception of rationality. The conception of the reasonable, for Scanlon, 'presupposes a certain body of information and a certain range of reasons which are taken to be relevant, and goes on to make a claim about what these reasons, properly understood, in fact support'.[147] According to Scanlon, 'deciding whether an action is right or wrong requires a substantive judgment on our part about whether certain objections to possible moral principles would be reasonable'.[148] Although this point is interesting, I do not propose to consider Scanlon's account of morality in detail, for so doing would require a book unto itself. In the context of my study, his account of the structure and inherent qualities of reasons is the really crucial element of his contractualism.

Concerning desires, Scanlon states:

> Desires are commonly understood in philosophical discussion to be psychological states which play two fundamental roles. On the one hand, they are supposed to be motivationally efficacious: desires are usually, or perhaps always, what move us to act. On the other hand, they are supposed to be normatively significant: when someone has a reason (in the standard normative sense) to do something this is generally, perhaps even always, true *because* doing this would promote the fulfilment of some desire which the agent has.[149]

The claim which Scanlon is concerned with in *What We Owe to Each Other* is that 'reasons for action can or must derive their justificatory force from the agent's desires [in the sense given above]'.[150] This claim is normatively significant, argues Scanlon, because it is based on the premise that moral and practical reasoning relies on the presence and motivating power of desires. Scanlon's argument is that, in fact, the language of desires cannot support the motivational role it is commonly assigned within an account of justification for action:

> [W]hen we consider the various states that might be identified as desires we find none that can play the general role in justification commonly assigned to desires – that of states which are independent of our practical reasoning and which, when they occur, provide reason for doing what will promote their fulfilment. Many of our reasons do have subjective conditions, but these turn out, on closer inspection, to be rather misleadingly described by the terminology of desire and desire fulfilment.[151]

Ultimately, Scanlon formulates an argument in support of his central contention concerning the nature of reasons and motivation which is *structural*. He argues for the centrality of 'maxims', or 'principles specifying the adequacy or inadequacy of various considerations as reasons for one or another judgment-sensitive attitude'.[152] Thus, Scanlon claims that 'our practical thinking takes place within a framework of maxims and is concerned with adopting, interpreting, and modifying these principles as well as with deciding, within the framework they provide, whether we have sufficient reason for acting in particular ways'.[153]

This conception of the presence of maxims as a fundamental constituent of practical reasoning will therefore disallow the motivational effects traditionally attributed to conceptions of desire in the following manner:

> My claim is that reasons for action, intention, and other attitudes exhibit a ... complex structure. I do not mean to deny that deciding what to do is sometimes a matter of deciding which of several competing considerations one wants more or cares more about. My point is rather that when this is so in a particular case it is because a more general framework of reasons and principles determines that these considerations are the relevant ones on which to base a decision. Much of our practical thinking is concerned with figuring out which considerations are relevant to a given decision, that is to say, with interpreting, adjusting, and modifying this more general framework of principles of reasoning.[154]

Thus:

> The claim I am making here is a structural one. I am calling attention to familiar features of our practical thinking that, I argue, are naturally represented in terms of reasons and judgments but cannot be accounted for if we take practical reasoning to be a matter of balancing competing desires on the basis of their 'strength'.[155]

Notwithstanding the clear analogies between Scanlon's conception of the structural nature of practical reason and that of Kratochwil (which, I believe, renders Scanlon's account of the fundamental nature of reason and practical reasoning extremely useful and appropriate for my purposes), he has also presented a convincing argument as to why claims to motivational limits on reasoning, in the particular sense considered by Roberts, can be rejected. Thus, both Roberts and Scanlon have cleared the way for an account of why reason, and reasonableness, can be conceptualised as objective and authoritative, and why it may therefore legitimately ground a constructivist understanding of international relations.

I now consider Roberts' account of why reason can properly be thought of as objective, and draw together the various conceptions of reasonableness and practical reasoning I have considered herein into one coherent account of the structure of normative reasoning.

Roberts, Rawls, Kratochwil: The structure of normative reasoning

My extended analysis of Roberts' consideration of the potential claims to necessary limitations on reasoning – and the systematic rejection of such through considered counterarguments (which, as we saw in the case of claims to motivational limits on reasoning, involved reliance on Scanlon's complex account of the nature of practical reasoning as being fundamentally bound up with the ideas of judgement-sensitive attitudes and a motivationally sufficient normative structure for reasoning about action) – has cleared the way for a consideration of *how* accounts of reasoning and reasonableness can be thought of as both objective and authoritative.

Roberts claims:

> [I]f there are no necessary theoretical, practical or motivational constraints on our reasons, then we can draw either of two conclusions. This implies that either reasons need not necessarily be constrained within the contexts that they initially arise or not all contexts are necessarily limited, local and particular. If either conclusion is warranted, and if they are not equivalent it may be that both are, then reasons need not be partial and subjective.[156]

Roberts' central claim is that, *if* reasons need not be partial and subjective, then the potential exists for them to be impartial and *objective*. His understanding of objectivity is explicitly contrasted with the conception of objectivity at the heart of logical positivism (i.e. the conception of objectivity as 'somehow corresponding to, or giving a proper account of, some set of facts'[157]) as well as the conception of objectivity assumed by Platonic foundationalism (i.e. objectivity 'as a matter of faithfulness to an independent order of moral facts that enjoy a special epistemic status'[158]). *Contrary to* these conceptions, the conception of objectivity which Roberts applies in the case of practical reason is fleshed out as follows:

> We are quite used to the idea of objective judges or referees, and their objectivity is a matter of taking all relevant factors into consideration, of weighing available evidence and argument and of coming to impartial or unbiased decisions. On this everyday understanding, objectivity is taken to be undermined by partiality, bias, subjectivity, arbitrariness and idealisation and reinforced by their opposites.[159]

Thus:

> Minimising partiality is the task of an ongoing process of critical and practical reflection that kicks in whenever we have reason to suspect that our reasons may be partial in ways that we had not anticipated.[160]

This task – the task of minimising partiality – is, claims Roberts, a 'central feature' of Rawls' constructivism and is inherent within the ideas of the original position and a conception of reflective equilibrium 'as an account of critical and reflective reason'.[161] It is also, argues Roberts, crucial to an understanding of how reason can be thought of as *authoritative* without reliance on any external factor. Roberts' most fundamental claim:

> I want to suggest that practical reasoning can be thought of as 'a way of proceeding'. This... involves marshalling the reasons about which we are currently most confident and exposing them to critical reflection concerning their partiality in the light of challenges and alternative reasons. Note that the 'aim' of proceeding this way is not to identify a 'pattern laid up in heaven' but simply to reassure ourselves of the ongoing objectivity of our reasons, where objectivity is taken to mean something like 'does not rely on any partial assumptions or ways of reasoning of which we are currently aware'.[162]

Armed with this account of the objectivity and authority of reasons, therefore, Roberts claims that political constructivism need not be constrained by the boundaries of a particular culture, and need not 'start from within a certain political tradition', as we have seen Rawls claiming. Rather, political constructivism in its pure or 'primary' form can be seen as a broader form of justificatory theory and can transcend *all* claims to limitations or boundaries to practical reasoning. Roberts' own account of political constructivism, and the regulatory role played by reflective and authoritative reason at the heart of such, is therefore formulated thus:

1. *In the construction of principles of political justice political constructivism draws only on general and abstract resources, which will include conceptions of society and person,* and so does not rely on, nor is it derived from, any particular conception of the good or of moral facts.

...

2. *Political constructivism also draws on an account of objectivity as impartiality or non-subjectivity.*

...

3. *Political constructivism involves an account of reflective and critical practical reasoning that is concerned to continuously hold 1 to the standard of 2,* with the effect that no conception or assumption at 1 can ever be more than provision.[163]

What we have in Roberts' account of the objectivity and authority of practical reasoning is a tool for the justification of political principles which is capable of the following:

1. *Transcending cultural boundaries*: Roberts argues that Rawls' assertion in *Political Liberalism* (and, by extension, *The Law of Peoples*) that political constructivism is inextricably tied to the conditions inherent within a particular culture (in Rawls' case, political liberalism) can be shown to be false, and that, through an analysis of the most basic requirements of sound practical reasoning, a constructivist theory can build an account of reasoning and of reasonableness (which, in Roberts' theory, we can deduce as being the willingness to engage in reasoning with others in a *practical* and *reflective* manner) which is not constrained by any limitations (whether they be theoretical, practical, or motivational in nature). By establishing the potential objectivity (in the sense outlined above) and, therefore, authority of practical reason, Roberts has effectively argued that constructivism can generate principles of justice *applicable and appropriate to international relations*.
2. *Grounding the combined account of public/practical reason I explored in the last chapter*. As I will set out in detail below, the 'constraints of practicality' identified by Roberts, and more broadly the starting points for the conceptions of the reasonable and practical reason developed by Rawls, function in a remarkably similar way to the fundamental conditions and requirements placed on normative reasoning by Kratochwil. Therefore, and in order to generate a theory capable of understanding the effects on practical reasoning generated by the presence of intersubjective normative social structure in international relations, I reiterate my argument that political constructivism should engage with the sophisticated account of practical reasoning – and its accompanying insights into the epistemological, legal and institutional elements which are requisite to any proper

account of justice in IR – developed by Kratochwil. Additionally, the stipulation in Roberts' account of constructivism that practical reasoning draw on 'abstract and general resources', including conceptions of society and the person, coupled with the requirement that reasoning recognise and respond to the fact of reasonable pluralism, means that a minimally demanding interpretation of the Rawlsian conception of reasonableness has been located. Public reason will be the natural consequence of a recognition of the constraints of practicality on the part of agents. McKinnon's claim that Rawls' theory is too demanding has been dispelled by Roberts.

3. *Ultimately, overcoming the poststructuralist critique.* As we saw in Chapter 1, the claim by Walker and Ashley was that the very foundations of the traditional discipline of IR were prefaced on illegitimate processes of dichotomisation and the unjustified privileging of one category (i.e. state; politics) over its counterpart (i.e. interstate; international). Walker and Ashley showed that the textual homogeneity and epistemological rigidity with which political knowledge was called on could be shown via deconstructive theoretical techniques to be shaky and infirm. However, and in keeping with many poststructuralist philosophies, Walker and Ashley offered very little in the way of a *reconstructive* alternative to what they perceived to be an illegitimate foundationalist discipline. What I have attempted to prove herein, however, is that a philosophical constructivism, grounded in a *legitimate* conception of the reasonable and a robust conception of normative reasoning (which accounts for both a Rawlsian account of the normative significance of the idea of public reason and the Kratochwilian account of the intersubjective processes by which normative social structure conditions practical reasoning) *can* reconstruct a legitimate and viable account of the nature of international relations capable of answering the poststructuralist challenge.

In my contention, Roberts' account of the nature of practical reasoning is to be preferred over McKinnon's in formulating a theory designed to transcend poststructuralism, for the following reasons:

1. On Roberts' interpretation, the conditions of reasonableness do not require that agents accept the fact of permanent pluralism *because* they accept that their judgement, and the judgment of others, is necessarily burdened. Rather, the constraints of practicality dictate that we begin from where we find ourselves in contemporary

international relations – that is, in a world characterised by a vast plethora of divergent doctrines which appear, at least prima facie, to be reasonable. By grounding an account of practical reason and reasonableness in the conditions of practicality, Roberts effectively dispels McKinnon's argument that a Rawlsian conception of reasonableness requires too great a uniformity of belief among, and is too demanding on, agents. The requirement that reasoning reflect the practical conditions of the world imposes minimal restrictions on agents which, I would argue, cannot be said to be over-demanding (and which also justifies the importance of Kratochwil's theory to a constructivist account of international relations, given the requisite acceptance of a contemporary international world infused with normative social, institutional and legal structure);

2. Once McKinnon's critique of Rawls' conception of reasonableness is dispelled, my claim is that an account of the requirements of practical reason which *avoids* reliance on substantive arguments concerning the importance of congruence and nonsubservience to a conception of the person (and peoples), and necessitates complex considerations regarding the attributes and evaluative preferences required to be possessed by agents (as I have considered above) should be preferred. In my contention, an account of practical reason predicated on minimal yet robust criteria, which can be shown to be both objective and authoritative (as Roberts shows), will be more appropriate to international relations than an account which relies on arguments concerning substantive conceptions of value (along with the relatively thick conception of the agent as possessing the various skills and attributes identified by McKinnon, which necessarily accompanies her conception of practical reason). The latter are far more theoretically risky and prone to the charge that they rely on acceptance of a liberal metaphysics and a liberal conception of the person. For my purposes, and in the context of international relations, therefore, the Rawlsian conception of reasonableness will be more appropriate;
3. Finally, Roberts (along with Scanlon) has also dispelled McKinnon's concerns regarding motivational adequacy. By effectively challenging the claim that there are necessary motivational limitations on reason, Roberts through Scanlon presents a convincing argument as to *how* the structure of practical reason contains the tools necessary to establish sufficient motivational adequacy. Therefore, the motivation of agents to act according to good (i.e. reasonable) reasons – and therefore the commitment of agents to engaging with others on publicly available terms – has been accounted for.

We are now in a position to offer a categorical statement of the structure of normative reasoning in international relations:

1. *We begin with an appropriate conception of the reasonable.* In Rawls, as we saw, the conception is bound up with the idea that 'it is by the reasonable that we enter as equals the public world of others and stand ready to propose, or to accept, as the case may be, fair terms of cooperation with them'.[164] Through an exposition of Rawls' account in *Political Liberalism* and *The Law of Peoples*, and through McKinnon's analysis of Rawls' conception of the reasonable, we came to identify the constituent elements of the idea: Agents are reasonable when they (1) they have the capacity for a sense of justice; (2) accept the consequences of the burdens of judgement; and (3) subscribe to a (full or partial) reasonable comprehensive doctrine.[165] McKinnon offered an extensive analysis of the requirement that agents accept the consequences of the burdens of judgement as a constituent element in the concept of the reasonable, which, she claims, necessarily leads agents to practise toleration and to respect the limits of public reason. For McKinnon, however, the requirement that agents accept the consequences of the burdens of judgement is too demanding, in that it requires too high a degree of uniformity of belief as to the causes of the fact of permanent pluralism. McKinnon suggests that 'an account of why ideal people accept the permanence of pluralism can be given which does not rely on specifying that they accept the burdens of judgment'[166]: the 'many flowers' explanation of the fact of permanent pluralism. The problem is, claims McKinnon, that such a view 'leaves constructivism without a motivational story to explain why stage 2 people could be motivated by stage 1 reasons to practice toleration and exercise public reason'.[167] McKinnon's suggested account of the motivation of agents to accept such reasons, as considered in detail above, is her account of the value placed on self-respect by agents, and the recognition that self-respect can be achieved in a vast plethora of distinct ways. This recognition, claims McKinnon, is less demanding than Rawls' burdens of judgment stipulation, as it does not require that agents accept the fact of permanent pluralism (the key to understanding their motivation to exercise public reason) on the basis of a uniformity of belief.

I have attempted to show through an analysis of Roberts' interpretation of Rawls' conception of reasonableness that McKinnon's critique is unsustainable and, ultimately, that Rawls' conception of reasonableness is more appropriate to an account of political constructivism capable of transcending poststructuralism than McKinnon's. Roberts presents an account of the conditions of practical reasoning which, I argue, is (1) genuinely uncontroversial and less demanding on agents in McKinnon's sense than McKinnon's insistence that agents accept the intrinsic value of self-respect (even the minimal and adaptable account of self-respect she develops); (2) effectively dispels arguments concerning the existence of necessary limits on reasoning, and therefore clears the way for an account of the objectivity and authority of practical reason; and (3) through arguments originated by both Roberts and (as we saw in detail) Scanlon, presents an account of the motivational adequacy of reason capable of augmenting the account of normative practical reason developed by Kratochwil. What Roberts presents, therefore, is an account of the nature of reason, and an interpretation of Rawls, which can justify the claim that agents will be motivated to engage in public justificatory debate in order to construct principles of justice which transcend cultural boundaries.

2. *From Roberts' minimal account of the constraints of practicality, and Rawls' account of reasonableness, we can construct a conception of normative reasoning appropriate to international relations*. Such an account, as I have argued, should combine Rawls' account of the normative significance of public reason with Kratochwil's conception of the nature and conditions of practical reasoning within the context of normative structure. To recall:

a. Both Rawls and Kractochwil conceive of the *resources* of practical reasoning in a remarkably similar way. For Rawls, the idea of the realistic utopia in *The Law of Peoples* depends, as we have seen, on the 'facts of social conduct as historical knowledge and reflection establish them'.[168]

b. In framing their arguments and proposals within the limits of public reason, agents are envisaged by Rawls to draw on the 'plain truths now widely accepted, or available, to [agents] generally'[169] – that is, publicly available ideas, methods of inquiry and means of reasoning, or those resources which are publicly available and uncontroversial. This is a requirement of reasoning which can properly be said to be public. Notice that it adheres with Roberts' stipulation in his analysis of the constraints of practicality that practical reason begin with where we are now.

c. Similarly, Kratochwil's account of the contextualising nature of topoi, or commonplaces (which characterise the starting-points, orientation and pathways followed by tracts of practical reasoning anchored around the intersubjective stabilisations of meanings which Kratochwil claims are embodied and expressed through the language of norms) are inherently bound up with the concept of an 'enthymeme', or 'rhetorical proof' which, Kratochwil claims, must start with 'things as they really are'.[170] The very concept of topoi, and the manner in which they influence the way intersubjectively established norms will affect the course of practical reasoning, links Kratochwil's account of the conditions of normative reasoning with shared ideas inherent in the background conditions of society. As Kratochwil states: commonplaces built in to rhetorical proof will express 'some shared interpretation of actions on the basis of certain practical experiences'.[171]

d. Public reason and Kratochwilian practical reason both cohere with Roberts' conception of reasonableness as being grounded in the 'constraints of practicality'. Moreover, the path-dependent and norm-oriented nature of practical reason in Kratochwil coheres with the limits of public reason in Rawls. Tracts of reasoning anchored around intersubjective meanings fixed via common understandings is, in its very essence, a *public* and *shared* expression of the development of normative structure in international relations. The crucial strength of Kratochwil's theory, however, is that it links public justificatory debate with an explanation of the development of sophisticated accounts of practical, legal and institutional reasoning, and a complex account of social epistemology, which I have argued is essential to a true understanding of the nature and conditions of philosophical reasoning in international relations.

e. In keeping with the requirements of objective and authoritative reason as identified by Roberts, a combined account of public/practical reasoning can be *reflective* and *self-critical.* Normative social structure is not a fixed concept – the stabilisation of meaning is fluid and can be considered and revised depending on how circumstances might change or how new puzzles may arise and may need to be solved (as we saw in Kratochwil's scrabble analogy). What Kratochwil provides us with is a means by which to link everyday and 'commonplace' ideas and principles, and those of a more specialised but nevertheless practical nature, with an account of the stabilisation of intersubjective meanings and the construction of normative structures through pathway-dependent practical reasoning.

This conception of normative reasoning, in my view, can function as a robust, legitimate grounding for a theory of political justification which has the potential to overcome the challenge of poststructuralism.

Conclusion: Poststructuralism and Beyond

I have argued in this book that poststructuralism, of the form developed by Ashley and Walker (among others), represents a viable and continuing challenge to the traditional foundations and methodologies of the discipline of International Relations. In Chapter 1 I attempted to set out the manner in which poststructuralism attempts to deconstruct the structures and practices (e.g. logocentrism and textual homogenisation) by which the discipline of IR has traditionally sought to establish and perpetuate a dominant theoretical approach (one synonymous with modernism), with accompanying methodological preconceptions, to its analysis of the nature of international relations. In successfully deconstructing the foundations upon which these processes of rationalisation[1] and textual homogenisation rest, the poststructuralists create the conditions required for a radical reanalysis of the fundamental nature of international relations and (just as significantly) allow us to reimagine the theoretical possibilities which flow from the opening of traditionally closed categories of knowledge about such. This, as I have argued, is an extremely worthwhile task and has, I believe, paved the way for the softening of previously static disciplinary boundaries which IR consciously sought to establish between itself, on the one hand, and parallel disciplines such as political theory and International Law on the other, leading to the beginnings of a move towards a more fluid disciplinary outlook and, ultimately, a more unified form of International Theory (as we saw in the Introduction, in the passages quoted from Wendt and Snidal's important article).

But how can we move past the poststructuralist *critique* of IR to a form of international theorising which genuinely *overcomes* the problems highlighted by Walker and Ashley in a legitimate and satisfying manner? This is the question I have attempted to answer in this book.

Poststructuralism by itself simply does not seem to allow for much by way of 'post-poststructuralist' *re*constructive theory. By beginning with genuinely legitimate predicates designed to take seriously the unique conditions of international relations, and in proceeding to construct a conception of practical reason which encompasses those elements of the various forms of constructivist international theory which I believe speak most clearly to the very heart of the nature of world politics, the conditions for a method of theorising about international relations which genuinely overcomes the challenge of poststructuralism will have been achieved. To that end, I have tried to show that traditional IR, by itself, does not possess the tools required for a genuinely *re*constructive theory, and is by itself too immersed in its own trenchant insistence on various theoretical and methodological exclusions to be truly able to overcome the challenge set down by the poststructuralists (I did this through my analysis of the constructivisms of Wendt and Kratochwil in Chapter 2). It is only by embracing the sophisticated conceptions of public reason (as we saw in Rawls), institutional reason (as we saw in Buchanan) and an account of the nature of practical reasoning with norms (as we saw in Kratochwil) that we will possess the tools needed for a holistic conception of normative reasoning, grounded in the minimal yet legitimate and robust conception of the reasonable worked out by Roberts (with influences from Scanlon and Rawls), with which we can overcome the challenge of poststructuralism. As I have stated before, but which bears repeating, I am very well aware that the poststructuralists themselves would dismiss this project in its entirety. However, given the vast potential for a sophisticated understanding of the nature of international relations (and its various normative elements) which flows from the concepts and structures I have attempted to construct in this book, and given my arguments that such concepts and structures represent an entirely legitimate, minimally grounded, robust approach to the problem of theorising about the international, I would (naturally) reject such a rejection. It is easy (although sometimes vastly liberating) to break down walls; it is far more difficult to rebuild them in a secure, inclusive, constructive and mutually acceptable manner.

Notes

Introduction: The 'Enormous Creative Potential of Practical Reason'

1. Friedrichs, J., and Kratochwil, F., 'On Acting and Knowing: How Pragmatism can Advance International Relations Research and Methodology', *International Organisation*, 63, 2009, pp. 701–731, p. 710
2. Snidal, D., and Wendt, A., 'Why There is International Theory Now', *International Theory*, 1(1), 2009, pp. 1–14
3. Ibid., p. 2
4. Ibid., p. 3
5. Ibid., p. 4
6. Ibid. The 'four decades ago' remark refers to a piece entitled 'Why There is no International Theory', written by Martin Wight in 1966, in which Wight laments the absence of a unified and authoritative International Theory.
7. Ibid.
8. Ibid., p. 5
9. Ibid.
10. Ibid., p. 6
11. Ibid.
12. Ibid.
13. I use the term 'responses' in a conceptual sense. Kratochwil's major expression of his critical constructivism (*Rules, Norms and Decisions*) was published in 1989, comfortably before much of the work in critical and poststructuralist theory in IR surfaced. It is instructive to note that Wendt's form of constructivism – whose major expression was published in 1999 – was taken far more seriously by the discipline of IR than Kratochwil's had been a decade earlier. IR simply did not possess the tools to cope with Kratochwil's radical position at that time. Wendt's challenge was couched in theoretical terms far more aligned with the familiar terrain of IR, and thus it was an easier and safer position for IR to seriously engage with.
14. These terms are fleshed out in detail in Chapter 2, but the essence of the distinction between conventional and critical constructivism is the fact that critical constructivism divorces itself far more radically from the ontological, epistemological and methodological commitments of the traditional discipline of IR.
15. 'On Acting and Knowing', p. 701.
16. Ibid.
17. Ibid., p. 704
18. Ibid., p. 705
19. I examine such a position herein – that of Allen Buchanan.
20. Ibid., p. 710. Friedrichs and Kratochwil advocate a pragmatic approach to the study of international relations rooted in the idea of 'abduction'. Essentially, they claim that '(social) science is, or should be, above all a more conscious

and systematic version of the way by which humans have learned to solve problems and generate knowledge in their everyday lives' (Ibid.) – in other words, that the understandings and knowledgeable processes involved in reasoning about action contain enormous potential to ground a pragmatic understanding of the nature of world politics. While I do not necessarily follow Friedrichs' and Kratochwil's precise methodology as advocated in 'On Acting and Knowing', I do believe that the combined constructivism I advocate *can* function as a pragmatic solution to the problems identified by poststructuralism and other critical forms of theory. *If* traditional structural analyses and rigid methodological boundaries have been shown to be illegitimate by the poststructuralists (as I claim they have), and *assuming* that we do not wish to employ metaphysical conceptions of independent moral or theological orders in order to ground a conception of international ethics, a constructivist alternative which legitimately grounds a robust understanding of international relations in the minimal and legitimate predicates of the conditions of practicality and the ideas of reasonableness and public reason *is*, in essence, a pragmatic solution to the poststructuralist challenge. I am very well aware that Walker and Ashley would likely dismiss my attempt to overcome their critique of International Relations theory as yet another attempt to privilege the status of the rational being in a 'theoretically unimaginative' manner. I would obviously disagree with any such dismissal. It is easy to deconstruct and problematise attempts to ground claims to an authoritative understanding of world politics; far harder to reconstruct meaningful and useful theoretical knowledge if one flat-out refuses to acknowledge the existence of *any* legitimate foundations (constructivist, foundationalist or otherwise) for such. Thus, I believe, the theories of Walker and Ashley have not particularly evolved beyond their initial incarnations and, ultimately, have nowhere else to go.
21. Which Kratochwil distinguishes from his conception of normativity – the latter being bound up with the effects on practical reasoning provided by the presence of norms.
22. Columbia, 1993.
23. Harvard, 1999 – including 'The Idea of Public Reason Revisited'.

1 Inside/Outside: Walker, Ashley and the Poststructuralist Critique of IR

1. Ashley, R.K., 'The Achievements of Post-Structuralism', in Smith, S., Booth, K., and Zalewski, M. (eds) *International Relations Theory: Positivism and Beyond*, 1996, Cambridge, p. 241
2. Cochran, M., *Normative Theory in International Relations*, Cambridge, 1999, p. 121
3. Brown, C., *Sovereignty, Rights and Justice: International Political Theory Today*, Polity Press, 2002
4. This 'monologue' includes the classical Realist heroes of Thucydides, Machiavelli and Hobbes.
5. Walker, R.B.J., *Inside/Outside: International Relations as Political Theory*, Cambridge, 1993, Chapter 2

6. Connolly, C., *Political Theory and Modernity*, Oxford, 1988
7. The title of Der Derian and Shapiro's book on the subject, *International/Intertextual Relations* (Lexington, 1989) gives a good indication of the perceived importance of a textual monologue to the theory of IR.
8. Particularly Wendt, A., *Social Theory of International Politics*, Cambridge, 1999
9. Phrases coined by Reus-Smit, C., 'Constructivism', in Burchill, S., and Linklater, A. (eds) *Theories of International Relations*, Palgrave, 2005
10. Walker, *Inside/Outside*, p. 5
11. Referenced in note 9 above.
12. Walker, R.B.J., *After the Globe, Before the World*, Routledge, 2010, p. 13
13. Ibid., pp. 43–44
14. Ashley, R.K., 'Living on Border Lines: Man, Poststructuralism, and War', in Der Derian, J. and Shapiro, M.J., (eds) *International/Intertextual Relations*, Lexington, 1989
15. Gregory, D.U., foreword to Der Derian and Shapiro (eds), *International/Intertextual Relations*, p. xvii
16. Ashley, 'Living on Border Lines', p. 261
17. Ibid.
18. Ashley, R.K. and Walker, R.B.J., 'Speaking the Language of Exile: Dissident Thought in International Studies', *International Studies Quarterly*, 34(3), September 1990, p. 261
19. Ashley, 'Living on Border Lines', p. 262
20. Der Derian, J., 'Boundaries of Knowledge and Power in IR', in Der Derian, J., and Shapiro, M.J. (eds) *International/Intertextual Relations*, Lexington, 1989, p. 6
21. Walker, *Inside/Outside*, p. 47
22. George, J., *Discourses of Global Politics: A Critical (Re)Introduction to International Relations*, Rienner, 1994, p. 192
23. George, *Discourses of Global Politics*, p. 193
24. Doyle, 'Thucydidean Realism' discussed in George, *Discourses of Global Politics*
25. Walker, *Inside/Outside*, p. 29
26. Ashley, 'Living on Border Lines'
27. Ibid., p. 286
28. Ibid., p. 287
29. Ibid., p. 288
30. Ibid., p. 289
31. Ibid., pp. 292–293
32. Ibid., p. 294
33. Ibid., p. 297
34. Ashley, 'The Achievements of Post-Structuralism', p. 244
35. Walker, *Inside/Outside*, p. 6
36. Ibid., p. 62
37. Ibid., p. 66
38. Walker, R.B.J., 'A Dirty Dozen: What is at Stake in Contemporary Claims about Sovereignty', October 2005, unpublished paper presented at SAID workshop, p. 1
39. Ibid., pp. 4–5
40. Walker, *Inside/Outside*, p. 73

41. Ibid., p. 86
42. Walker, 'A Dirty Dozen', p. 5
43. Syracuse, 1981
44. Princeton, 1983
45. Pogge, T.W., 'Liberalism and Global Justice: Hoffmann and Nardin on Morality in International Affairs', *Philosophy and Public Affairs*, 15(1), Winter 1986, pp. 67–81, p. 70
46. Ashley, R.K. and Walker, R.B.J., 'Reading Dissidence/Writing the Discipline: Crisis and the Question of Sovereignty in International Studies', *International Studies Quarterly*, 34(3), 1990, 367–416, pp. 382–383
47. Rorty, R., 'Human Rights, Rationality and Sentimentality', in Shute, S. and Hurley, S. (eds) *On Human Rights: The Oxford Amnesty Lectures 1993*, Basic Books, 1993: 'Philosophers like myself, who think of rationality as simply the attempt at such coherence, agree with Rabosi that foundationalist projects are outmoded' (p. 117)
48. Ashley and Walker, 'Reading Dissidence/Writing the Discipline', p. 390
49. Ibid., p. 388
50. Ibid., p. 389
51. Ibid., p. 390
52. Cochran, *Normative Theory in International Relations*, p. 134

2 Overcoming the Poststructuralist Critique? Ontology and Epistemology in the Constructivist Theories of Wendt and Kratochwil

1. Chronologically, while there has been much overlap between the key events in the development of poststructuralist and constructivist theories in IR, poststructuralism was generally established enough to allow constructivism to form as a theoretical *response* to it.
2. The terms 'conventional' and 'critical' constructivism were coined by Ted Hopf in 'The Promise of Constructivism in International Relations Theory', *International Security*, 23(1), Summer 1998, pp. 171–200. Christian Reus-Smit further subdivided constructivist theories into three distinct approaches; 'systemic', 'unit-level' and 'holistic' in 'Constructivism', in Burchill, S. and Linklater, A. (eds.), *Theories of International Relations*, Palgrave, 1996. Alexander Wendt can be read as embodying many of the characteristics of systemic constructivism, while Kratochwil's approach is more holistic.
3. Ibid., p. 47
4. Particularly Chapter 1 of *Social Theory of International Politics*.
5. Hopf, 'The Promise of Constructivism in International Relations Theory', p. 181
6. As Reus-Smit claims, '[t]hough theoretically elegant, this form of constructivism suffers from one major deficiency: it confines the processes that shape international societies within an unnecessarily and unproductively narrow realm'; 'Constructivism', p. 199
7. Particularly illuminating is Kratochwil's important essay 'Constructing a New Orthodoxy? Wendt's "Social Theory of International Politics" and the

Constructivist Challenge', *Millennium*, 29(1), 2000, pp. 73–101; and reproduced in Kratochwil's *The Puzzles of Politics: Inquiries into the Genesis and Transformation of International Relations*, Routledge, 2011. It should be noted that, following Kratochwil's and others' observations and critiques of his claims in *Social Theory of International Politics*, Wendt reformulated his conception of the relationship between the mind and scientific methodology to a certain extent (see his '*Social Theory* as Cartesian Science: An Auto-Critique from a Quantum Perspective' in Guzzini, S. and Leander, A. (eds) *Constructivism and International Relations: Alexander Wendt and his Critics*, Routledge, 2006). In this paper, Wendt advocates a 'non-foundational', 'quantum' approach to the problems of epistemology identified in his earlier work, and states thus (on p. 216):

> When applied to social science the 'non-foundational' aspect of quantum theory points in two directions. First, we need to take more seriously the complementarity of Explanation and Understanding. On the one hand, this means that the *Methodenstreit* between positivists and interpretivists is based on a false, classical premise. In quantum theory it would be absurd for the 'particle guys' to fight with the 'wave guys' about who has the truth, since the knowledge each offers is understood to be inherently partial, and so must be complemented with the other for a complete description. The 'Hobbesian' epistemological mentality one often sees in the social sciences today assumes that either Explanation or Understanding must constitute The One True Description, which from a quantum perspective is simply not the case. Instead, what we need is an 'epistemological Westphalia', in which positivists and interpretivists recognise the other's contribution to their shared goal of comprehending social life. More specifically, given that social science today is dominated by the positivist concern with the particle aspect of social life, what this means is taking the wave aspect – consciousness and meaning – seriously as well. In retrospect I do not feel I did that in *Social Theory*, where, despite my concern with the role of ideas in international life, I never mentioned consciousness and treated meaning as an object. To take consciousness and meaning seriously would require answering some hard methodological questions, given that consciousness is unavailable to objective, third-person inquiry. In particular, it would require coming to grips with the epistemological specificity of second- and perhaps even first-person knowledge as ways of apprehending the social – in short, with the distinct requirements of a 'science of the subjective'.

The revisions set out in '*Social Theory* as Cartesian Science' certainly constitute an interesting development in Wendt's constructivism and achieve a new level of abstraction in his metatheoretical considerations. However, I choose here to focus on Wendt's primary arguments in *Social Theory of International Relations* since, firstly, the position set out in '*Social Theory* as Cartesian science' does not present a radical departure from *Social Theory of International Politics* in the senses relevant for my purposes and, secondly, from the contextual perspective of my analysis of IR's responses to the challenge of poststructuralism, Wendt's position in *Social Theory of International Politics* represented the key expression of IR's attempt to deal with the metatheoretical issues which the poststructuralists had identified as needing to be addressed. Further, it allows a way in to an analysis of the holistic form of constructivism, and ultimately the sophisticated conception of practical reason, advocated by Kratochwil. Despite Wendt's (self-acknowledged) move towards a more 'postmodern anti-foundationalism' in his reformulation of the basis on which scientific methodology relates to ontology, he is still explicitly advocating a scientific (albeit quantum-based) methodological approach to the study of international relations and is still, therefore, operating from a perspective which perpetuates the traditional borderlines of the discipline (as Guzzini and Leander remark in the very same volume which contains '*Social Theory* as Cartesian Science':

> [H]e [i.e. Wendt] makes his argument for a theoretical heterodoxy by consciously staying within the *disciplinary* orthodoxy. For Wendt accepts the narrow confines for the discipline erected by Kenneth Waltz, as well as the narrow borders of the classical self-understanding of international society itself. In other words, to undermine more legitimately two key theoretical positions in IR, methodological and ontological individualism and materialism, he consciously stays within the identity-defining parameters of the discipline, including its reference to states as the main organising principle.
>
> (Guzzini, S., and Leander, A., 'Wendt's Constructivism: A Relentless Quest for Synthesis', in *Constructivism and International Relations: Alexander Wendt and his Critics*, pp. 73–74)

Therefore, although Wendt's latest work does go some way towards an attempt to divorce his methodological assumptions from the more traditional limits of the types of theory Wendt's constructivism is attempting to counteract, the fact that he is still concerned with 'explaining consciousness in scientific terms' ('*Social Theory* as Cartesian Science'; p. 189) means, I contend, that the analysis of the limitations of Wendt's constructivism set out below, particularly when contrasted with that of Kratochwil, remains valid. One final point is that I am aware that Wendt is working on a new book entitled *The Limits of International Relations*, due for publication in mid-2015, which may well progress his theory further.

8. Stephan, H. R., 'Review of *Constructivism in International Relations: The Politics of Reality*', Maja Zehfuss, 2002, Cambridge, In-SPIRE, July 2004, p. 2
9. McGraw-Hill, 1979
10. *Social Theory of International Politics*
11. A logic that remains immutable, given the permanency of the *systemic* nature of international relations. Waltz is therefore able to counter arguments concerning the end of the Cold War and the accompanying transformations of the nature of world politics (and thus an end to the relevance of neo-Realism) by asserting the argument that the end of the Cold War served as an internal, rather than a structural, transformation, and thus the key tenets of Realism which flow logically from structural claims

remain relevant to the post-Cold War era (particularly given the existence of nuclear weapons which determine a permanent logic of self-help). See Waltz, K., 'Structural Realism after the Cold War', *International Security*, 25(1), 2000, pp. 5–41

12. As Barry Buzan claims, '[n]eo-realists focus on structure at the system level, but even Waltz freely acknowledges that this mode of analysis has to be accompanied by a unit-level theory in order to get a complete explanation of events'; 'The Timeless Wisdom of Realism?', in Smith, Booth and Zalewski (eds.), *International Theory: Positivism and Beyond*, Cambridge, 1996, p. 51
13. I will, however, argue below that methodological differences serve to create competing characterisations of the ontological status of international relations, but the point is simply that it is fair to assume that *any* account of world politics which purports to be constructivist will embody the key claims identified here. For the development of my argument concerning the debate between Wendt and Kractochwil, it is necessary that I begin my analysis of constructivism with the conventional variety.
14. Hopf, 'The Promise of Constructivism in International Relations Theory'
15. Ibid., p. 172
16. Ibid.
17. Ibid., p. 174
18. Ibid., p. 175
19. Ibid., p. 177
20. Ibid., p. 178
21. Ibid., pp. 180–181
22. Ibid., p. 182
23. Reus-Smit, 'Constructivism', p. 196
24. *Social Theory of International Politics*, p. 10
25. Wendt, A., 'Constructing International Politics', *International Security*, 20(1), Summer 1995, pp. 71–81, p. 73
26. Ibid.
27. Kratochwil, F., 'Constructing a New Orthodoxy?', p. 77; contains a quote from *Social Theory of International Politics*, p. 94
28. Wendt, A., 'Anarchy is What States Make of it: The Social Construction of Power Politics', *International Organisation*, 46(2), Spring 1992, pp. 391–425, pp. 394–395. Emphasis in original.
29. Finnemore, M. and Sikkink, K., 'Taking Stock: The Constructivist Research Program in International Relations and Comparative Politics', *Annual Review of Political Science*, 2001, pp. 391–416, p. 393
30. Wendt, 'Anarchy is What States Make of it', p. 395
31. Kratochwil, 'Constructing a New Orthodoxy?', p. 76
32. *Social Theory of International Politics*, p. 96
33. Koslowski, R., and Kratochwil, F., 'Understanding Change in International Politics: the Soviet Empire's Demise and the International System', *International Organisation*, 48(2), Spring 1994, pp. 215–247, p. 215
34. Price, R., and Reus-Smit, C., 'Dangerous Liaisons? Critical International Theory and Constructivism', *European Journal of International Relations*, 4(3), 1998, pp. 259–294, p. 265

35. Wendt, 'Constructing International Politics', p. 74
36. Fischer, M., 'Feudal Europe, 800–1300: Communal Discourse and Conflictual Practices', *International Organisation*, 46(2), Spring 1992, p. 430
37. Hopf, 'The Promise of Constructivism in International Relations Theory', pp. 181–186
38. Ibid., p. 183
39. Price and Reus-Smit, 'Dangerous Liaisons?'
40. *Social Theory of International Politics*, p. 47
41. Osterud, O., 'Antimonies of Postmodernism in International Studies', *Journal of Peace Research*, 33(4), 1996, pp. 385–390
42. *Social Theory of International Politics*., pp. 49–50
43. The sources particularly relevant for an analysis of Wendt's epistemology are Chapter 2 of *Social Theory of International Politics* ('Scientific Realism and Social Kinds'); Wendt, A., 'On Constitution and Causation in International Relations', *Review of International Studies*, 24, 1998, pp. 101–118; and the Forum on *Social Theory of International Politics, Review of International Studies*, 26(1), January 2000, pp. 123–180.
44. *Social Theory of International Politics*, p. 51
45. Ibid.
46. Ibid., p. 56
47. Ibid., pp. 75–76
48. Ibid., p. 57
49. Ibid., p. 77
50. Wendt, A., 'On the Via Media: a Response to the Critics', *Review of International Studies*, 26(1), 2000, pp. 165–180; p. 173
51. Ibid., pp. 170–171
52. As characterised most succinctly in IR by Hollis, M., and Smith, S., *Explaining and Understanding International Relations*, Oxford, 1990
53. Wendt, 'On Constitution and Causation in International Relations', p. 101
54. Wendt, 'On the Via Media', p. 165
55. Wendt, 'On Constitution and Causation in International Relations', p. 103
56. Ibid., pp. 102–103
57. Ibid., p. 106
58. Smith, S., 'Wendt's World', *Review of International Studies*, 26(1), 2000, pp. 151–163, p. 153
59. Wendt, 'On Constitution and Causation in International Relations', p. 115
60. Ibid.
61. Smith, 'Wendt's World', p. 153
62. Ibid., p. 154
63. Ibid., p. 156
64. Ibid., p. 157
65. Kratochwil, 'Constructing a New Orthodoxy?', p. 75
66. Ibid.
67. Specifically the processes whereby the world becomes characterised as a set of unitary states with predetermined interests, due to the structural requirements of anarchy.
68. *Social Theory of International Politics*, pp. 58–59
69. Ibid., p. 59
70. Kratochwil, 'Constructing a New Orthodoxy?', p. 91

71. Ibid., p. 95
72. *Social Theory of International Politics*, p. 61
73. Ibid., p. 73
74. Ibid., p. 68
75. Dixon, J., and Dogan, R., 'The Conduct of Policy Analysis: Philosophical Points of Reference', *Review of Policy Research*, 21(4), 2004, pp. 559–579, p. 561
76. Ibid., p. 560
77. Guzzini, S., 'A Reconstruction of Constructivism in International Relations', *European Journal of International Relations*, 6(2), 2000, pp. 147–182
78. Ibid., p. 159
79. Ibid., pp. 59–60
80. Giddens, A., *The Constitution of Society: Outline of a Theory of Structuration*, Berkeley, 1984, pp. 249–250
81. Guzzini, 'A Reconstruction of Constructivism', p. 162
82. Kratochwil, F., *Rules, Norms, and Decisions: On the Conditions of Practical and Legal Reasoning in International Relations and Domestic Affairs*, Cambridge, 1989, p. 7
83. Kratochwil, F., and Ruggie, J., 'International Organisation: A State of the Art or an Art of the State', *International Organisation*, 40(4), 1986, pp. 753–775, p. 764
84. Ibid., p. 765
85. Ibid., p. 768
86. Kratochwil, 'Constructing a New Orthodoxy?', p. 88
87. Kratochwil and Ruggie, 'International Organisation', p. 770
88. Kratochwil, 'Constructing a New Orthodoxy?', p. 90
89. Frost, M., *Ethics in International Relations: A Constitutive Theory*, Cambridge, 1996
90. Kratochwil, *Rules, Norms, and Decisions*, pp. 31–32
91. Kurki, M., 'Causes of a Divided Discipline: A Critical Examination of the Concept of Cause in International Relations Theory', available online at www.globalpolitics.net, p. 5
92.

    > Sense I. Here that which is 'caused' is the free and deliberate act of a conscious and responsible agent, and 'causing' him to do it means affording him a motive for doing it. Sense II. Here that which is 'caused' is an event in nature, and its 'cause' is an event or state of things by producing or preventing which we can produce or prevent that whose cause it is said to be. Sense III. Here that which is 'caused' is an event or state of things, and its 'cause' is another event or state of things standing to it in a one-one relation of causal priority.

    Collingwood, R.G., *An Essay on Metaphysics*, Oxford, 1998/1940, p. 285
93. Ibid., p. 296
94. Kratochwil, 'Reflections on Theory and Practice', available online at http://hdl.handle. net/1814/1876, p. 1
95. Kratochwil, *Rules, Norms, and Decisions*, p. 25
96. Ibid., p. 24. Emphasis in original.
97. Skinner, Q., 'Hermeneutics and the Role of History', *New Literary History*, 7(1), 1975, pp. 209–232, p. 209

98. Chicago, 1970
99. Skinner, Q., 'Conventions and the Understanding of Speech Acts', *The Philosophical Quarterly*, 20(79), 1970, pp. 118–138
100. Oxford, 1975
101. Strawson, P.F., 'Intention and Convention in Speech Acts', *The Philosophical Review*, 1964, pp. 439–460
102. Kratochwil, *Rules, Norms, and Decisions*, p. 25
103. Kratochwil, 'Reflections on Theory and Practice', p. 2
104. Ibid.
105. Ibid., p. 3
106. Ibid., p. 8
107. Kratochwil, 'Constructing a New Orthodoxy?', pp. 100–101
108. Ibid., p. 101
109. Ibid.
110. Kratochwil, 'Reflections on Theory and Practice', p. 3

3 Constitutive Political Theory: Mervyn Frost and the Role of Norms in International Political Theory

1. His holistic theory presents an account of the role of agency in the determination of norms constitutive of social practices, and the effect of these norms on the justification and limitations of action.
2. The position I focus on most significantly in this book is that of John Rawls.
3. Particularly, the theory developed in Frost, *Ethics in International Relations*.
4. Ibid., p. 142
5. Kratochwil, however, relies on an embedded conception of the normative conditions of practical reasoning which I will claim is crucial in understanding the constructed nature of international relations and which thus should be taken seriously by the constructivist positions I explore herein.
6. This method was first developed by Rawls in his early work and has been utilised by Ronald Dworkin in the field of jurisprudence (and in the manner in which Frost employs it), *Taking Rights Seriously*, Duckworth, 1981.
7. Frost, *Ethics in International Relations*, p. 101.
8. Frost, M., *Constituting Human Rights: Global Civil Society and the Society of Democratic States*, Routledge, 2002, p. 47
9. Frost, *Ethics in International Relations*, p. 77–78
10. Ibid., p. 78
11. Ibid., p. 60
12. Ibid., p. 47
13. Frost, *Constituting Human Rights*, p. 3
14. Frost, *Ethics in International Relations*, p. 79
15. Frost, *Constituting Human Rights*, p. 7
16. Ibid., p. 21.
17. Frost, *Ethics in International Relations*, p. 105
18. Ibid., pp. 111–112
19. Ibid., p. 112

20. Frost, *Constituting Human Rights*, p. 48
21. Frost, *Ethics in International Relations*, Chapter 5
22. Ibid., p. 97
23. Frost, *Constituting Human Rights*, p. 48
24. Frost, *Ethics in International Relations*, pp. 138–139
25. Frost, *Constituting Human Rights*, p. 5
26. Frost, *Ethics in International Relations*, pp. 143–155
27. Ibid., p. 151
28. Frost, *Constituting Human Rights*, p. 66
29. Frost, *Ethics in International Relations*, p. 143
30. Ibid., p. 97
31. Ibid.
32. Cochran, *Normative Theory in International Relations*, pp. 107–108
33. Hegel, *The Philosophy of History*, Prometheus, 1991, p. 9
34. Sutch, P., 'Human Rights as Settled Norms', *Review of International Studies*, 26(2), 2000, p. 228
35. Frost, M., 'Mervyn Frost Replies to Peter Sutch's "Human Rights and Settled Norms" ', *Review of International Studies*, 26(3), 2000, p. 479
36. Frost, *Ethics in International Relations*, p. 90
37. Cochran, *Normative Theory in International Relations*, p. 109
38. Ibid., p. 110
39. Frost, *Constituting Human Rights*, p. 47
40. Ibid., p. 48
41. Ibid., p. 49
42. Frost, *Ethics in International Relations*, pp. 99–100
43. Sutch, P., 'Global Civil Society and International Ethics: Mervyn Frost's Restatement of Constitutive Theory', 26(3), 2000, pp. 488–489
44. Brown, C., *International Relations Theory: New Normative Approaches*, Columbia, 1992, p. 64
45. Daniels, N., 'Wide Reflective Equilibrium and Theory Acceptance in Ethics', *The Journal of Philosophy*, 76(5), 1979, p. 258

4 Beyond Coherence: Rawls' Conception of Public Reason

1. Walker, R.B.J., 'Democratic Theory and the Present/Absent International', *Ethics & Global Politics*, 3(1), 2010, p. 4.
2. Rawls, *Political Liberalism*, p. xxvii
3. Ibid., p. 47
4. Ibid., p. Xliii of 'Introduction to the Paperback Edition'; and p. 12
5. Note that Rawls claims in his later work that justice as fairness is but one formulation of a political conception of justice, not necessarily the correct one. According to Rawls' own commitments, there are a variety of different expressions of a freestanding political conception of justice which could *all* be the basis of an overlapping consensus among reasonable comprehensive doctrines. Nevertheless, it remains the conception of justice which Rawls himself affirms.
6. Ibid., p. xxx
7. Ibid., p. 10

8. Ibid.
9. Ibid., p. 51
10. The rational is, in my contention and at least insofar as Rawls conceptualises it, the simpler and more intuitive of the two concepts.
11. Ibid., p. 50
12. Ibid., p. 51
13. Ibid.
14. Ibid.
15. Ibid., p. 52
16. Ibid., pp. 53–54
17. Ibid., p. 54
18. Ibid.
19. Ibid.
20. Ibid., pp. 55–56
21. Ibid., pp. 56–57
22. Ibid., p. 58
23. ibid., p. 59
24. Ibid.
25. Ibid.
26. Ibid., pp. 60–61
27. Unless, as will be seen below, we can do so in ways which 'uphold the ideal of public reason'.
28. Ibid., pp. 66–67
29. Ibid., p. xix
30. Ibid., p. 224
31. Ibid., pp. 224–225
32. Ibid., p. 225
33. Ibid.
34. Ibid., pp. 226–227
35. Ibid., p. 227
36. Ibid., p. 247
37. Ibid., p. 248
38. Ibid., p. 10
39. 'The Idea of Public Reason Revisited', in Rawls, *The Law of Peoples*, p. 140
40. Rawls states at pp. 49–50 of *Political Liberalism*: 'The reasonable is an element of the idea of society as a fair system of cooperation and that its fair terms be reasonable for all to accept is part of its idea of reciprocity.... the idea of reciprocity lies between the idea of impartiality, which is altruistic (as moved by the general good), and the idea of mutual advantage understood as everyone's being advantaged with respect to one's present or expected situation as things are'.
41. O'Neill, O., *The Philosophical Review*, 106(3), July 1997, pp. 411–428
42. Ibid., p. 415
43. Ibid. Emphasis in original.
44. Ibid.
45. More specifically, O'Neill charges Rawls with shifting between *modal* and *motivational* conceptions of reasonableness.
46. Ibid., p. 418
47. Ibid., p. 422

48. Ibid., pp. 422–423
49. Ibid., p. 419
50. That is, if it can be shown that Rawls' conception of public reason can be contextually appropriate in grounding a theory of international political constructivism, Effect 1 above will have been disproved.
51. Rawls, *Political Liberalism*, p. 49. In other words, the capacity for a sense of justice.
52. Rawls, *The Law of Peoples*, pp. 54–55
53. Ibid., pp. 55–57
54. A full discussion of the category 'decent' is included below.
55. Rawls, *The Law of Peoples*, p. 88
56. Ibid., p. 14
57. Ibid., p. 87

5 Contemporary Moral Foundationalism: Buchanan's Conception of Normative Reasoning and the Role of Institutions in Political Justification

1. Buchanan, 'The Egalitarianism of Human Rights', p. 682
2. Buchanan, A., *Human Rights, Legitimacy, and the Use of Force*, OUP, 2010, p. 54
3. Chiefly *Human Rights, Legitimacy and the Use of Force*.
4. The first essay in Buchanan's 2010 work, entitled 'Justice, Legitimacy and Human Rights', is a reproduction of an essay by Buchanan originally published in 2000. In this chapter, Buchanan makes explicit reference to Rawls' paper 'The Law of Peoples'. It is clear, from Buchanan's assertions regarding the content of the Law of Peoples, that this chapter focuses on the earlier version of 'The Law of Peoples', published in 1993 in *On Human Rights: The Oxford Amnesty Lectures*, Shute, S., and Hurley, S. (eds)., Basic Books, 1993 (aside from the acknowledgement at FN 1 of 'Justice, Legitimacy and Human Rights' acknowledging that 'Rawls expanded his views in a work entitled *The Law of Peoples* published by Harvard University Press in 1999'). Note Buchanan's claim that according to one possible interpretation of the structure of the Law of Peoples, 'there is a radical discontinuity between *Political Liberalism* and "The Law of Peoples" '. Thus, Buchanan's chapter appears to ignore Rawls' claims in the later version of *The Law of Peoples*; chiefly the key assertion that determination of the Law of Peoples is developed from *within*, and as an extension of, political liberalism (see p. 55 of *The Law of Peoples*). Notwithstanding, and possibly because of, this apparent lack of scholastic rigour (Buchanan's 2010 collection explicitly states the 'thematic interconnections' between the essays contained therein, and thus, presumably, their continuing theoretical relevance), the chapter nevertheless contains important insights, both into Rawls' conception of the reasonable in international relations, as well as Buchanan's own ideas concerning the ability of reasonableness to do the justificatory work, as well as its formulation, at the international level.
5. Teson, F.R., *A Philosophy of International Law*, Boulder, 1998
6. Moellendorf, D., 'Constructing the Law of Peoples', *Pacific Philosophical Quarterly*, 77(2), 1996, pp. 135–144

7. Tan, K.C., 'Liberal Toleration in Rawls's Law of Peoples', *Ethics*, 108, January 1998, pp. 283–285
8. Buchanan, *Human Rights, Legitimacy, and the Use of Force*, p. 14
9. Ibid.
10. Ibid., p. 15. Quoting *Political Liberalism*, p. 49, and pp. 49–50.
11. Buchanan, *Human Rights, Legitimacy, and the Use of Force*, p. 16. I am ever aware that Rawls got round this problem in *The Law of Peoples* by claiming that his international thought developed out of, and as an extension of, political liberalism; but it is worth considering Buchanan's arguments here as they give a key insight into his own ideas about the proper basis for a theory of international justice.
12. Ibid., p. 17
13. Ibid., p. 18
14. Ibid., pp. 18–19
15. Ibid., p. 19
16. Ibid., p. 20
17. Ibid., p. 21
18. Ibid.
19. Ibid.
20. Ibid., pp. 21–22
21. Ibid., p. 22
22. Ibid., pp. 22–23. Emphasis in original.
23. Ibid., p. 25
24. Ibid.
25. Ibid., p. 28
26. Ibid., p. 26
27. Ibid., pp. 26–27
28. Ibid., p. 27
29. Ibid., p. 28
30. 'Equality and Human Rights', citation at p. 68
31. 'The Legitimacy of the International Order', citation at p. 72
32. Ibid., pp. 85–86
33. Ibid., p. 86
34. Ibid., p. 53
35. Buchanan, *Justice, Legitimacy, and Self-Determination: Moral Foundations for International Law*, Oxford, 2007, p. 86
36. Ibid.
37. Ibid., p. 87
38. Buchanan, *Human Rights, Legitimacy, and the Use of Force*, pp. 87– 88
39. Ibid., p. 89
40. Ibid., p. 90
41. Ibid.
42. Ibid., p. 91
43. Ibid.
44. Buchanan claims: 'Certain rights are properly called human rights because the duties they entail provide especially important protections for basic human interests, given the standard threats to those interests in our world.' Ibid., p. 116
45. Ibid., p. 93

46. Ibid., p. 95
47. Ibid., p. 96
48. Ibid.
49. Ibid., p. 79
50. Ibid., p. 114
51. Ibid., p. 116
52. Buchanan, *Justice, Legitimacy, and Self Determination*, p. 88

6 Philosophical Constructivism and Critical Constructivism Combined: Kratochwil's Account of the Conditions of Practical Reasoning and the Rawlsian Conception of Public Reason

1. Rawls, *The Law of Peoples*, p. 19
2. Ibid., p. 57
3. Kratochwil, *Rules, Norms and Decisions*, p. 11
4. Ibid., pp. 11–12
5. Ibid., pp. 21–28
6. Ibid., p. 21
7. Ibid., p. 23
8. Ibid.
9. Ibid., p. 24
10. Ibid.
11. Ibid.
12. Ibid.
13. Ibid.
14. Ibid., p. 25
15. Ibid.
16. Ibid.
17. Ibid., p. 26
18. Ibid., p. 27
19. Ibid.
20. Ibid., p. 29
21. Ibid., p. 30
22. Ibid., p. 31
23. Ibid., pp. 31–32. Emphasis in original. This passage was cited in Chapter 2. However, for ease of reference, I recount in here.
24. The fact that Kratochwil's account of normative reasoning is framed as a solution to the 'problem of adducing consent' is thus an effective route by which to link the normative theories of Kratochwil and Rawls.
25. Kratochwil, *Rules, Norms and Decisions*, p. 33. Emphasis in original.
26. Ibid.
27. Hence the applicability of public reason to international relations. The key claim, as has been cited above but reproduced here: 'The idea of public reason for the Society of Peoples is analogous to the idea of public reason in the domestic case when a shared basis of justification exists and can be uncovered by due reflection.'

28. Kratochwil's conception of moral reasoning (as we will see below) is not formulated in a way which necessarily answers the key question 'Why should agents in international relations be concerned with reasonableness and public reason?' As an example, Kratochwil states the following on p. 91 of *The Puzzles of Politics*:

    > International law is a secular construct and thus is distinguishable from morality, religion or mythical elaborations that endow the interaction of states with some ultimate meaning. This meaning is defined in either a philosophy of history or in a mechanical interpretation such as the balance of power. After all, it was no accident that the legal conceptualisation of international relations attained importance when the 'right way of life' as an organising principle of political life had to be abandoned.

29. Kratochwil, *Rules, Norms and Decisions*, p. 215
30. Although legal reasoning constitutes a distinct branch of practical reasoning, for the reasons discussed below.
31. Kratochwil, *Rules, Norms and Decisions*, p. 34
32. Ibid., p. 35
33. Ibid.
34. Ibid.
35. Ibid.
36. Ibid., p. 36
37. Ibid.
38. Ibid., pp. 37–38
39. Ibid., p. 38. Emphasis in original.
40. Ibid., Emphasis in original.
41. Ibid., p. 41
42. Ibid., p. 39
43. Ibid., pp. 42–43
44. Ibid., p. 207.
45. Kratochwil, *The Puzzles of Politics*, p. 127
46. Kratochwil, *Rules, Norms and Decisions*, p. 217.
47. Ibid., p. 218. Emphasis in original.
48. Ibid.
49. Ibid., p. 219
50. Ibid., pp. 219–220
51. Ibid., p. 226
52. Ibid., p. 223
53. Ibid., pp. 226–227
54. Ibid., p. 227
55. As we have seen, a distinction can be drawn between legal and non-legal institutional reasoning by the specific topoi which inform the context in question, and by the effect on reasoning provided by the norms in question, themselves contextualised through the presence of a variety of 'commonplace' meanings.
56. This is not to argue that, in every respect, legal reasoning is coterminous with practical reasoning. It is not even to argue that the only distinction between legal and practical reasoning is the incorporation of specifically

legal topoi in the case of the former. It is simply to argue that the function and role of topoi in both legal and practical reasoning are comparable, and therefore that the analysis of the importance of topoi to *legal* reasoning undertaken in detail by Kratochwil can be considered relevant to a consideration of practical reasoning more generally.

57. Kratochwil, *The Puzzles of Politics*, p. 90
58. Kratochwil, *Rules, Norms and Decisions*, p. 227
59. Ibid., p. 229. Emphasis in original. Kratochwil also states (at p. 237): '[T]he "characterisation" of an act is decided and supported on the basis of common-sense judgments which marshal wide assent to such evaluations'.
60. Ibid. Emphasis in original.
61. Ibid., p. 228. Emphases in original.
62. Ibid., p. 229. Emphasis in original.
63. Ibid., p. 236
64. Ibid., p. 238
65. Kratochwil, *The Puzzles of Politics*, pp. 131–132
66. Rawls, *The Law of Peoples*, p. 57
67. The norms selected by Rawls are as follows (found at p. 37 of *The Law of Peoples*):

    1. Peoples are free and independent, and their freedom and independence are to be respected by other peoples.
    2. Peoples are to observe treaties and undertakings.
    3. Peoples are equal and are parties to the agreements that bind them.
    4. Peoples are to observe a duty of non-intervention.
    5. Peoples have the right of self-defence, but no right to instigate war for reasons other than self-defence.
    6. Peoples are to honour human rights.
    7. Peoples are to observe certain specified restrictions in the conduct of war.
    8. Peoples have a duty to assist other peoples living under unfavourable conditions that prevent their having a just or decent political and social regime.

68. Kratochwil, *Rules, Norms and Decisions*, p. 138
69. Ibid., p. 139
70. Ibid.
71. Ibid.
72. Ibid., p. 142
73. The distinction between the utterance's *il*locutionary force, as opposed to its *per*locutionary effect, is important. Bruce-Hall claims of Kractochwil's considerations of the institution of promising:

    > The duty-imposing character of promises results from the performance of the promise as a speech act, not from the expectation of the hearer that the promise will be kept. Kratochwil draws upon Hume's assertions that in promising 'the hearer's expectation ... must be based on the belief that, *Ceteris Paribus*, the act will be performed even if the hearer does change his mind (i.e. his inclinations, etc.). It is because this

> expectation is so strong, that people rightly come to rely on promises in a way they don't on statements of intent'.

In Bruce-Hall, R., ' "Trust Me, I Promise": Kratochwil's Contributions toward the Explanation of the Structure of Normative Social Relations', in *On Rules, Politics & Knowledge*, Palgrave Macmillan, 2010, pp. 62–63. Bruce-Hall cites the quote of Hume in Kratochwil, *Rules, Norms & Decisions*, p. 147.

74. Kratochwil, *Rules, Norms and Decisions*, p. 147
75. Ibid., pp. 148–149
76. Rawls, 'The Idea of Public Reason Revisited', p. 155
77. Rawls, *The Law of Peoples*, p. 23
78. Ibid., p. 24
79. Ibid., p. 25
80. Rawls defines the 'Society of Peoples' on p. 3 of *The Law of Peoples* as 'all those peoples who follow the ideals and principles of the Law of Peoples in their mutual relations'. This is effectively the same as conceptualising the 'Society of Peoples' as 'all those peoples who are willing to engage with other reasonable peoples through the use of public reason, predicated on publicly available terms'. This is because, in agreeing to engage with other reasonable peoples on publicly reasonable terms, a people will accept and follow the 'ideals and principles of the Law of Peoples'.
81. Given their shared histories of *reasonable* engagement with one another.
82. This is due to the fact that Kratochwil does not have necessary recourse to a foundational idea of moral egalitarianism which, as was noted above, relies on a thick liberal conception of morality in order to remain vindicated. Thus, while Buchanan's conception of a standard of legitimacy, while sophisticated and interesting insofar as it is based on a conception of public reason and the requirement that agents have recourse to publicly available predicates as the focus of argument on political matters, the fact that it is *not* intimately bound up with the constructive processes by which normative social structures – and thereby the path of practical reasoning – are imbued with meaning mean, in my contention, that Kratochwil's theory is more *appropriate* in the context of a true understanding of international relations – with all the corresponding epistemological implications considered above.
83. Rawls, *Political Liberalism*, pp. 66–67
84. To recall, Rawls states:

> [L]iberal political values are of two kinds: (a) The first kind – the values of political justice – fall under the principles of justice for the basic structure: the values of equal political and civil liberty; equality of opportunity; the values of social equality and economic reciprocity; and let us add also values of the common good as well as the various necessary conditions for all these values; (b) The second kind of political values – the values of public reason – fall under the guidelines for public inquiry, which make that inquiry free and public. Also included here are such political virtues as reasonableness and a readiness to honour the (moral) duty of civility, which as virtues of citizens help to make possible reasoned public discussion of political questions.
>
> (*Political Liberalism*, p. 224)

85. Ibid., pp. 224–225
86. Davis, J.W., 'From Logic to Logics: The Relationship of Particular Cases to General Patterns in Social Life', *On Rules, Politics & Knowledge*, p. 45
87. Rawls, *Political Liberalism*, p. 224
88. Rawls, *The Law of Peoples*, p. 155
89. Rawls, *Political Liberalism*, p. 224
90. Rawls fleshes out the liberal principle of legitimacy at p. 217 of *Political Liberalism*:

    > [O]ur exercise of political power is proper and hence justifiable only when it is exercised in accordance with a constitution the essentials of which all citizens may reasonably be expected to endorse in the light of principles and ideals acceptable to them as reasonable and rational. This is the liberal principle of legitimacy. And since the exercise of political power itself must be legitimate, the ideal of citizenship imposes a moral, not a legal duty – the duty of civility – to be able to explain to one another on those fundamental questions how the principles and policies they advocate and vote for can be supported by the political values of public reason. This duty also involves a willingness to listen to others and a fairmindedness in deciding when accommodations to their views should reasonably be made.

91. Kratochwil, *Rules, Norms and Decisions*, p. 31
92. Rawls, *Political Liberalism*, pp. 212–213
93. Ibid., pp. 53–54
94. To recall, the idea of a political conception of justice is 'a moral conception worked out for a specific kind of subject, namely, for political, social, and economic institutions'. *Political Liberalism*, p. 11
95. Defined in *Political Liberalism* as 'a society's main political, social, and economic institutions, and how they fit together into one unified system of social cooperation from one generation to the next' (p. 11).
96. Rawls, *The Law of Peoples*, p. 62
97. Such requirements stated thus:

    > 1. First, the society does not have aggressive aims, and it recognises that it must gain its legitimate ends through diplomacy and trade and other ways of peace. Although its religious or other underlying doctrine is assumed to be comprehensive and to have influence on the structure of government and its social policy, the society respects the political and social order of other societies. If it does seek wider influence, it does so in ways compatible with the independence of other societies, including their religious and civil liberties. This feature of the society's comprehensive doctrine supports the institutional basis of its peaceful conduct and distinguishes it from the leading European states during the religious wars of the sixteenth and seventeenth centuries. 2. The second criterion has three parts. (a) The first part is that a decent hierarchical people's system of law, in accordance with its common good idea of justice, secures for all members of the people what have come to be called human rights. A social system that violates these rights cannot specify a decent scheme

of political and social cooperation. A slave society lacks a decent system of law, as its slave economy is driven by a scheme of commands imposed by force. It lacks the idea of social cooperation.... Among the human rights are the right to life (to the means of subsistence and security); to liberty (to freedom from slavery, serfdom, and forced occupation, and to a sufficient measure of liberty of conscience to ensure freedom of religion and thought); to property (personal property); and to formal equality as expressed by the rules of natural justice (that is, that similar cases be treated similarly). Human rights, as thus understood, cannot be rejected as peculiarly liberal or special to the Western tradition. They are not politically parochial.... (b) The second part is that a decent people's system of law must be such as to impose *bona fide* moral duties and obligations (distinct from human rights) on all persons within the people's territory. Since the members of the people are viewed as decent and rational, as well as responsible and able to play a part in social life, they recognise these duties and obligations as fitting with their common good idea of justice and do not see their duties and obligations as mere commands imposed by force. They have the capacity for moral learning and know the difference between right and wrong as understood in their society. In contrast to a slave economy, their system, of law specifies a decent scheme of political and social cooperation. A decent hierarchical society's conception of the person, as implied by the second criterion, does not require acceptance of the liberal idea that persons are citizens first and have equal basic rights as equal citizens. Rather it views persons as responsible and cooperating members of their respective groups. Hence, persons can recognise, understand, and act in accordance with their moral duties and obligations as members of these groups. (c) Finally, the third part of the second criterion is that there must be a sincere and not unreasonable belief on the part of judges and other officials who administer the legal system that the law is indeed guided by a common good idea of justice. Laws supported merely by force are grounds for rebellion and resistance. It would be unreasonable, if not irrational, for judges and other officials to think that the common good idea of justice, which assigns human rights to all members of a people, is being followed when those rights are systematically violated. This sincere and reasonable belief on the part of judges and officials must be shown in their good faith and willingness to defend publicly society's injunctions as justified by law. The courts serve as a forum for this defence.

(*The Law of Peoples*, pp. 65–67)

98. Ibid., p. 67
99. Ibid., pp. 67–68
100. Rawls, *The Law of Peoples*, p. 16
101. I would argue that the recourse to specialised discourses which themselves rely on specialised topoi is consistent with the requirements of public reason insofar as topoi represent generally accepted commonplaces, or 'common-sense understandings', of the specialist discourse in question.

7 The Concept of the Reasonable in International Political Justification: A Rejoinder to the Poststructuralist Critique

1. As well as the accompanying requirement for a sophisticated social epistemology, itself bound up with the need for a conception of institutional reasoning and an institutional component in any account of political justification, as identified by Buchanan.
2. Rawls, *The Law of Peoples*, pp. 121–122
3. And, by virtue of the passages entitled 'Non-ideal theory', with unreasonable or 'burdened' peoples, although these societies do not qualify as members in good standing of the Society of Peoples.
4. Rawls, *Political Liberalism*, pp. 49–50
5. Ibid., pp. 53–54
6. Ibid., p. 54
7. McKinnon, C., *Liberalism and the Defence of Political Constructivism*, Palgrave Macmillan, 2002, pp. 35–36. It is instructive to note that, in McKinnon's contention, it is not only the elements of Point 2 which speaks to the idea of the reasonable in the conception of the person employed by Rawls. Point 7 (a reasonable moral psychology) and Points 8 and 9 (social cooperation guided by publicly recognised rules, and the terms of such can be reasonably accepted by persons) also speak to the idea of the reasonable employed within Rawlsian constructivism. Points 8 and 9 essentially form the bedrock of the idea of public reason in political justification and do not, strictly speaking, constitute elements of Rawls' conception of the person.
8. Ibid., p. 36. McKinnon states: 'When Rawls claims that his conception of the person is an idea of practical reason he means that this conception provides the context in which practical reason is used to address the task of finding fair terms of social co-operation'.
9. Element (b), the acceptance of the consequences of the burdens of judgement, is fundamental to McKinnon's analysis of Rawls and she considers it in greater detail than the other elements of the concept of the reasonable. I consider such below.
10. The capacity for a conception of the good is not a constituent of the reasonable. The reasonable essentially characterises the way reasonable persons conceive of and approach their political relationship with others. The capacity for a conception of the good is internal to a person (although element (c) of the concept of the reasonable regulates the way a person connects with their own conception of the good in a reasonable manner) and relates to that person's ability to be moved by considerations of value. McKinnon states at p. 36:

    > *Persons possess the capacity for a conception of the good*: This is 'the capacity to form, to revise, and rationally to pursue a conception of [their] rational advantage or good'. Persons' conception of their own advantage will be informed by their conception of the good, which specifies what they take to be valuable in human life.

11. Ibid., pp. 36–37
12. The argument appears to be that so long as persons have a *capacity* for a sense of justice, they will be sufficiently motivated to *act* from such. It is

interesting that Rawls conceives of the reasonable as including the *capacity* for a sense of justice rather than simply *a* sense of justice, and is presumably indicative of an attempt by Rawls to conceive of the requirements of reasonableness in a manner which is less, rather than more, demanding on its subjects. The issue of whether the reasonable fosters enough motivational force in order to compel reasonable persons to engage with one another within the limits of public reason, and upon publicly acceptable terms – as well as the issue of the 'demandingness' of a conception of the reasonable – is important. I consider it below.

13. Rawls, *The Law of Peoples*, p. 23. Insofar as decent non-liberal peoples are reasonable, and given the character of a decent society as fleshed out by Rawls and considered above, it is safe, I believe, to state that a decent non-liberal people essentially embodies variations on these three characteristics. Therefore, rather than a 'reasonably just constitutional democratic government', they may form a decent consultation hierarchy or some analogous form of society. The presence of 'common sympathies', and a moral nature, is not, I believe, necessarily confined to liberal peoples. There is no reason I can see why a decent non-liberal society could not exemplify both and, as we have seen, decent peoples are certainly conceived of as possessing a moral nature by Rawls.
14. Ibid., p. 25
15. McKinnon favours the latter formulation. She claims that a conception of political justification formulated in terms of principles which agents *could not reject* (rather than those which agents 'are likely to accept') provides for a justification with 'critical power'. See p. 46 of *Liberalism and the Defence of Political Constructivism.*
16. To recall the principle of toleration, Rawls states at p. 16, FN 8 of *The Law of Peoples*: 'The main points of this conception of toleration can be set out in summary fashion as follows: (1) Reasonable persons do not all affirm the same comprehensive doctrine. This is said to be a consequence of the 'burdens of judgment'. (2) Many reasonable doctrines are affirmed, not all of which can be true or right as judged from within any one comprehensive doctrine. (3) It is not unreasonable to affirm any one of the reasonable comprehensive doctrines. (4) Others who affirm reasonable doctrines different from ours are reasonable also. (5) In affirming our belief in a doctrine we recognise as reasonable, we are not being unreasonable. (6) Reasonable persons think it unreasonable to use political power, should they possess it, to repress other doctrines that are reasonable yet different from their own'.
17. McKinnon, *Liberalism and the Defence of Political Constructivism*, pp. 39–40
18. Ibid., p. 40
19. Rawls, *Political Liberalism*, p. 56
20. McKinnon, *Liberalism and the Defence of Political Constructivism*, p. 41
21. Ibid., pp. 41–42
22. Ibid., p. 43. This flows from Rawls' statement in 'The Idea of Public Reason Revisited' that 'public justification is not simply valid reasoning, but argument *addressed to others*'.
23. The key and interconnected concepts of demandingness and motivational adequacy are discussed at length by McKinnon in *Liberalism and the Defence*

of Political Constructivism. Regarding motivational adequacy, she states at pp. 20–21 as follows:

> [F]ormal questions of motivational adequacy *per se* relate to whether a justificatory reason *could be* motivating for a person, and here there is a split between externalists [i.e. those who argue that practical reasons can be motivating *even despite* the fact that an agent does not have a present motivational commitment to act according to the reason in question, and would not acquire such even by deliberating from his/her present motivational commitments], and sub-Humean and deliberative internalists [i.e. those who argue that a practical reason is only motivationally adequate for an agent if that agent already has a motivational commitment to act according to it (the 'sub-Humean' version of internalism), or else could acquire one by deliberating soundly from his/her present motivational commitments (the 'deliberative' form of internalism)] on the other. But questions of demandingness relate to what it would take for a reason for which people *could* act to become a reason for which they *do* act: the split here is between sub-Humean internalists on the one side, and externalists and deliberative internalists on the other. Given a sub-Humean internalist account of motivational adequacy, justificatory reasons are not demanding because persons must already have a motivational commitment to act for the reasons for them to be considered adequate in the first place. Deliberative internalist accounts make justificatory reasons more demanding than this because reasons must be accepted in virtue of sound deliberation from a person's present motivational commitments, and sound deliberation is not something that all persons are presently committed to. The question of demandingness also arises for externalist accounts of motivational adequacy, where the worry about demandingness is that the changes that would have to be wrought in members of the constituency in order for them to acquire the appropriate motivational commitments are radical, deep and wholesale.

Regarding demandingness, McKinnon states as follows at p. 21:

> When I say that a theory of justificatory value is too demanding I shall mean that it requires an objectionably high degree of uniformity along some dimension by reference to which justificatory reasons might become motivating. My claim will not be that justificatory reasons should be undemanding, because one test of the critical power of justificatory reasons is whether they make demands of members of the constituency, and rightfully so. Rather, the important question is what level of demandingness is objectionable.

These concepts – motivational adequacy and demandingness – are, I would argue, even more cogent and complex at the international level than the domestic. The far wider range of reasonable pluralism – and far greater range of reasonable peoples with fundamentally differing characteristics – makes the task of presenting practical reasons to reasonable peoples in such a way that (a) they will be motivated to act according to them and (b) the reasons given will not place too high a level of demandingness on their recipients all the more difficult. I do believe, however, that Kratochwil has provided an account of practical reasoning which can explain the way in which reasoning *with norms and with intersubjective normative structure* will not be either too demanding, or else motivationally inadequate. As I have argued all along, theorists such as McKinnon would be wise to engage more fully with Kratochwil's work.

24. Ibid., pp. 44–45
25. Ibid., p. 47
26. Rawls states at p. 412 of 'Justice as Fairness: Political not Metaphysical' (*Collected Papers*, Harvard, 2001):

    > Liberalism as a political doctrine supposes that there are many and conflicting and incommensurable conceptions of the good, each compatible with the full rationality of human persons... As a consequence of this supposition, liberalism assumes that it is a characteristic feature of a free democratic culture that a plurality of conflicting and incommensurable conceptions of the good are affirmed by its citizens.

27. McKinnon, *Liberalism and the Defence of Political Constructivism*, p. 48
28. Ibid., pp. 48–49
29. > The second reading of this connection is suggested by something striking in Rawls' recasting of 'Justice as Fairness: Political not Metaphysical' in Lecture I of *Political Liberalism*. Here, all reference to incommensurability as the consequence of reason's burdened operation is removed. Instead, in Lecture II, we get an account of the permanence of pluralism in terms of the six burdens of judgment... none of which make mention of incommensurability. Instead, pluralism is claimed to be permanent because burdened reason operating in conditions of freedom prevents convergence on beliefs (especially beliefs about values).

    Ibid., p. 49
30. Ibid., pp. 49–50
31. Ibid., pp. 51–52
32. Ibid., p. 53
33. Ibid., pp. 53–54
34. Ibid., p. 54
35. Ibid.
36. Ibid., p. 58
37. Ibid., p. 59
38. Ibid., pp. 59–60
39. Ibid., p. 60
40. Ibid., p. 68
41. McKinnon, *Liberalism and the Defence of Political Constructivism*, p. 68
42. Ibid., p. 73
43. Ibid. Contains a quote from Rawls, *A Theory of Justice (2nd Revised Ed)*, Oxford, 1999, p. 440
44. Ibid., pp. 73–74
45. Ibid., pp. 74
46. Ibid., p. 76
47. Ibid., pp. 76–77
48. McKinnon states as follows regarding the nature of practical reasoning:

> Practical reason is the capacity to set ends and deliberate about means to these ends. When a person sets herself an end, rather than just discovering herself with this end, she endorses reasons for the pursuit of that end according to which she takes the end to be appropriate for her. Similarly, when a person reasons practically about the best means to her ends, she considers the extent to and way in which the various means over which she is deliberating will further her ends, and she endorses reasons for the adoption of the set of means which she takes to be the most effective with respect to the realisation of her ends. Ibid., pp. 84–85

49. Ibid., p. 83
50. Ibid.
51. Ibid., pp. 83–84
52. Ibid., p. 84
53. Ibid., p. 85
54. Ibid., p. 86
55. Ibid.
56. Ibid.
57. Ibid., p. 87
58. Ibid., pp. 87–88. McKinnon states:

> Weakly evaluative judgements are appropriate grounds for choosing between options both of which an agent values, both of which she cannot pursue, but neither of which are *evaluatively significant* for her. A choice or decision has evaluative significance for a person when action for the reasons she evaluates forms part of, or is excluded by, the self-conception at the heart of her self-respect. To say that weak evaluation relates to decisions lacking evaluative significance is thus to say that, although the person cares (although not necessarily deeply) about which reason she eventually endorses, she does not conceive of this assessment as part of her conception of herself as a certain sort of person. Ibid., p. 88

59. Ibid., p. 89
60. Ibid.
61. Ibid., p. 92
62. Ibid., p. 93
63. Ibid., pp. 93–94
64. A person with a robust self-conception has a vocabulary of worth of a greater depth and articulacy than a person with a fragile self-conception. A person whose congruence supports her confidence in her abilities to pursue her plans, and her assurance that these plans are the right ones for her, possesses the capacity to make more fine-grained and resolute strong evaluations of reasons than a person whose limited congruence leaves her plagued by self-doubt and the spectre of regret for a life ill-planned. Ibid., p. 95
65. It is only assessments of reasons underlying questions of *basic* justice which are, by necessity, strongly evaluative. Assessments of reasons underlying questions concerning, for example, specific governmental policies which do not speak to matters of basic justice can be quantitative or weakly evaluative in nature.

66. Ibid., p. 96
67. McKinnon claims that a commitment to public reason entails a commitment to toleration:

    The scope of public reason – that is, the constituency of people with whom public reasoning is appropriate – maps the limits of toleration. All others with whom a person is committed to engaging with in public reason governed debate she is also committed to tolerating. Toleration requires a person's principled refusal to use force or coercion to change the views of others, where she has reason to disapprove of those views. To be in a position to engage in public reason with another person therefore requires toleration of that person. Ibid., p. 102

68. Ibid.
69. In my contention, the phrase 'reasonably expect' would be more appropriate than 'expect' at this point. The point throughout is that persons can act as they choose – but in terms of practical reasoning concerning questions of basic justice, a commitment to framing justificatory debate within the limits of public reason is a necessary condition of the concept of the reasonable, both in international relations and in domestic affairs.
70. Ibid., p. 103
71. Ibid., pp. 103–104
72. Ibid., p. 105
73. Ibid., p. 115
74. Ibid., p. 116
75. Ibid., p. 119
76. To recall, I stated above: 'Objectivity' in the sense that, in order to be accepted by decent non-liberal societies, the principles which constitute the Law of Peoples must overcome the charge of ethnocentrism or cultural bias. This...flows from the fact that it would be unreasonable to expect decent non-liberal peoples, in equal standing with liberal peoples in the Society of Peoples, to reasonably accept as reasonable a corpus of principles which they reasonably deem to be peculiarly liberal-centric in nature.
77. Rawls, *The Law of Peoples*, p. 25
78. We saw in *Political Liberalism* that this is the 'distinctive moral power' of the idea of reasonableness. See Rawls, *Political Liberalism*, p. 51.
79. Rawls, *Political Liberalism*, p. 53
80. Rawls, *The Law of Peoples*, p. 55
81. Ibid., p. 16
82. It should be clear, at this stage, that Rawls at times appears to forget that he has included decent peoples within the ambit of the description he gives of reasonable peoples. Thus, given that he has previously stated: 'This account of the Law of Peoples conceives of liberal democratic peoples (*And Decent Peoples*) as the actors in the Society of Peoples' (*The Law of Peoples*, p. 23, emphasis added), it is odd that he goes on to describe the three elements of liberal peoples only. However, given his exposition of the political nature of decent peoples later on in *The Law of Peoples*, and the fact that they are conceived of as both reasonable and rational, it seems clear that decent peoples will also possess the three characteristics attributed to liberal peoples here,

with the substitution of a 'decent consultation hierarchy' in place of a 'just constitutional democratic government'.

83. Ibid., p. 23
84. Scanlon opens his chapter on 'reasons' in *What We Owe To Each Other* with the claim: 'I will take the idea of a reason as primitive' (Harvard, 1998, p. 17). When I describe the concept of the reasonable as 'primitive', I do not mean that it cannot be broken up into, and described by reference to, its constituent elements, as clearly it can. I mean instead that it is 'primitive' in a normative sense; its normative significance cannot be explained by recourse to any external normative concept, and its constituent elements are imbued with normative significance by virtue of the fact that they are constituent elements in the concept of the reasonable. Thus, as we have seen in the theories of Rawls and McKinnon, different constructivist theories can conceptualise the constituent elements of the concept of the reasonable in distinct ways, but in each the constituent ideas will retain their normative force by virtue of the fact that they are constituent elements of the concept of the reasonable.
85. Rawls, *Political Liberalism*, p. 51
86. As we have seen above, McKinnon begins her analysis of the idea of self-respect by considering Rawls' development of the concept in *A Theory of Justice* (Harvard, 1971). The concept of a primary good is noticeably and intentionally missing from Rawls' later works, in which, as is well documented at this stage, he explicitly attempted to move away from the requirement of substantive judgements about value in the constructive apparatus of his theory of justice.
87. Roberts, *Political Constructivism*, Routledge, 2007
88. Ibid., p. 112
89. Ibid.
90. Ibid.
91. Ibid., p. 113
92. Ibid.
93. Ibid.
94. Ibid.
95. Ibid., p. 114
96. Ibid.
97. Ibid.
98. Ibid.
99. Ibid., pp. 114–115
100. Ibid., p. 115
101. Ibid.
102. Ibid., p. 116
103. Ibid.
104. Ibid.
105. Environments are not static, according to Roberts, and are themselves subject to fluid processes of change and adaptation.
106. Ibid., p. 117
107. Ibid., p. 118
108. Ibid., pp. 118–119. Emphases in original.
109. Ibid., p. 119

110. Ibid.
111. Objective in this context means reasoning which is not constrained by limitations which would render it partial or subjective, or grounded in partial or subjective assumptions. We shall see Roberts' account of the objectivity and authority of practical reason below.
112. Ibid., p. 120
113. Ibid.
114. Ibid.
115. Ibid., p. 121
116. Ibid.
117. Ibid.
118. Ibid., p. 122
119. Ibid., p. 123
120. Ibid., p. 124
121. Ibid., p. 125
122. In the context of my study, arguments concerning the motivational conditions of reasoning – and which contain claims to the motivational limits on reasoning – are of chief importance because, if sustainable, they would negate my claim that a Rawlsian conception of reasonableness can justify the claim that reasonable agents would be motivated to accept reasons to respect the limits of public reason.
123. The latter because it addresses the question: '*Why* would agents be motivated to agree to abide by principles of justice so long as others also agree to do the same?' My argument in response to this question is that the motivational work is done by the concept of the reasonable (i.e. the idea that agents are willing 'to propose principles and standards as fair terms of cooperation and to abide by them willingly, given the assurance that others will likewise do so'), and *not* the idea of public reason (which, as we have seen, arises out of but is *not* equivalent to the concept of the reasonable), and that therefore issues of motivation *in this sense* are properly addressed to the more general concept rather than the idea of public reason.
124. Ibid.
125. Ibid.
126. Ibid., pp. 125–126
127. Ibid., p. 126
128. Ibid.
129. Ibid., pp. 126–127
130. Ibid., p. 127
131. Ibid.
132. Ibid., p. 128
133. Referenced in note 99
134. Scanlon, *What We Owe to Each Other*, p. 18
135. At least in terms of traditional conceptions of the role of interests as part of the motivation of agents to act pursuant to moral or normative considerations.
136. Ibid., p. 19
137. Ibid.
138. 'Judgment sensitive attitudes' are described as 'attitudes that an ideally rational person would come to have whenever that person judged there

to be sufficient reasons for them and that would, in an ideally rational person, "extinguish" when that person judged them not to be supported by reasons of the appropriate kind'. Ibid., p. 20

139. Ibid.
140. Ibid., p. 21
141. Ibid. One means of accounting for the latter requirement, that agents be predisposed to unreflectively *think* of the particular proposition or intended course of action at the relevant moments, is, I suggest, Kratochwil's account of the effects of norms upon agents' practical reasoning and, in particular, his account of the contextualising role of topoi or commonplaces upon such. The establishment of a particular commonplace, or indeed an analogy in the Kratochwilian sense, could, I suggest, provide agents with a predisposition to think of a particular proposition or course of action at analogous moments.
142. Ibid., p. 22
143. Scanlon, *What We Owe to Each Other*, pp. 33–34
144. Ibid., p. 23
145. Ibid., p. 35
146. Ibid. Scanlon says of belief: 'Belief is not merely a matter of judgment but of the connections, over time, between this judgment and dispositions to feel conviction, to recall as relevant, to employ as a premise in further reasoning, and so on' (Ibid.)
147. Ibid., p. 192
148. Ibid., p. 194
149. Ibid., p.37
150. Ibid., p. 41
151. Ibid., p. 49
152. Ibid., p. 53
153. Ibid.
154. Ibid., pp. 52–53
155. Ibid., pp. 53–54
156. Roberts, *Political Constructivism*, p. 131
157. Ibid.
158. Ibid.
159. Ibid., pp. 131–132
160. Ibid., p. 132
161. Ibid. Roberts claims:

> Rawls lays out the original position as his first stage [of his constructivist justificatory theory, anchored around an account of objective reasoning]. This is intended to be an objective point of view from which to judge proposed principles of justice. In laying it out, Rawls is clear that he is attempting to identify a choice situation that, as far as possible, screens out partial and subjective influences on choice and thus prevents the justification of principles from being made for partial reasons. This is the role of the veil of ignorance that screens knowledge of conceptions of the good position in society, natural endowments, etc. As a second stage, Rawls nests this choice situation within a broader notion of reflective equilibrium as an account of critical and reflective reason.

The role of this process of reflection is to demonstrate to ourselves, and others, that the original position, and therefore the principles of justice, actually does not depend on subjective reasons (Ibid.).

162. Ibid., pp. 134–135.
163. Ibid., pp. 138–139. Emphasis in original.
164. Rawls, *Political Liberalism*, p. 53
165. McKinnon, *Liberalism and the Defence of Political Constructivism*, p. 35
166. Ibid., p. 46
167. Ibid.
168. Rawls, *The Law of Peoples*, p. 16
169. Rawls, *Political Liberalism*, p. 225
170. Kratochwil, *Rules, Norms and Decisions*, p. 217
171. Ibid., p. 218

Conclusion: Poststructuralism and Beyond

1. I.e. theoretical techniques designed to foster a conception of world politics which seeks to erase the presence of contingency in favour of rational order, the order of fixed, immutable sovereign spaces with definable limits.

References

Ashley, R.K., 'Living on Border Lines: Man, Poststructuralism, and War', in Der Derian, J. and Shapiro, M.J. (eds) *International/Intertextual Relations*, Lexington University Press, 1989

Ashley, R.K., 'The Achievements of Post-Structuralism', in Smith, S., Booth, K., and Zalewski, M. (eds) *International Relations Theory: Positivism and Beyond*, Cambridge University Press, 1996

Ashley, R.K., and Walker, R.B.J., 'Speaking the Language of Exile: Dissident Thought in International Studies', *International Studies Quarterly*, 34(3), September 1990

Ashley, R.K. and Walker, R.B.J, 'Reading Dissidence/Writing the Discipline: Crisis and the Question of Sovereignty in International Studies', *International Studies Quarterly*, 34(3), 1990

Austin, J.L., *How to do Things with Words*, Oxford University Press, 1975

Beitz, C., *Political Theory and International Relations*, Princeton University Press, 1979

Beitz, C., *The Idea of Human Rights*, Oxford University Press, 2011

Brown, C., *International Relations Theory: New Normative Approaches*, Columbia University Press, 1992

Brown, C., *Sovereignty, Rights and Justice: International Political Theory Today*, Polity Press, 2002

Buchanan, A., *Justice, Legitimacy, and Self-Determination: Moral Foundations for International Law*, Oxford University Press, 2007

Buchanan, A., 'The Egalitarianism of Human Rights', *Ethics*, 120(4), July 2010

Buchanan, A., *Human Rights, Legitimacy, and the Use of Force*, Oxford University Press, 2010

Buzan, B., 'The Timeless Wisdom of Realism?' in Smith, Booth and Zalewski (eds) *International Theory: Positivism and Beyond*, Cambridge University Press, 1996

Cochran, M., *Normative Theory in International Relations*, Cambridge University Press, 1999

Collingwood, R.G., *An Essay on Metaphysics*, Oxford University Press, 1998/1940

Connolly, C., *Political Theory and Modernity*, Oxford University Press, 1988

Daniels, N., 'Wide Reflective Equilibrium and Theory Acceptance in Ethics', *The Journal of Philosophy*, 76(5), 1979

Der Derian, J., 'Boundaries of Knowledge and Power in IR', in Der Derian, J., and Shapiro, M.J. (eds) *International/Intertextual Relations*, Lexington University Press, 1989

Dixon, J., and Dogan, R., 'The Conduct of Policy Analysis: Philosophical Points of Reference', *Review of Policy Research*, 21(4), 2004

Dworkin, R., *Taking Rights Seriously*, Duckworth Publishers, 1981

Finnemore, M. and Sikkink, K., 'Taking Stock: The Constructivist Research Program in International Relations and Comparative Politics', *Annual Review of Political Science*, 2001

Fischer, M., 'Feudal Europe, 800–1300: Communal Discourse and Conflictual Practices', *International Organisation*, 46(2), Spring 1992

Forst, R., *The Right to Justification*, Columbia University Press, 2007

Forum on *Social Theory of International Politics, Review of International Studies*, 26(1), January 2000

Friedrichs, J., and Kratochwil, F., 'On Acting and Knowing: How Pragmatism can Advance International Relations Research and Methodology', *International Organisation*, 63, 2009

Frost, *Constituting Human Rights: Global Civil Society and the Society of Democratic States*, Routledge, 2002

Frost, M., *Ethics in International Relations: A Constitutive Theory*, Cambridge University Press, 1996

Frost, M., 'Mervyn Frost Replies to Peter Sutch's 'Human Rights and Settled Norms', *Review of International Studies*, 26(3), 2000

George, J., *Discourses of Global Politics: A Critical (Re)Introduction to International Relations*, Rienner, 1994

Giddens, A., *The Constitution of Society: Outline of a Theory of Structuration*, Berkeley, 1984

Guzzini, S., 'A Reconstruction of Constructivism in International Relations', *European Journal of International Relations*, 6(2), 2000

Guzzini, S., and Leander, A., 'Wendt's Constructivism: A Relentless Quest for Synthesis', in Guzzini, S. and Leander, A. (eds) *Constructivism and International Relations: Alexander Wendt and his Critics*, Routledge, 2006

Hegel, G.W.F., *The Philosophy of History*, Prometheus, 1991

Hoffman, S., *Duties Beyond Borders*, Syracuse, 1981

Hollis, M., and Smith, S., *Explaining and Understanding International Relations*, Oxford University Press, 1990

Hopf, T., 'The Promise of Constructivism in International Relations Theory', *International Security*, 23(1), Summer 1998

Koslowski, R., and Kratochwil, F., 'Understanding Change in International Politics: the Soviet Empire's Demise and the International System', *International Organisation*, 48(2), Spring 1994

Kratochwil, F., 'Reflections on Theory and Practice', available online at http://hdl.handle.net/1814/1876

Kratochwil, F., *Rules, Norms, and Decisions: On the Conditions of Practical and Legal Reasoning in International Relations and Domestic Affairs*, Cambridge University Press, 1989

Kratochwil, F., 'Constructing a New Orthodoxy? Wendt's 'Social Theory of International Politics' and the Constructivist Challenge', *Millennium*, 29(1), 2000

Kratochwil, F., and Ruggie, J., 'International Organisation: A State of the Art or an Art of the State', *International Organisation*, 40(4), 1986

Kratochwil, F., *The Puzzles of Politics: Inquiries into the Genesis and Transformation of International Relations*, Routledge, 2011

Kuhn, T., *The Structure of Scientific Revolutions*, Chicago University Press, 1970

Kurki, M., 'Causes of a Divided Discipline: a Critical Examination of the Concept of Cause in International Relations Theory', available online at www.globalpolitics.net

McKinnon, C., *Liberalism and the Defence of Political Constructivism*, Palgrave, 2002

Moellendorf, D., 'Constructing the Law of Peoples', *Pacific Philosophical Quarterly*, 77(2), 1996
Nardin, T., *Law, Morality and the Relations of States*, Princeton University Press, 1983
O'Neill, O., 'Political Liberalism and Public Reason: A Critical Notice of John Rawls, Political Liberalism', *The Philosophical Review*, 106(3), July 1997
Osterud, O., 'Antimonies of Postmodernism in International Studies', *Journal of Peace Research*, 33(4), 1996
Pogge, T.W., 'Liberalism and Global Justice: Hoffmann and Nardin on Morality in International Affairs', *Philosophy and Public Affairs*, 15(1), Winter 1986
Price, R., and Reus-Smit, C., 'Dangerous Liaisons? Critical International Theory and Constructivism', *European Journal of International Relations*, 4(3), 1998
Rawls, J., *Political Liberalism*, Columbia University Press, 1993
Rawls, J., *A Theory of Justice (2nd Revised Ed)*, Oxford University Press, 1999
Rawls, J., *The Law of Peoples*, Harvard University Press, 1999
Rawls, J., 'Justice as Fairness: Political not Metaphysical', *Collected Papers*, Harvard University Press, 2001
Reus-Smit, C., 'Constructivism', in Burchill, S., and Linklater, A. (eds) *Theories of International Relations*, Palgrave, 2005
Roberts, P., *Political Constructivism*, Routledge, 2007
Rorty, R., 'Human Rights, Rationality and Sentimentality', in Shute, S. and Hurley, S. (eds) *On Human Rights: The Oxford Amnesty Lectures 1993*, Basic Books, 1993
Scanlon, T., *What We Owe to Each Other*, Harvard University Press, 1998
Skinner, Q., 'Conventions and the Understanding of Speech Acts', *The Philosophical Quarterly*, 20(79), 1970
Skinner, Q., 'Hermeneutics and the Role of History', *New Literary History*, 7(1), 1975
Smith, S., 'Wendt's World', *Review of International Studies*, 26(1), 2000
Snidal, D., and Wendt, A., 'Why There is International Theory Now', *International Theory*, 1(1), 2009
Stephan, H. R., 'Review of *Constructivism in International Relations: The Politics of Reality*', Maja Zehfuss, Cambridge University Press, 2002, In-SPIRE, July 2004
Strawson, P.F., 'Intention and Convention in Speech Acts', *The Philosophical Review*, 1964
Sutch, P., 'Global Civil Society and International Ethics: Mervyn Frost's Restatement of Constitutive Theory', 26(3), 2000
Sutch, P., 'Human Rights as Settled Norms', *Review of International Studies*, 26(2), 2000
Tan, K.C., 'Liberal Toleration in Rawls's Law of Peoples', *Ethics*, 108, January 1998
Teson, F., *The Philosophy of International Law: Human Rights Approach*, Boulder, 1998
Walker, R.B.J., *Inside/Outside: International Relations as Political Theory*, Cambridge University Press, 1993
Walker, R.B.J., 'A Dirty Dozen: What is at Stake in Contemporary Claims about Sovereignty', October 2005, unpublished paper presented at SAID workshop
Walker, R.B.J., 'Democratic Theory and the Present/Absent International', *Ethics & Global Politics*, 3(1), 2010
Walker, R.B.J., *After the Globe, Before the World*, Routledge, 2010

Waltz, K., *Theory of International Politics*, McGraw-Hill, 1979
Waltz, K., 'Structural Realism after the Cold War', *International Security*, 25(1), 2000
Wendt, A., 'Anarchy is What States Make of it: The Social Construction of Power Politics', *International Organisation*, 46(2), Spring 1992
Wendt, A., 'Constructing International Politics', *International Security*, 20(1), Summer 1995
Wendt, A., 'On Constitution and Causation in International Relations', *Review of International Studies*, 24, 1998
Wendt, A., *Social Theory of International Politics*, Cambridge University Press, 1999
Wendt, A., 'On the Via Media: a Response to the Critics', *Review of International Studies*, 26(1), 2000
Wendt, A., '*Social Theory* as Cartesian Science: an Auto-Critique from a Quantum Perspective', in Guzzini, S. & Leander, A. (eds) *Constructivism and International Relations: Alexander Wendt and his Critics*, Routledge, 2006

Index

Ashley, Richard, 5, 6, 8, 15–16, 17, 35–7, 40, 43, 50, 70
  and the 'celebratory register of freedom', 37–9
  and the critique of logocentrism, 20–3, 27–9, 59, 239
  and intertextuality, 26–7, 239

Buchanan, Allen
  and critique of Rawls' conception of public reason, 10, 119–31, 141–2, 144–5
  and the Modest Objectivist View, 131–41
  and social epistemology, 135–41, 167, 172–3, 177

constitutive theory, 74–89
constructivism, 1–2
  conventional, 1–2, 44–9
  critical, 1–2, 61–71
  political, 2, 94, 182, 187–8, 216–17, 229

Friedrichs, Jorge
  and engaging with epistemology, 5–6
Frost, Mervyn, 66
  and constitutive theory, 9, 74–89

Kratochwil, Friedrich
  and critical constructivism, 1–2, 6, 8–9, 43–4, 58, 59–60, 63–5, 69–71, 72–4, 145, 146, 170–1
  and engaging with epistemology, 5–6
  and norms, 9, 32, 43, 64–6, 68, 72, 74, 75, 89, 145–6, 150–6, 158–63, 168, 179–81, 182–3, 184, 187, 242–3
  and practical reason, 4, 7, 10–11, 18, 145–6, 150–69, 179–81, 182–4, 186–7, 216, 229, 238–9, 242–3
  and pragmatism, 5, 59–60, 148–9
  and Rawlsian public reason, 11, 94, 150, 162, 165–8, 169–73, 178–81, 182–3, 229–30, 239, 243
  and the role of topoi in normative and legal reasoning, 10–11, 152–3, 154–63, 179, 187, 242–3

McKinnon, Catriona
  and critique of Rawls' conception of reasonableness, 11, 188, 189–91, 193–8, 201, 212–13, 218–20, 240, 241
  and the personal bases of self-respect, 11, 188, 200–12, 218, 219, 241, 242
  and practical reason, 189–91, 193–5, 200–1, 204, 205–13, 218–20, 240, 241

O'Neill, Onora, 108–13, 226, 227

poststructuralism, 5, 6, 8, 15–39, 40, 43, 50, 59, 70, 93–4, 239, 244

Rawls, John
  and Kratochwilian practical reason, 7, 11, 182–4, 186, 216, 217, 229–30, 238–9, 242, 243
  and political constructivism, 2, 94, 182, 187–8, 216–17, 229
  and public reason in *Political Liberalism*, 9–10, 95–113, 117, 120–1, 122–4, 128, 162, 169–78, 182, 187, 189, 191–3, 197–8, 201, 214–16, 218–19, 238, 241
  and public reason in *The Law of Peoples*, 9–10, 95, 113–17,

120–2, 124, 162, 165–6, 167–8, 169–78, 182, 184–6, 187, 191, 201, 213–16, 218, 238, 241, 242
and reasonableness, 11–12, 18, 94–5, 119, 125–7, 129–31, 141–2, 144–5, 150, 182–3, 184, 186, 187–9, 191–6, 201, 212–20, 226–7, 240, 241–3
reasonableness, 97–101, 182–243
reasoning
legal, 151–6, 157, 158–9
limitations on, 224–35
with norms, 145–69
practical, 4, 7, 10–11, 18, 145–6, 150–69, 179–81, 182–4, 186–7, 189–91, 193–5, 200–1, 204, 205–13, 216, 218–20, 229, 238–9, 240, 241, 242–3
public, 93–117, 169–73, 178–81
public in the domestic context, 9–10, 95–113, 117, 120–1, 122–4, 128, 162, 169–78, 182, 187, 189, 191–3, 197–8, 201, 214–16, 218–19, 238, 241
public in the international context, 9–10, 95, 113–17, 120–2, 124, 162, 165–6, 167–8, 169–78, 182, 184–6, 187, 191, 201, 213–16, 218, 238, 241, 242
public and practical combined, 11, 94, 150, 162, 165–8, 169–73, 178–81, 182–3, 229–30, 239, 243

Roberts, Peri
and 'the constraints of practicality', 12, 220–4, 238, 242, 243
and limitations on reasoning, 12, 188, 201, 204, 224–9, 236–8, 239–40, 241–2, 243

Scanlon, Thomas
and motivational limitations on reasoning, 12, 228, 229, 230–5, 240, 242
Snidal, Duncan
and 'International Theory', 2–4

Walker, R.B.J., 5, 6, 8, 15–16, 17, 35–7, 40, 43, 50, 70, 143
and the 'celebratory register of freedom', 37–9
and the critique of logocentrism, 19–20, 22–3, 27, 29–31, 59, 93–4, 239
and intertextuality, 19–20, 24, 25, 29–34, 239
Waltz, Kenneth, 26–9, 44–5, 47, 48
Wendt, Alexander, 1–2, 46–8
and causation and constitution, 53–61, 63, 65, 66–7, 89
and 'International Theory', 2–4
and 'scientific realism', 42, 49, 50–3, 54–61, 63,
and social constructivism, 1–2, 8, 17, 42–3, 45, 49, 62, 63

Printed and bound by CPI Group (UK) Ltd, Croydon, CR0 4YY